Broken Porzelan

Broken Porzelan

Katie (Katharina Krämer) Bering

iUniverse, Inc.
New York   Bloomington

Broken Porzelan

iUniverse books may be ordered through booksellers or by contacting:

iUniverse
1663 Liberty Drive
Bloomington, IN 47403
www.iuniverse.com
1-800-Authors (1-800-288-4677)

Because of the dynamic nature of the Internet, any Web addresses or links contained in this book may have changed since publication and may no longer be valid. The views expressed in this work are solely those of the author and do not necessarily reflect the views of the publisher, and the publisher hereby disclaims any responsibility for them.

ISBN: 978-1-4502-4092-5 (pbk)
ISBN: 978-1-4502-4091-8 (cloth)
ISBN: 978-1-4502-4093-2 (ebk)

Library of Congress Control Number: 2010909997

Printed in the United States of America

iUniverse rev. date: 8/13/2010

Contents

Credits

Book Cover Painting by Katie Krämer Bering
Art Teacher - Sherie McKay Gladu
Graphic Designer of Cover - Anthony Loncaric
Editing - Laurie Tansey & Alexandra Gayowsky
Photo Editing - Jackileen R. Rains
Danube Swabian culture information from Frank Schmidt

I dedicate this book to my Mother
Katharina Hühn
For Her Love, Endurance and Strength

To My Dear Mother

In the Spring of your life, the world was at war:
When you were young and beautiful, life was a bore.

In the Summer of your life, you had children to raise:
I recall, you never received much praise.
It was in fashion then to be stern as a mother
For you never spoke of our father.

In the Autumn of your life, you reached out for love once more, I guess.
For the years passed ever so with bitterness.

In the Winter of your life, as I see you slowly fading away,
I desperately, with gratitude, want to say,
My heart for you has a magic wand.
I believe to have a Mother is the greatest bond.

Forever, with Love Katie

Acknowledgments

For my husband Bill, for his quiet support and kindness throughout my journey of writing this book. Words cannot express my deeply felt love and appreciation.

I also would like to thank family, friends, especially Jackileen, Ann, Jane, and Martha, and neighbours for their support and believing in me.

Prologue

It is Monday morning February sixteenth two thousand and four, when I finally take the long drive into the Soo for a very different reason than my usual once a week shopping trip. Today, I will stay in town and not return home for the next five days.

The highway is usually well groomed, but today the snow is falling down with great speed and the accumulation on the pavement lends itself to some treacherous driving at times. But the beauty of the vast fields glistening all in white and the hills peeking through in the distance makes my ride very tranquil. Listening to my favourite CD *"Wien, Wien nur Du allein"* by James Last, I start to plan my day. As I approach the sign that tells me I am within the city limits, I breathe a little easier knowing that the sixty kilometers of snow covered roads are behind me. Within minutes I spot the red brick house as I turn the corner. My mind twirls around to my past just like the wind blowing the snowflakes all around me. I push the car door open as I spot a large shaded sign that reads:

BROCKWELL CHAMBERS
BED AND BREAKFAST

The name suits this old house, for it is named after the street it sits on "Brock Street." I take a deep breath, I feel a little uneasy, but continue. My eyes focus on the beauty and grandeur of this old building. A foundation strong enough to hold up a three storey, over one hundred year old house gives me reason to believe that some things do last. I continue to walk toward the house and listen to the crunch of the dry snow with every step I take.

Standing on the porch and pushing my hood back on my shoulders, I feel a sense of peacefulness. Walking closer to the oak door, I ring the door bell. In a moment, the door opens and Maria greets me.

"Hello, Maria. I'm so glad to see you," I say cheerfully. Maria is not herself as she quietly invites me in. She holds her head and explains to me, "I have a terrible headache; you know, the kind that makes you feel nauseated."

"Oh dear, it sounds like a migraine." "Yes, I think so," she replies. "Come follow me, I'll take you upstairs." I've been here before. My eyes barely focus on the stairs before me, as I want to feast my eyes on this grand design of woodworking of years gone by. Maria patiently waits for me at the top of the red carpeted stairs that are leading to the four guestrooms. When I finally catch up to her, in her strong Dutch accent, she says, "Take any room you like for they are not rented out till this weekend and you will be gone by then." Maria excuses herself and slowly starts walking down the stairs. With her head turning back in my direction, she adds apologetically, "I am so sorry Katie, but if you need anything, Roy, my husband, will be downstairs." I nod my head and say "Thank You" to her.

The spacious hall I stand in is surrounded by beautiful paintings in brown and gold frames. The four guestrooms are identified by color: blue, green, burgundy and yellow. Each one decorated differently, but elegantly presented, just like Maria herself. I chose the green room. I turn the golden knob, as I peek around the corner and my eyes fixed mostly on the large mirror in front of me. Quietly, I close the door and place my suitcase on the bench underneath the mirror. I stand still in front of the long length mirror for a while. Gently, my fingers move my silvery hair away from my face. As I remove my long black coat, the rest of the room comes into focus. Oh, how beautiful, elegant, warm and cosy this color of green feels. The fireplace gives the room a feeling of warmth. It is the absolute perfect setting to write. But this is not just ordinary writing. I am here to write about my childhood, times of family, war and hardship. Instantly, my mood changes, and I feel my eyes warming with tears waiting to flow. But, I push back. Not yet...

Slowly, deep in thought I unpack, placing my writing pad and my special pen carefully on the desk. On the night table, the bottle of Champagne I brought from home, a box of Laura Secord Chocolates, and a picture of myself at the age of twelve years old. For so long now, I have dreamt of finishing this book but something always comes along to hold me back. Something more urgent, or perhaps it is my own deep rooted conscience too fragile to follow my heart as I would have to dig deep into the soul of forgotten dreams. In any case, the story of my life which has been silenced for so long has to surface, not by boring conversations, but in this book. With my pen carefully held in my fingers, I start to write.

Untimely Birth

I was born to my Mother on a Thursday afternoon on August 12th, 1937, with only a midwife and my *Oma* (Grandmother) present. My birth was the easiest of my Mother's two deliveries before me. Easiest definitely in the delivery but far from a joyful welcome for my Mother, not that any of this was intentional, but rather it was the timing of my birth. My Oma cleaned the afterbirth and wrapped me in a clean warm blanket. She took me to my Mother's bed. Mother lay listless and limp, and only said, "Oh, another girl," as she held me in her arms. My Oma told me this story many times and each time she did so, she'd remember something more. I never tired of hearing stories of my childhood. Oma added and said, "Ya, I stood at the foot of your Mommi's bed, and I watched her so unhappy. I had tears in my eyes for you."

There was reason to worry, for in three short years, our Mother brought four girls into this world. The first born Margaret named after our father's Mother, and thirteen months later twins, Suzanna, named after our Mother's Mother, and Therezia after my father's Grandmother, were born. My Mother named me Katharina, after her own name. In those days the Godparents' names were the ones mostly given to the child. My sisters preceded me, and had taken the names of family members, and so Mommi's name was left to give to me. Giving

1

us girls traditional names in our culture was actually more important than our birthdays. We celebrated our Namesake day, not our birthdays. Mine fell on November the twenty fifth every year. When my Mother learned she was pregnant with me, our Mother's and Father's marriage was in deep trouble.

"Can you imagine?" Oma told me, "Your Mommi threw your *Dati* (Father) out. She packed his bags and told him to never come back again." "But why?" I questioned. "Your Dati made a big mistake." Oma continued, "I pleaded and explained to *Kati.* (my mother's short name) to please forgive him, that in time you will forget. But, your Mommi's mind was made up, and so after many tries your Dati gave up and left us all behind."

Mommi and Dati met in unusual circumstances. First of all, our father was only nineteen years old and our Mother a mature twenty four year old when they married. Our Mother was the youngest of sixteen children, a close family with Mother being the youngest and one of two girls, the rest all boys. Our father, you could say, was an only and pampered child. He had a younger sister, but she died in her teens. His Mother then focused solely on him. And of course marrying an older woman caused doubt, not only for our Father's Mother, but for our Grandmother as well.

"Your Father was a kind man and treated your Mother with respect and I liked him. But, you know," Oma continued, "*Joshi* (Father's short name) being a good looking man, always dressed in a suit every day for work, was trouble. Your Mommi with so much work raising you girls, she didn't have the energy or the time," Oma explained.

Our Father worked in the downtown square in *Groß Kikinda.* (Groß meaning large) as a salesman for a fabric store, which was owned by his family. My parents, Katharina Huhn and Josef Krämer, married on August 14th, 1934, in their home city of Kikinda, Jugoslavia. I've never actually seen a wedding picture of my parents, but was told their wedding to be modest, yet beautiful. Our Father with strikingly good looks, a face with strong features, dark hair and full lips, our Mother with small features, flawless skin, perfectly shaped white teeth and dark wavy hair. They were married only a short three years and divorced in 1937, the year I was born.

Mother told me this story only once, as we sat together on two lawnchairs, a rare moment talking about my Father. Mother went on to share with me after so many years of silence, on that unforgettable afternoon. I cleared my thoughts quickly, so I would not miss one single word that I was anxiously waiting to hear. Mother cleared her throat, as she calmly told me. After I threw your Father out, he was misled by someone who indicated that I was ready to take him back. Your Father arrived one afternoon with two black Horses and a black lacquered carriage. He stood in the doorway, dressed in his best navy blue suit so good looking and attractive, Mother smiled a little as if she visualized him standing next to us at that moment. The look on his face, I knew he was happy. "What are you doing here?" I asked him, sarcastically. "I heard you want me back," he said. "Oh, you did." I started to laugh, you know that kind of laugh that makes you feel like a fool and then said to him, "You're mistaken if you think so." Mother explained, shaking her head, "Oh, Käthe, I was so hurt and I wanted to hurt him back." "When I found them together that afternoon so many years ago," she continued, "I was so worked up that all the way home I couldn't breathe." She stopped talking. "Tell me more Mother." Reluctantly, she told me.

"Well, I found a note in his suit pocket one afternoon and it was from a girl. You know, men," she tried to make light of it, but I could tell even after all those years that a part of her still hurt, "the note read, Joshi, please meet me in the vineyard tomorrow, at one in the afternoon, okay?" My Mother looked away, almost apologizing to me and said, "I went to the vineyard and found them there, lying on the grass between the rows of the grapes." she stopped talking and I didn't ask any more questions.

But, she did tell me this. "I did something that bothers me to this day." she explained. The girl that your Father met that day worked downtown next to the tailor shop, where your'e Father worked. I knew the girl's father. Being so angry, I walked downtown, and told the young girl's Father what she did with my husband. Oh, Käthe, oh, he hit that girl so hard and humiliated her, in front of that store so everyone could hear and see. I wanted to stop the Father but he wouldn't listen. I heard that he disowned this young girl as well. Oh, it was awful. It was something I should have never done." Mother took my hand and said, "Your Father was very good to me. In spite of everything, I want you to know that." Her voice trailed off.

At that moment, how that afternoon must have changed the once happy and trusting woman, my Mother, and us girls, forever.

A Doll for Katharina

My first recollection of my childhood came when I was only four years old. My first Christmas memory was a visit from Krampus. Krampus dressed in red to resemble a devil and chains part of the scaring tactics when he entered the room. The reason for his visit was mainly to scare children to be good for the Christmas Season. If we were good, hopefully we would receive a small gift when Kristkindl came to our house on Christmas morning. The anticipation of Krampus coming, and it was to be tonight, made me shiver all over. I didn't like Krampus at all. Mommi summoned us girls into the long hallway, where we stood all in a row, waiting for Krampus. "Now," Mommi reminded us, "answer all his questions when Krampus talks to you." I jumped as I heard the chains rattling outside the door. By the time Krampus asked my older sister *Grete* (Margaret) a question, I started to shake from fright. I ran over to my Mother and wrapped my little arms around her leg. Mommi tried to push me away, but stopped when I started to cry. That night, too frightened to fall asleep, I tiptoed to my sister Grete's room and crawled into bed with her. I was so quiet that she didn't know I was there.

As I walked into the kitchen the next morning for breakfast, everyone was already by the table waiting for me. "What's the matter Käthe? Didn't you like Krampus last night?" my Mother said smiling. I shook my head, "No", with a pouty look on my face. Everyone in the room was snickering and laughing at me. With every moment passing I became more embarrassed and didn't like it at all that my family thought I was a scaredy cat. I ate my breakfast in silence with my head down. As soon as I was done, I said my thank you, as always, and walked directly to my room.

Later in the day as we, the twins and I, played in our favourite spot in the sunny hallway, Susi whispered to me, "Käthe, don't be scared of Krampus. It's *Hans Onkel* (Uncle John) all dressed in red." "No! Really!?' surprised, I raised my voice. "Shhh, shhh." She put her finger over her lips. "Mommi wouldn't like it if she knew I told you." "Well, how do you know?" "Grete told me and I recognized Hans Onkels voice." Well hearing this wonderful news put my confidence back intact. The day ended happy and I never told this secret to anyone ever. Although I didn't understand how long it would be until Christmas, our traditional celebrations were a sure sign that the Christmas season had begun.

Four weeks before Christmas an Advent wreath of evergreens was hung from the ceiling over the dining table with four candles placed on the wreath. The candles were held in place with a steel clamp that was connected to the wreath. On the first Advent Sunday one white candle burned and left on for awhile. We'd gather around the wreath and while we watched the candle, said a short prayer as a Family. I loved the smell of evergreens in the house. On the second week, this procedure was repeated with one more candle lit, leaving the fourth one for last. Of course we knew then it was Christmas.

There was one more tradition. Mommi planted wheat kernels in a shallow glass bowl, about the same time as the wreath appeared. I remember watching these gentle green perfectly straight grasses grow to the height of a drinking glass which was placed in the middle of the bowl. Mommi informed us when this wheat grew tall that we would have a blessed and good year. I remember sitting by this bowl for hours and I could swear I saw these grasses grow right in front of me. The bowl of wheat stayed in the kitchen and was watered sparingly. When it reached about six inches high to the top of the glass we knew then it was Christmas. I was convinced that the four weeks before Christmas determined my fate of being worthy of good things to come to me throughout the whole year.

While we waited anxiously for Christmas, we'd pass the time outside playing in the courtyard. By this time enough snow had fallen on the ground for us to make snowballs. Once in awhile one of those snowballs would be too hard and hurt on contact. But, we knew if we fought amongst ourselves that we'd end up in our bedrooms and playing would be over for all of us. If one of us got hurt, we'd try to take care of ourselves and never ever tattle on each other. My Mother put the scare in us, for she was strict most of the time. Oma was very different from my Mother. When Mother yelled at me and scolded me, I found my Oma's lap warm and comforting. She gently stroked my hair, and spoke these words. "There, there, my sweet child, it'll be ok, you'll see."

After my Father and Mothers divorce, my Oma, Mothers Mother and Mother's Brother, Hans moved in, the only family I ever knew.

In those few weeks before Christmas, Mommi and Hans Onkel paced the floor together and spoke of war, Partisans and Russians. Words I hadn't heard before. The worry was just not in their faces, but also in their tone of voice. Our house most of the time was orderly and happy. Hans Onkel, Oma and Mommi talked endlessly, when they worked in the kitchen together. Their admiration for one another made us feel secure in our daily lives.

We children were totally unaware that in the 1940s our family had grave concerns and deeply troubled over the world at war. More and more people in our city heard of the horrible devastation throughout Europe. The news spread quickly of a troubled future ahead for us folks that lived for centuries in the old Jugoslavia and spoke German, called Donau Schwaben. The reason for this concern was mostly because we were of German descent.

The day before Christmas, I woke to the excitement buzzing around the house. The smell of cinnamon, cloves, vanilla and lemon reached every corner of the house. I loved that spicy aroma, the smell of fresh cookies baking in the oven, and my Mother's delicious nut and poppy seed strudels, for we couldn't wait to indulge in this wonderful baking. It must have been then that my love of the Christmas spirit began.

On cold afternoons, I took my wooden spinning top that our Hans Onkel made for us and went to play. We also passed the time with a game that needed a long piece of string, or a heavy piece of wool thread. Only two could play Cat's Cradle, making formations and taking the string from each other's hands and creating new ones. We didn't have any toys. When I asked Mommi if and when I'd get a toy her answer was always the same, "Oh someday, my child, you will get one, just be patient."

On Christmas Eve the preparations were anything but calm in our house. Mommi was far too busy with last minute doings. For one of us to get her attention was not too good. I knew all I had to do was follow my sisters and imitate everything they did and I would be okay. Finally, Christmas Eve was here. Our Aunt from my Father's side joined us for this festive evening. Nanna, a teacher by profession and also a spinster, was very educated, Mommi told us. Nanna played the piano. Most of the time our piano was closed, but not on Christmas Eve.

We knew by the knock at the door that it was Nanna. She was so happy to see us, as she gave us a kiss on the cheek, and handed us a beautifully wrapped bar of expensive chocolate. The way our eyes lit up to Nanna, it was clear to see our admiration for her, as we thanked her politely. Mommi made us change into our floor length nightgowns earlier. Mommi made the matching nightgowns with warm and soft fabric, the style a simple yoke with a round collar. The color was off white, with three buttons in front for us to easily slip into and pull over our heads. We lined up by the piano and waited to sing for our family. Nanna moved the piano chair just exactly into place and sat down. When Nanna nodded her head we knew that was our cue to sing. We had been practicing and we started singing the first song, *Oh Tannenbaum.* then, *Leise Riselt der Schnee.* Mommi, Hans Onkel and Oma stood directly across from us. The pride in their faces was clear to see, as we harmonised every tone with our childlike voices and finished our singing with, *Stille Nacht. Heilige Nacht.* definitely the song I liked the most.

Nanna clapped her hands, "Oh my, the singing is even better than last year." With a smile, Nanna gave each one of us one more hug and a kiss, as we politely said "Good night" to her. Mommi with her hands together, stooped down, looking at us, "Time for bed, girls. You know Kristkindl is coming in the morning and you need your sleep." "Okay Mommi," we agreed immediately. Hans Onkel grabbed my hand and I skipped all the way to my room. Hans Onkel let go of my hand, then fluffed my pillow and pulled the feather duvet on one side, so I could jump in. "Okay now," he said, as he stroked my cheek, "have a good sleep now, sweet child." My uncle was a gentle man and I loved him very much. He smiled at me as he closed the door behind him.

I pressed my hands together tightly, like I did every night. It is a sin to go to bed and not say a prayer, so I always did. Tonight, I ended my prayer not with my usual Amen, but with selfish wants. "Please God, could I please have a doll this Christmas. I will be so good, I promise. Please God," I pleaded.

Christmas Morning 1941.

Susi came and woke me. "Good Morning Käthe," she said. "Did you have a good sleep?" "Yes I did," I answered. "And you?" "Me too," she said, as she stretched her arms up to the ceiling. We took turns washing our hands and faces in the basin that stood on the dresser next to my bed. The basin had to be filled with fresh water the night before, one of Mommi's strict orders. We had to be careful not to spill water on the wooden cabinet, for it left a mark. We girls wore our hair in braids most of the time, but not today. On special occasions, such as Christmas, we'd fuss and brush each other's hair until shiny and most of the waves from the braids slightly softened. Mommi finished by pulling the hair straight back from our forehead, secured with a clip, so a large bow that matched our dresses was tied, the finishing touch. Mommi worked hard to make us white crisp pinafores, with ruffles along the side of the opening by the shoulders down to the waist, with a large bow in the back. These pinafores were worn over hand-me-down dresses. Every two years or so Grete was fitted for a new dress when she outgrew it and it was handed down until the dress fit me. That year my dress was pink. I peeked as Mommi ironed them, and they hung in a row on hooks. The pink was the smallest, so I knew it was mine.

Mommi called for breakfast. We opened the door and there it was. Sometime last evening, the Christmas tree was decorated. Perhaps Nanna stayed and helped too. The most beautiful Christmas tree I ever saw. So much glitter. I stared with my mouth half open and just couldn't get enough of the beautiful view. Susi kept tugging at me, "Come already, Mommi is waiting," she said. Christmas morning we indulged in coffee cake. This morning it was cherry coffee cake. It was so delicious. The sugar oozed out of the uneven parts of the cake. Hot milk with a bit of strong coffee for flavour with lots of sugar was served. I didn't like milk, hot or cold, but the cake made up for it. Mommi cut the pieces so large that when offered another piece I felt one was more than enough for me.

Back in our rooms, the beds had to be made. I was barely tall enough to reach halfway across my bed to straighten the duvet. My little hands pulled and fussed with the duvet, just to have to start all over again. My sisters took pity on me at times and came to help. When I looked at any one of them with this pouty helpless look on my face they gave in and came to help. Mommi's strict orders to get ready with our underclothes, also meant clean hands and face. After checking each other's leggings to make sure they looked straight, we walked out into the hall where Mommi finished dressing us with our outer clothes. One by one, our dresses carefully held and slipped over our heads. The pinafores, so crisp and white, after slipping our arms through completed the outfit. The bow for our hair with long ribbons of the matching color as the pinafores was the finished look.

Oh, how I loved my pink dress. I slid my hands up and down the fabric, I loved that slippery feel. We thanked our Mother for the pinafores, for we thought that was our Christmas gift. As we were admiring each other's dresses, Hans Onkel let it slip, and said something about a toy. "Kristkindl is bringing us a toy, is she?" Our anxious pleas were beginning to upset our Mother. Oma finally spoke up and said to her daughter, "Nah, Kati, see how happy they are. Why don't you give them a present? Please, come on, I beg you."

The anticipation of getting a toy never changed from year to year. Up to now, we were told next year, every year, but had never received one yet. The excitement, the heart pounding out of our chests and the glow in our eyes, was heart-warming. Finally, Mommi, with a deep sigh, observing our anticipation had no choice but to give in and say, "Okay, okay I'll go and get them." We immediately ran to the couch, like the regimented children we were, and sat in a row, Grete on one end and me on the other. With our hands in our laps, and our legs together, we patiently waited for our Mother to return.

After a few minutes, Mother came in with two long boxes on her arms. Hans Onkel was behind her carrying two more, the boxes large and slender and different colors. Mother bent over Grete and placed the box in her hands. "Thank you, Mommi," Grete said. Mommi moved over one step to Susi, then to *Medi*, (our nickname for Therezia) and then it was my turn. After all the thankyous were said, we untied the bows and opened the boxes. Oh, my, what a beautiful doll! Our dolls were in different colors of clothing, mine a beautiful soft pink. I was speechless, oh, the doll was so beautiful. I was beside myself. Hans Onkel, Oma and Mommi were sitting across from us, observing our reaction, for this wonderful and generous gift. Mother didn't want to spoil us, and she didn't.

"Take good care of your dolls," she added as we excused ourselves and headed for our rooms. I however was so happy with my Mother that I turned back and gave my Mother a quick kiss. Although we didn't kiss often in our family, it felt right. When I returned to my room, my sister was already playing with her doll. I sat on my bed with my box beside me, I started to undo the bow and opened the box, and there she was. The most beautiful doll I had ever imagined. I slid my fingers behind her head and gently took her out of her box. The *porzelan* head (porcelain), the eyes brown just like mine, and pink lips, rosy cheeks and long dark eyelashes, with hands so dainty and porzelan too. Oh, what a gorgeous outfit she wore. I moved the jacket to the side, which was pink brocade. A white blouse made from lace fabric under the jacket, a long skirt and even underwear, socks, shoes and gloves. Her body felt soft and flexible, and all body parts moved.

I found out many years later that Mommi and Hans Onkel worked very hard to save the money to buy these dolls. Our Mother worked in a brick factory, just outside the city limits. The work was hard, especially in the summer, for the temperature was not only extremely hot and humid outside but inside where the bricks were fired, the heat was unbearable. Mommi left early in the morning way before we girls woke for our day. It was unusual for a woman to work outside the home at that time, but being divorced and on her own, gave Mommi no choice but to make money elsewhere. Hans Onkel worked for a farmer as often as he could. Hans Onkel had health problems, and was not well enough to keep a full time job. And of course our Oma tended to the housework. Our house was so clean most of the time, with Oma down on her hands and knees scrubbing the floors often.

Every night, I carefully laid my doll next to me. First, I'd look and admire her, then talk to her, then hug and kiss her; till we closed our eyes together and we fell asleep. Every morning my doll laid in my arms exactly as I placed her the night before, I lifted her up over my face and said good morning and placed a kiss on her cheek. I lingered on with this warm feeling with my new doll and loved mornings.

A week later, Susi and Medi were already playing in the hallway when I joined them. Dressing and undressing our brand new dolls. I never tired of repeating the same play for hours. The rays of a January sun streaming into the French door and the warmth of a winter's afternoon made playing very peaceful for me. In between our play with our dolls and talking to each other we became aware of Mommi and Hans Onkel still pacing the floor. It definitely gave me some concern and I wondered why? Children pick up on these things, especially when more and more often words of war surfaced, but of course I didn't know what that meant.

I was quickly distracted when Oma called me to come to the kitchen. My feet froze, as I heard a loud crunch from the direction of the French door. Hans Onkel stepped on my doll's head. My body paralysed for a moment and my face filled with pain. My eyes full of tears, I stepped closer and closer to my doll. With my hands over my mouth and looking down, I saw my doll's head broken. My heart dropped as I stared and bent over my doll. My tears so thick, I could hardly see. I picked my doll from the floor, sobbing as I held my doll close to my heart. Hans Onkel kneeled next to me and apologized. "I am so sorry Käthe, I didn't mean to do it." I didn't hear my Uncle's pleas, except my own cries of pain. Hans Onkel picked me up and held me tightly in his arms. He kept wiping my tears and stroking my hair. "Please stop crying Käthe, please, I will try to fix the doll," he whispered in my ear. I managed to nod my head just a little. I couldn't stop the constant flow of tears until much later. Hans Onkel held me in his arms until I fell asleep on his chest.

When I woke the next morning, my doll laid next to me tucked in my arm. Hans Onkel did the best that he could to glue the head back together, but my beautiful doll didn't look the same. For the longest time that morning in bed I lay and asked myself the never ending question,"Why did I leave her, why?" I silently started to cry again. Although my doll didn't look the same as before, it didn't hold me back from playing endlessly with my sisters. Only once in awhile as my finger stroked over the cracks and I watched my sisters play with their perfect dolls, I became sad, and wished, and wished.

My Mother's lack of concern for my feelings was obvious when comments of blame surfaced. I heard Mommi say to Oma, "Well, she shouldn't have left the doll lying in the hallway." Oma came to my defence and quickly reminded my Mother, "She's only four years old, Kati. Besides, she was obeying and only followed my orders. You know she listens so well." It became troublesome to me and made me withdraw. My Mother a strict Mother and on many occasions my Grandmother talked on our behalf trying to change our Mother's mind about being so hard on us girls. My Mother never actually hit me. For punishment she made me kneel on corn in the corner for a certain amount of time, probably only fifteen minutes or so, but it seemed forever to me. I didn't mind the punishment as much as the embarrassment that I minded more. It meant I was bad, the corner was bad, and that I committed a sin.

But, when Mommi was patient with me, took my hand and we walked together into the city and stopped at the bakery for a treat, a piece of delicious torte, or a *Sladele* (sherbet), instantly life was normal again, forgiven and forgotten.

That winter was a tragic time for our family, especially our Mother. Apparently, when we girls played in the snow, we forgot our red ball in the yard, the ball visible from the French door. That evening my sister, Medi, somehow in her nightgown and no shoes, went outside to retrieve the ball. Sometime later, Mommi found Medi outside the door, lying in the snow, cold and shivering. Our Mother never could figure out how she opened that door, but somehow she did. What actually happened remained unknown to us.

The next morning, we were told not to disturb Medi for she was sick and needed to rest. After a few days, I was allowed to see her. She stretched her hand out to me; she felt so warm and looked so pale. We didn't talk much, and Medi soon fell asleep and I left the room. Medi was sick for a week or so and Mommi spent a lot of time in her bedroom, with damp towels periodically taken in and out of her room. Medi's condition worsened, and when the doctor finally came, it was too late. Medi died that winter.

The mood in the house was so different. I remember Mommi, Hans Onkel and Oma standing with their backs by the wood stove. All I heard, their cries and tears running down their faces. Confused, I pulled on my Mother's dress and asked why they were crying. She didn't answer or pay any attention to me, so I turned away and sat on my wooden chair close by sitting on my hands, staring and just observing. Mommi's voice broken and could hardly get the words out as she grabbed her brother's hand and asked him this question. "Please Hans, we need to tell Joshi, he should know, he'll want to come to the funeral." Their crying made me feel uncomfortable, and I didn't like the feeling in the house. Mother was on edge with everyone, and I wondered why.

Hours later, a tall, dark, good looking man entered and stood in the doorway. Mommi and the man greeted each other with a quick hello. After a bit of silence, the tall man asked my Mother, "Is this little Käthe?" "Yes." my Mother answered. I watched his every move as he slowly walked over to me. He picked me up in silence and held me for a while. Without a word he leaned over and placed a kiss on my forehead. He lingered with his eyes a little longer, and then gently put me down.

I found out many years later that the tall man was my Father. As it turned out it would be one of only two times I saw my Father, and each time, I didn't even know it.

The funeral was extremely sad, but for me a big confusion and I didn't understand. It was not only cold outside, but the black colors worn that day, reflected the mood of sad feelings. A procession of relatives and neighbours walked behind our Mother. Hans Onkel told me later for our Mother did not let us girls go along for she felt it was too cold and way too sad. Leading the procession was the priest with a large cross and two altar boys. It was mostly silent, except for the crunching of the snow and the cries of sorrow. When they came to a stop, the prayers began with the priest and then everyone joined in. Mommi held a hankie in her hand, sobbing, listening to everyone around her doing the same. Oma, Hans Onkel and Mommi were clutching to each other with extreme sorrow faces as they opened the gate to our Courtyard. I was glad when they arrived home, for I was worried, tired and wanted to sleep.

Another tradition for families in mourning was a black band about two inches wide worn on the arm above the elbow for one year. Dark clothing, along with a dark babuschka for ladies, and dark brimmed hats for men, especially for the older grownups, was worn as well. Going down any street, we always knew, we had to be extra friendly to people like that, even if we didn't know them. It meant respect to the dead. So Mommi, Hans

Onkel and Oma wore these bands it seemed forever. Usually children our age didn't wear these bands and were not expected to follow this tradition yet.

Spring finally came. The exterior of our modest home, small in size, beige stucco design with brown trim around the windows, the houses close together, with the sidewalk adjacent to the house with a wrought iron fence around the entire property. Houses had stucco siding, so they could be painted often and kept clean. The French door opened up to the long porch in the back of the house. The porch was as long as the entire house, with an overhang that was supported by several large pillars. The four foot stucco wall enclosed the porch. From the porch we directly walked down a step into the courtyard. The back yard consisted of packed down dirt with grass growing here and there. A homemade chicken wire that was held together with posts for strength, kept the chickens, geese and ducks in one area in the back. On the opposite side a weathered little woodshed, the outhouse, stood alone.

Next to the old cherry tree our wrought iron gate with a circular and curved pattern, was strong, and black in color and the only entrance to our house. I remember the gate well, but it was the porch where the family gathered every evening, that I remember most, especially when the wide ledges lined up on the porch with flower pots filled with red and white geraniums and greens of ivy hanging down the wall, an absolutely beautiful sight.

It was a time to perhaps ponder over the future, and what it might hold for our family. Our evenings out on the porch became my most relaxing time of day. It was a time to talk, to laugh, to cry, to dream, and just to have fun, wind down, and just be a kid listening to family talk before bed. Oh, and that sweet gentle smell filled the air from the big old cherry tree in full bloom, made the nostrils suck in breaths so deep, that it filled every part of the body and made daydreaming effortless.

That spring was my turn to visit Nanna. Every one of my

sisters had their turn already, except for me. Mother thought I was too young to stay overnight with anyone. But Nanna wouldn't take no for an answer. So, reluctantly Mommi arranged the day and time with Nanna. It seemed we took forever, but we finally arrived at Nanna's gate. The sidewalk leading up to the house was so narrow that we walked in single file with Mommi in front, and I followed. The air filled with a unique powerful scent which I knew to be roses that grew all along the sidewalk and in the flower bed in front of the house, with every color possible. I had to be careful to walk in the middle, for the thorns, if allowed to come near, hurt.

Nanna stood on the porch, waiting to greet us. When we reached the steps, my Mother handed me the small cloth bag, and in an irritated voice she said to me, "I expect you to remember your manners and wash your feet before bed. Do you hear me?" Before I could answer her, she walked away, and I along with Nanna waved goodbye to Mommi, as she disappeared around the neighbour's house.

Nanna took my bag from me and walked to the guestroom with me behind her. It was my first time here.

Oh, but Nanna's house was so fancy, I thought. Not at all like our house. Nanna's voice soft and I liked the way she talked to me. She made me feel special. "Now Käthe", she said, "I want to make you feel comfortable, so come and sit here." She picked me up and sat me on the piano stool next to her. "I know you have a good singing voice, let me play a song, and then we will sing together. Okay, Sweetie?" I nodded with my head, yes. We had an absolute wonderful afternoon and evening. We played a board game called *Mensch ärger dich nicht* (The game of Sorry), a challenging game that I enjoyed very much. I even won a few games. Nanna also made chicken paprikasch, with dumplings, so delicious, and a thick slice of bread to dunk in the red paprika juice, very satisfying.

When evening came and it was time to go to bed, I remembered everything Mommi told me. I washed my feet, my face and my hands. Nanna stood by my bed waiting for me, with my nightgown in her hands. "Käthe you are a very good girl and you have good manners, I like that," she said, slipping the nightgown over my head. As she undid my braids and brushed my long hair, she asked, "Would you like to come back again sometime, Käthe?" Without hesitation my answer was yes. Nanna noticed the sad look on my face, "Don't worry, I will talk to your Mother, okay, my child." She stroked my cheek and I felt her warmth. The bed was so high that a stool was needed to jump on the bed. Nanna waited for me to jump up and lay myself in the middle of the bed so she could tuck and cover the duvet around my body. "Now don't you fall out of this bed, she laughed," as she said that. She kissed my forehead and walked to her own bed, which was in the next room, and left the door open just a crack.

The bed so white and the sheets so slippery, oh I liked that feeling. I said my prayer and ended with blessing my whole family, especially this night and I fell asleep. The morning came too soon for we barely finished breakfast and started to play when Mommi knocked at the door. Mommi didn't like it that I wasn't happy about going home. Mommi scolded me on the way home. I withdrew and said nothing. Nanna was the only relative that our Mother spoke to after the divorce. Perhaps Mother felt uncomfortable around Nanna, because Nanna was a sophisticated woman, and our Mother was not.

On many evenings our porch turned into a gathering of neighbours. It was not unusual for several languages to be spoken; Hungarian, Serbian and our dialect of German, Schwovisch. Communicating in these three languages was normal in everyday living used without effort. Folks discussed war and politics for hours, with many different conflicting opinions. Old men sat on benches, smoking their long pipes and discussing politics for hours on end. It was a way of life, those afternoons when we played out in front of our house, knowing that someone knew at all times of our whereabouts. Having a wooden homemade bench in front of our house became a place to not only rest in between play on lazy afternoons, but a chance to watch various birds. The turtle dove was a regular, always busy looking for food on the ground while making a humming sound. From time to time I observed another bird. This bird, somehow awkward looking, white and large, especially the wing span. The bird sat on a high post for hours without moving, perhaps this is why I watched when it finally did fly from one post to another, my head turning and following every inch of that flight. Mother explained to me that the bird was large because it brought babies into the world and flew to different houses to deliver babies and was named *The Storch.* (stork). I was fascinated with this bird and believed this delightful explanation for quite some time.

For centuries in Kikinda, located in the regent of Banat in the north upper section of Jugoslavia, our neighbours lived in harmony, trading goods, such as fruits and vegetables, and cattle and much more. Most folks grew their own vegetables. Some traded their crops for goods needed that they didn't have, like fabric, machinery or other goods. The area around our city was entirely farmland, with agricultural villages nearby working and cultivating every available inch of fertile ground. Wood of any kind was scarce, for I don't remember seeing a forest or clumps of trees ever. Most homesteads planted only fruit trees in their yards. Ornamental trees, such as linden or agazi (locust) trees grew along streets on both sides all the way into our city. The land as far as the eye could see was totally flat. Although our family did not farm anymore like our Grandparents, we did own enough land to plant a garden that grew every vegetable possible. I learned to eat different vegetables such as celery root. Mommi grated this root and made a salad similar to our coleslaw. My Mother also planted our own poppies for her poppy seed strudel. These small black seeds when harvested were stored in tins in a cool place until needed. Before Mommi used these little seeds for strudel, they had to be crushed by a machine that was only used for this one purpose. The poppies for baking were large and full of seeds, entirely different than the miles and miles of poppies in the fields that grew in between the wheat and barley. These poppies were of no use other than the beauty and splendour to the eye, especially when the wind gently moved the heads back and forth. Although the red color was dominant, white poppies did show through here and there.

I don't remember my Mother ever shopping for anything, except the occasional bag of sugar, flour and coffee. Oma made homemade soap on a regular basis. When the fat that couldn't be used for cooking was collected she made enough soap to last for a few months. The thick paste that looked milky was poured in a tray that had sections of a certain size. When it hardened the soap turned light beige, and cut into pieces. It was used for doing laundry and for hygienic purposes. The soap was slippery and lasted a long time.

Our neighbours sometimes referred to us as family. Every household spoke their Mother tongue, but out on the street, our family spoke these three languages fluently. Neighbours took pride in helping each other whenever the need arose, equally sharing happiness and sorrow. On an everyday basis, now these talks of war grew louder and louder with every week that passed. I, of course did not understand. We girls felt the tension around us but all we knew that something was different.

I remember on Sundays going to Mass with clean crisp clothes on and my little prayer book in my hand walking a fair distance with my sisters beside me and Hans Onkel not too far behind us. Mother didn't come with us on a regular basis but taught us to pray every night, although she herself didn't believe in regular church going. In our Church the children all sat in the front pews with parents and grownups further back. I loved the spicy, aromatic smell that was distinctly used only in church. When the *Glinglbeidel* (offering basket) was passed, we took turns with our one coin for the family. It was an honour to be the one that dropped the coin in this velvety pouch which was connected to a long handle. Going to Church every Sunday with my family was not only a good feeling but has been an enduring spirituality that has lasted throughout my life.

By now I turned six years old and quite interested in learning new things. I couldn't go to school yet, like my sisters, but one thing I could learn was to knit, like Grete, I thought. Mother praised Grete often, so maybe she could teach me how to knit when she came home from school. But before that could be done strands of wool had to be rolled into one big ball. I sat outside in the porch, with *Bengy* (our dog) snuggling next to me for hours practicing how to knit, pearl and straight stitches. Bengy, with his silky white hair, I loved to pet him and stroked him and told him every day that I loved him. Being alone most of the day Bengy became my playmate. We played for hours in the courtyard. He was a frisky dog, and had even more energy than I. Sometimes, we both fell to the ground and it seemed that meant he could lick me all over my face. I tried to turn my head every which way, but he was fast.

Finally the time came when I attempted to knit a pair of socks for myself. Winter was coming, and my feet usually cold, it seemed a perfect project. With Grete's help I could do it, I reassured myself. After some time of knitting with four needles, I reached the heel. It looked really good. I was proud of myself. My Mother didn't say much, except reminded me to finish whatever I started. Grete gave me instruction after school or the night before to keep me going for the day. It was time for the heel, and I was convinced I remembered everything Grete told me.

When Grete came home from school that afternoon and took a look at my sock she started to laugh. I became angry and lashed out at her, and hit her. I also threw my knitting to the ground. Mother appeared out of nowhere. She wasted no time, and hit me, hard. I was so hurt and surprised, for she never hit me before. I ran under the cherry tree and wet myself. I was crying so hard that I was gasping for air. My Oma not far away, scolded my Mother. "What are you doing hitting this child, shame on you Kati." Oma rushed over to me. "Come, my child," she said, and she took my hand and walked me to the house. Oma washed me down and put clean clothes on but nothing, not even Oma's caring nature, could take away the violated feeling I felt towards my Mother.

In the next few days, my distance and cold actions towards my Mother became noticeable. I avoided eye contact and did not talk to my Mother for a few days. But, when Mother had enough of my silent treatment and the days became normal and Mommi looked me straight in the eyes, and started imitating me and made a pouty face just like mine, I didn't want to give in, but I'd end up cracking a little smile, and then into a laugh, the heart softened, and once again I was happy. Mommi took me in her lap, and stroked my hair, and kissed me to make it all better and reminded me not to be so sensitive.

One evening, I couldn't fall asleep; I heard Oma and Mommi talking. At first I thought it was only family talk, but when my name came up, I heard more. They spoke of their concern, mainly of my sensitivity, "She is, (meaning me) very observant and understands right from wrong very well, for her age, be careful what you say to her," my Oma warned my Mother. I was troubled, and didn't like hearing this criticism, and became resentful of the opinion they had of me. And once again, I said nothing, and became withdrawn.

The cherries, one of our favourite fruit, had now ripened to a deep red color. Time to pick and we knew what that meant. Some of the fruit was taken to the market for money. The rest canned for the winter months. But picking and eating from the tree, was definitely the most fun. In the season of this delicious fruit, a traditional meal was prepared from scratch. My Grandmother started this meal in the morning when the house was empty and everyone left for the day and we were alone, just me and her, she started the dough. "Come and watch," she said, "so you can make strudel someday for your family." Oma started working the dough. It looked like a lot of work to me. After the dough rested for some time underneath the bowl, it was then transferred to a white tablecloth that Oma beforehand laid over a medium size table. The fat was melted and dribbled on the dough. I was so proud to help. The fun began as Oma and I started pulling the dough from underneath, until it reached over the entire table's edge and paper thin. The edges of the dough twirled around our hand and pulled off. The left over dough was used later for dumplings for soup. We both stood back for a moment and admired this work of art, especially when it stayed intact without a single tear. Oma explained to me that if the air in the house was warm, the easier the dough stretched. The squeezed pitted cherries, sugar and roasted breadcrumbs arranged evenly on the dough. Now it was time to roll up and bake. This procedure repeated at least four to five times.

By the time the strudel was completed it was lunchtime and we were hungry. "Well," Oma said, "we have to try this strudel, don't you think Käthe." I laughed and said, "Of course, Oma." With a devilish smile on her face, she added, "We have to taste it so we know if it is good enough for the rest of the family." When the strudel cooled, Oma cut two large pieces and placed them on a plate. With a well earned drink in one hand and the plate in another, we headed out to the porch. The sweet syrup from the cherries melting in my mouth, oh, so delicious, it was torture to wait till supper to have some more.

"Well, Käthe," Oma said, "now we will peel the potatoes for some soup. Okay?" "Yes, Oma", I said as I was quite happy to learn and pitch in, while I peeled the potatoes, Oma sautéed the onions. Just before serving time, the leftover dough from the strudel, was pulled in small pieces then added to make dumplings, gave the soup additional flavour and also thickened the broth. This time with my Grandmother, having quality time together, having fun and teaching me not only to cook traditional recipes, but just talking together, for we were not a kissing family, but a pat on the back and a squeeze here and there, enough to last forever.

With the table set, and when everyone had taken their seats, Oma and I served the soup. I was so proud, for I helped with this delicious meal. After everyone's plate was full of soup, Oma and I sat down. Talking was not encouraged during our meals, so you could hear the scraping of the spoons loudly. The exceptional taste of the strudel made us smack our lips, and "mmm, mmm," was heard often. After cleaning up and doing the dishes, it was time to gather in the porch. But now, we held our stomachs, for all of the strudel was gone. Worth every bite, we all agreed. We looked forward to having this meal from season to season.

In our house, dessert was not served daily. As a treat, instead of candy, we sucked on a stick of wood which came from one of our trees in the backyard. Mommi cut the brown pieces of spindles carefully they came from the root part of the tree, not the branches. The tree was small in size and was never to be climbed on, strict orders. The piece of wood was pencil thin and had a flavour of vanilla. For hours I'd sit on one of the low branches of the cherry tree and sucked on this spindle of wood. Sugar in our house was used sparingly. Honey, especially clover honey was mostly used in cooking, of course on a slice of bread as well. Honey was also used in hot tea to nurse a cold along with a wool sock wrapped snugly around our neck until the cold was gone. This was a tradition in our house that we continued all our lives.

We lived a simple way of life in the 1940s. Perhaps folks were content with the same routine day in and day out. My Mother did not have luxuries like facial creams, so she used her creativity and knowledge of plants. Mommi used cucumber peels and rubbed the wet part all over her face every time she made cucumber salad for supper. On occasion Mommi scared us when she placed slices of cucumber on her eyes. She looked spooky. As far as travelling was concerned, it was almost nonexistent. First of all it was very costly, so our family could not afford it. Dressing up for Church, Name Sake Day and special holidays, such as Christmas we looked forward to and planned for with excitement for days. We enjoyed the beauty of nature, took pride in growing the biggest, most fragrant roses, carnations, sweet williams and blue cornflowers, the same for growing vegetables .I remember folks standing together for hours and discussing their crops, giving each other advice on their new discoveries. As long as there was food on the table and water to drink, Mommi often said "What more do we need?" Safety up to now was never a concern, so we continued as children do, noticing and observing.

That summer our gate had to be locked nightly. Our usual visits from neighbours needed to be announced. We girls were told when visitors came to the gate, to get our Mother first, before letting anyone in. Our gate was never locked before, and visitors always welcome. I didn't understand. However, one afternoon, as I held on to the bars of the gate, I saw several soldiers walking holding guns, on the opposite side of the street. I didn't say anything to my family, but instead, every day I went to the gate to check it out.

Many afternoons, when the sun was high in the middle of the sky, we'd find a cool place, preferably underneath a tree and played *Butsch, Butsch, Bodeloch.* This game we played with mud. Two of us made a team, and of course our dog, our constant companion, also stood around and watched. A paste of mud was made with earth and water for consistency, like pie dough, which was placed in one hand and worked to make a round disk about 3" wide and 1/2" thick. Then in the middle of the disk, we'd spit. With the arm up high, hugging the disc in the palm, we would throw the disc to the ground. If the disc split in the middle and burst, a perfect shot. After a throw, we'd gather around and observe the shape and size of the hole, before a winner was declared. The skill of *Butsch, Butsch, Bodeloch,* surpassed any toy. We didn't know it then, but only in that region of the world was the earth of perfect consistency to make this seasonal sport fun and never boring. We were never able to duplicate it in other places we lived. Playing tag was just for something to do. Great exercise filled our day and helped to make us competitive.

It was a fruitful year in 1943. The apricots were large and juicy. What wasn't sold or eaten was canned or cooked into jam. On warm afternoons for a midday snack we were given a slice of homemade crusty bread with a thick layer of jam on top. While the jam was still warm, that treat by far surpassed any other food for me. Harvesting everything from the garden became endless work for my family. We girls were expected to help with vegetables, such as beans and peas. Most of the housework rested on my Oma's shoulders, for Mother worked at the brick factory at least four days a week. Mommi's hours were long, many times the day ended for us before Mommi returned.

My Oma was a woman of strong bones, round face, and naturally round cheeks. Her blue eyes were large and clear with hardly any eyebrows which gave her face a certain character. The deep lines around the mouth and cheeks, a sure sign of being in the sun all the time, proved that her face and hands never experienced the luxury of creams; rather she took pride in hard work. She wore a full skirt, which reached all the way down to her ankles with a white, crisp apron on top. I remember so well, she'd hang on to the apron with her right hand and swang it back and forth. By the time evening came along the apron proved that a lot of work was done, for the apron was not white anymore. Her long brown hair, with very little silver showing through pushed back from her face, tightly braided and twisted around into a bun in the back of her head. I never saw my Grandmother with a different look. What I liked most about my Oma, definitely her warm blue eyes. Her bountiful body would embrace my small frame and I'd lose myself in her gentleness and warmth.

The peas, beans, cucumbers and beets now neatly stacked in glass jars and preserved to store in the cellar. Garlic braided and hung on rafters. Onions stored in wooden crates. To keep carrots and parsnips for months, moistened sand in wooden containers was used. Stacks of cut up cabbage placed in large crocks to make sauerkraut, with leaves of cabbage placed in between rows of kraut and ready to use for cabbage rolls. The crock was closed with a piece of wood large enough to cover the opening. A brick or two on top to keep the crock sealed, till perfectly cured.

The interior of our house was of simple style and modest furnishings, but clean and comfortable. To the right of the French door was a large long bench. It was the bench where we sat and put our shoes on and also stored our shoes underneath when we entered the house. Above the bench a brown long piece of wood with many hooks. This is where our hats hung in the summer and our warm clothes in the winter. A large opening with a cloth curtain pulled to one side was the entrance to our kitchen. The kitchen, a modest room with a wood stove, a large basin, and a small butcher block table, the table, uneven with many cuts and cracks, where all the preparations of our daily meals were prepared. As I looked in, the appearance of the kitchen looked clean and white and adjacent to the kitchen, our eating room. In the middle of the room, a wood table of timeless design sat, strong and plain. The wall, except for a long bench which was used as a standby for extra seating when company came, was bare.

At the end of a long hallway hung a large family portrait, with individual pictures, with Mommi in the middle, Grete on top, the twins on each side, and me on the bottom. Dressed in our holiday outfits of matching pinafores, and of course bows in our hair, grouped together in one intricate golden frame. The portrait must have been taken just before Medi died. Many years later, Mommi told me how hard it was for her to look at that picture every day. Medi looked so healthy and happy. "Oh the hardest of all," Mommi confided in me as she started to cry on the only occasion she let me see her feelings, "I couldn't go in her room for months."

Past the French door on the left, the bedrooms all in a row. The bedrooms had large ledges on every window to sit on. I especially enjoyed those afternoons, instead of taking a nap, I'd sit on the window sill with the warm rays of sunshine and soft wind blowing and moving the white lace curtains back and forth, with me in the middle of it all pretending to be a princess. I could daydream for hours. When my name was called from the other side of the door, it became an intrusion to me. On many occasions, I ran to my bed and pretended to be asleep, just to gain a few more minutes to dream.

My room, furnished with two single beds, a little pot underneath the bed for night time use only in white porzelan. On my bed laid a soft white thick feather duvet, a square fluffy pillow that rested against the headboard, and a small wooden cabinet in between the beds, with a basin of water on top. I didn't have a closet as such, but a wooden stand that held my few dresses in perfect shape. Drawers, well more like a box with a lid, where I stored my underwear. It wasn't much but we managed quite well. Mommi didn't allow candles in our room, but that didn't seem to be a problem. When the moon shone in our window, we managed to get around well. Privacy in our house was important, so it just made it easier for us to undress in the dark.

In early spring, three goats arrived at our gate. One for each one of us, Mommi told us to raise and play with. Oh, what joy, they were so small and loveable. One had little tassels hanging by the neck, the one we all wanted and argued over. I'd hang on to the neck of the goat with one hand, and used my other hand to fight Bengy off from licking my entire face. We girls had so much fun, playing with our goats and dog. Oma told me this story about our Mother which I loved hearing.

Oma started, "When your Mommi was just a child, she brought home every stray animal that she could find. Every week or so she just happened to find a stray somewhere in the neighbourhood, and of course brought the animal home, and

29

nursed the animal back to health. "Did she ever keep any?" I questioned Oma. "Of course what do you think? But, her real love was horses. Oma leaned over to me and with pride she said. "She was called by some in the area the horse whisperer." When anyone in the neighbourhood had a problem with taming a horse and they couldn't do it, your Mommi was called. Yup, she was that good," Oma said. So perhaps, this was the reason we were allowed to have animals as pets. I could tell Mommi loved animals, because she taught us to be kind and gentle to our pets.

That September Hans Onkel made plans to butcher a pig. It was a big occasion, when preparations for the long winter had to be made. The day of the delivery finally came, as usual on a Saturday and neighbours and friends came to help. The farmer delivered the pig alive, up to our gate. Oh what a commotion it was. Hans Onkel had a rope around the pig's neck and tried to pull this heavy animal past the courtyard into the back yard. The pig was huge. Our Oma stood by the entrance of the porch, "This pig has lots of fat, which we need for cooking." Our Mother nodded her head with agreement. My sisters and I could do nothing but watch. Mommi yelled and told us to close the gate to the porch, and make sure that our dog Bengy was with us.

The pig must have known its fate, because the squealing became louder with every moment. Mother was holding the rope now and Oma had another rope around the body. The circling of this large animal continued until hopefully it would tire soon and drop. Oma fell a few times. The pig strong, kept fighting, and showing little sign of giving up. By now a few neighbours came by to relieve Oma and Mother. The pig moved slower, the end in sight. Just then I looked over to Hans Onkel and he held the largest knife I had ever seen, the blade pointy and sharp. I looked away, but my curiosity made me turn back. The movement of the pig went on for a while, and then all of a sudden the pig dropped on its side. Hans Onkel and a neighbour leaped on top of the pig and the knife went into the air. At that very moment I turned away. I heard the loudest squeal, as I held my ears closed with my fingers and squeezed my eyes tightly so I wouldn't see anything. While a lot of scuffling went on and then, silence.

In a circle around the pig everyone stood, looking down, except for Mother. Mother was busy holding a bowl by the neck of the pig, to collect the blood that was gushing out. On the outside stove, Oma sautéed onions in a large cast iron pan. We could smell it all the way to the porch. Hans Onkel motioned with his arm for us to come out of the locked porch. "It is safe now," he said joyfully. It took all the grownups to move the pig to the area that was set up for the butchering.

On that evening we had fried onions and blood, which was considered by some a real delicacy. It was so good. Homemade bread and wine was enjoyed with this special snack. Even we children were allowed to drink wine. Drinking alcohol in our family was not a usual weekly habit, but today seemed different. Although we stored wine in our cellar, for a bottle to be opened for dinner was rare.

A celebration of song and dancing and much laughter carried through until the early morning. The accordion player was plenty loud enough for everyone to hear. I never saw my Mother and Oma dance before like they did that evening. I watched my Mother lead my Grandmother across the courtyard with movements of grace and style and in perfect step with the music. It made me extremely happy. At one point Mommi lost her *schlappe* (slipper) and without missing a beat continued the waltz barefoot. I realized quickly that dancing was not just in the feet, Mommi's hips moved back and forth with ease and it was attractive to watch. Mommi also knew the words to the song and sang every word of *Rote Rosen, Rote Lippen und Roter Wein* **(Red Roses, Red Lips and Red Wine).** It appeared my Mother had a happy side to her that I truly enjoyed. It was heart-warming for me as my Mother grabbed my hand and started twirling me around and taught me to dance a waltz. The happiness and laughter between neighbours and our family that evening was a vision, unforgettable. Bengy, our white long haired dog joined in too, especially the hopping part. I loved that kind of joy, not the butchering part, mind you.

For supper, Mother served sausages, mustard, sauerkraut and potato salad, with of course good hearty homemade bread. It was mouth watering, it was that good. The time had come and we had to say our goodnights and rushed off to bed. We complained and begged to stay up a little longer but our Mother stood firm and wouldn't give in to our pleas. We wanted this night to last a little longer, especially my older sisters. After our evening prayer is the first time I heard one of my sisters speak ill of our Mother.

This celebration took place every year, with neighbours helping each other until everyone in the neighbourhood had their butchering done for the winter. We girls, however, remained at home with Oma when Hans Onkel and Mother went to help neighbours. In the weeks that followed, our family made strings of sausages, some put in the smokehouse and some left to eat fresh, either way, a different taste but, equally delicious. Ham also smoked and hung in the cellar, ready to eat in the long winter months. The fat near the skin from the pig cooked down to make lard. The part of the fat with bits of meat, we cooked down separately and called Kramle, something special, a standard food that was enjoyed by everyone. The taste of Kramle, with a salty crunchy feeling to the texture, a classic food, for we never tired of eating it every week. Bits of Kramle stored in glass jars, stayed fresh for a long time. For supper, Kramle, a piece of bread and pickles was enjoyed on many occasions throughout the winter.

From one pig the cooked down lard, poured in a large crock, lasted all season. We didn't have butter, so the lard was used for everything, from spreading on bread, cooking and baking. Only for special cookies, Mommi bought butter. Even though a bakery was nearby, our family made our own bread. Only once in a while for buns, Mommi and I strolled down to the bakery together, and if Mommi was in a good mood, a Sladele in the summer or a piece of torte or squares in the winter was enjoyed by the two of us.

Along with the ham and sausages, a slab of bacon in one piece called speck, was cured, smoked and hung on rafters. We enjoyed this delicacy all year because it was smoked and didn't need refrigeration which we did not have back then. It was practical and delicious. Even on a hot summer day, speck, with a thick slice of bread, along with red ripened tomatoes and peppers from the garden, made a satisfying meal. When the watermelons and cantaloupes ripened and they were dropped into the deep well to cool before eating, my sisters and I ate this fruit every chance we had, with the juice running down all over our faces. The cracking sound when cutting meant a ripe and sweet melon. These melons were exceptionally sweet and large in size.

Before the winter a traditional celebration was held. It was to reap the hard work of the harvest of the season. It was now time to enjoy our labour of love, which began in early spring with the planting season and ended late into the fall with harvesting everything possible. You could say it was our Thanksgiving, like we celebrate in America and Canada. With the fruits, vegetables and meats stored away for the winter, it was now fitting to take some well earned time to celebrate. This celebration was called Peter and Paul Fest.

The Fest took place at the edge of the city in a large field. I remember walking on stubbles, for the field was now cut. In the summertime these fields grew poppies in between the wheat and corn by the thousands.The main attraction for the day had already begun in early afternoon. Young men and boys scouted about to find sticks, corn husks and logs to build a heaping pile of wood to be burned, the main attraction. When the pile reached about six feet, it was time to arrange tables and chairs in a circle. Everyone brought their favourite food. Many different recipes were exchanged from year to year. Something I looked forward to every year was actually not food, but a raspberry soda, something special. Only once a year I could enjoy this treat.

When the sun started to disappear and the cool wind in the air set in, the fire was lit. As the paper ignited the fine brush underneath the pile, it made a roaring sound with the crackling of the wood taking hold and the flames in no time at all shot up to the sky. The children stood around the fire with awe and excitement in our faces, including my sisters and me. The fire soon calmed down to red and yellow coals, and that's when the fun began. In the field, games of all different kinds were played, from soccer to handball to lawn bowling. But when the young men and boys took turns jumping over the mountain of flames, I became excited. Each time they landed their feet on the other side, a loud roar could be heard from the crowd.

One of our neighbouring young men took my hand "do you want to jump over this fire with us, Käthe, do you?" Well, I didn't want to pass up this opportunity of a chance to do something daring, so I quickly said yes. I looked back to ask my Mother, but Mommi was too busy to notice. Before I knew it, one young man held on to my one hand and another young man the other one. "Now, Käthe, hold on tight, we are going to take a run for it and when we tell you to jump, you jump, okay." I swallowed several times, "I will." The three of us holding on tight started to run, my eyes wide open, and all of a sudden I wasn't scared anymore. "Jump Käthe, jump!" they yelled as I leaped. We moved through the air like an airplane. I felt the warmth of the fire below me, mostly on the bottom of my feet, but the cool air on my bare skin, felt sharp as the wind blew my blouse away from my body. My hair was blowing away from my face and the air made a whistling sound in my ear. The smell of the fire was thick and made me gulp for air as we then landed far away from the fire on the other side. We laughed out loud as they let go of my hand. Full of praise for my bravery, they were.

"Could I go again?" I asked, almost begging. "Yes, sure you can later." This excitement was fun, and we repeated this jump many times that evening. Mother was socializing with the neighbours and didn't take much notice of me. I welcomed the freedom. I wasn't used to this new Mommi, not telling me what to do or say. Before the evening ended and the fire burned down to dark coals, one more treat was to come before the night was done.

Large steel mesh containers with long handles on each side was used to pop the popcorn. Two strong men were needed to turn the crate over the coals constantly until every kernel of popcorn, popped. The popcorn then poured into large bowls, for all to enjoy. When every kernel was eaten, it was now time to clean up and pack up. We walked home as a family, along with our neighbours. That night sleep came quickly, I was so tired.

The harvest time came to an end and it was time now to look forward to a different kind of work, with Mommi and Oma enjoying quiet times together to do some sewing. Everything we owned was made from scratch, such as underwear, blouses, dresses, coats and much more. Our neighbouring villages such as Molidorf, Topola, Masdorf, were mostly farmers and made fabric from hemp. It made it easy for our family to trade our goods for fabric, with the neighbouring town folk at the market. Most of the fabric was pure, and also soft to touch. It was soothing to me in the evenings to see my family sitting around the wood stove, with Mommi and Oma either mending socks or knitting some. Both of my sisters were doing their homework every night as I watched with envy and counted the days until I could join them and go to school too.

Living in Kikinda meant some pretty strong rainfalls in spring and late fall. Sitting on my windowsill and watching the large drops hit the sill, one by one, I found relaxing. However, when lightning filled the room with enough light to see everything, I became scared in my bedroom alone. My sisters and I ran from any room that we were in and huddled and grabbed each other from fright with every crack of the loudest thunder I ever heard. Sometimes the thunder was so loud that my whole body rose off the ground from fright. We would end up holding each other's hands until the storm passed. But as quickly as the rains came, that's how quickly they also were gone. With the sky so clear and blue afterwards and the air so clean, it made us forget our fright very quickly.

When the slow warm rains fell in the summer, the ones with no lightning or thunder, it was our turn and our shoes came off. It was time to play. We didn't have a pool or a lake nearby, but stepping in every puddle and the small ditches next to the sidewalk, which were filled with streaming water all the way home from the city square, turned into much laughter and fun for my sisters and me. On many of those rainfalls my sundress clung to me, as if it was part of my skin. We were soaked from head to toe, by the time we reached our gate, but we didn't care.

One afternoon in late fall, Grete, Susi and I walked to a park where they played soccer. It took a long time as I walked through a lovely park, called Plantosch Garden. At the end of the park the soccer field appeared. The young men with their soccer uniforms on were already in the field playing as we approached. I remember seeing a tall man, somehow familiar to me, playing out on the field. Several times that same man kept looking at us, but being so busy in the game we never spoke. Before the game was over, the three of us left. We took our time and enjoyed the walk home; then Grete, out of the blue, said this to Susi and me, "Did you know that man that kept looking at us is our Tati?" "No," we answered. I didn't know my Father and it didn't mean much to me at that time.

All the preparations for the winter months were in place, and we had plenty to eat. There was no reason for hunger, for our family worked hard and managed their crops well. However, the town folk became more and more worried about our fate in the war all around us.

Unfortunately, late October, in 1944, our world turned into a journey of years longing to return to our homeland, the only place we ever knew, where we made roots so deep that for some this loss never left for the remainder of their lives.

Destiny Unknown, Shipped and Condemned

In late October in the year 1944, friendly soldiers appeared at our gate. They asked to speak to our Mother. After talking sometime to the soldiers our Mother returned to the house. My Mother immediately turned to our Uncle without a word to the rest of us. "Come, Hans." she motioned calmly with a nod of her head, come, as they stepped in the dining room and closed the door. With grave looks on their faces they returned. This is what they said to us, all of us anxiously standing in one spot, waiting, while knowing this was no ordinary talk. "The soldiers came to give us the dreadful news, more like orders," Mommi said the news that we didn't want to hear. Mommi turned to Oma and said, "We have twenty four hours to leave our home. The sooner we leave the better." Our Grandmother became upset and excited and started rambling. "No, I am not leaving. I never heard of such a thing, no one can make us leave just like that." "Yes, Mother they can, and they did. They told us anyone staying here and refusing to leave will be slaughtered," "But why?" Oma questioned, "Because we speak German? No, that's impossible!" as she shook her head in total confusion.

"Mother please, come on, there is no time to waste. Maybe

in a few weeks we can come back and everything will be normal again." Mommi tried to reassure our Grandmother. In the meantime, Hans Onkel stood by the door looking over at us girls, still standing in the same spot waiting for an explanation. We knew it was serious, but didn't really understand. Noticing our worried faces, our Uncle came to reassure us that everything will be all right. We were not convinced and started to cry. The thought of our Oma being separated from us, was something we could not imagine or accept. We ran over to Oma and started grabbing her legs and arms, pleading for her to change her mind.

"We have to leave soon." Mommi said, "There are only so many trucks, wagons and trains available to take us away." We could tell Mommi was trying hard to pretend, but we knew she was deeply worried. "We will take only the things we need for a few days, for we will return soon." Our family still divided in the decision to leave. Hans Onkel ran to the cellar and brought the large crock of hardened lard with fried pork chops in between up to the door. Mommi grabbed a feather duvet and started throwing things like a little money, underclothes, hats and mitts in the middle. The duvet then folded, hobo style, with two corners tied, and crossed over to the other corner and tied. Our Grandmother could not comprehend or understand the magnitude of this decision, and we girls felt the same. But there was no time to waste, and reluctantly Oma started to move towards the door.

With our coats, hats, mitts and shoes on, we walked out to the Courtyard. My sisters and I were totally confused with leaving so abruptly and couldn't concentrate and just kept inching our bodies closer to the outside gate. Mommi turned back and locked the door with our large key. We didn't lock our house often in the past, but we knew the hiding place where Mommi placed the key so that when we return we will know how to get back in. Our dog Bengy was so happy to see us. We told him we loved him and us girls stroked him and kissed him but he wouldn't calm down. Bengy clung to us like never before, it was horrible to have to force and pry his hands and legs from us until finally we had to slam the door. Dogs have a way of knowing when something is wrong, for Bengy started to bark, and we never seen Bengy jumping at the gate the way he did that day. His anxious bark could be heard far too long and made us feel lonesome already and we barely left.

Mother gave one more order, as she gave the iron gate one more tight twist on the lock. "We will be walking fast," she said, as she swung the duvet over her shoulders, "Come on, no dawdling. You know I can't pay attention to all of you at the same time. Keep your eyes on us and follow me," as we stepped out to the street. It was then I heard in the distance, a faint crackling sound that was not familiar, but for some reason totally unknown to me, frightening. As I looked in between two houses, a large piece of sky seemed to be sprinkled with dust of red and yellow clouds. As I became older and understood, I realized the barrage of the crackling sound was indeed the enemy lines of fire so fierce and close that it formed the red sky, that I saw that day we left Kikinda.

We started walking, our Hungarian and Serbian neighbours embracing our family, weeping as we hurried along. One Hungarian neighbour could not believe it, used some profane words to describe his disgust, "Just because you speak German? My God! We've been neighbours and friends for so many years. Be safe, hurry back." We just nodded our heads, as we kept walking faster away from our home. With more people coming out of their houses, with wall to wall people, by the time we reached the trucks, I became lost.

The reason was, as we entered the city square, I looked up and a man was hanging from the tree. It was then I stopped as I heard someone nearby say that this is an example what happened when you stay. I was momentarily startled and lost sight of my family. I couldn't see my family, with so many people, one couldn't see too far. I became frantic, and as I looked around every available truck filled quickly, the crowds became less in numbers, I started to shake. Finally, I stopped walking around, and stopped looking for my family, stood still and started crying. It wasn't long, before a soldier came along and asked me if I was lost.

"Yes," I said wiping my tears. Without hesitation, he grabbed hold of me and threw me on his shoulders, as he rushed to catch the first wagon that was filled and ready to leave. He asked my name. "*Käthe Krämer.*" "Okay." He was out of breath as we reached the wagon. The truck started to leave just then. This young soldier was running as fast as he could with me bouncing up and down and holding his hand fearfully tight. We caught up to the truck, but the door was closed. The soldier banged on the door with his fist until it opened. "Wait!" he said to the driver. "There is a little girl here. She lost her family." The soldier took one step up and leaned over far enough, "Käthe do you see your family?" I looked as fast as I could, but I didn't recognize anyone. "No," I said. Quickly he dashed to the next truck.

"Don't worry," he said, "we will find them." The next truck full and ready to leave, but my family was not on that truck either. The third and fourth truck had already left. So, we moved on to the next truck, but by this time, there was only one vehicle left. I was losing hope to find my family. Exhausted and totally out of breath, the soldier said, "Käthe look in this truck." Exhilarated with joy, I jumped off the soldier's neck and worked my way through the aisle to be with my family. I never even looked back to thank the young soldier. This neglect of mine bothered me from time to time and lingered on.

My family was so happy to see me, especially my Oma, but not my Mother. After a long pause, Mommi changed her mind and gave me a squeeze. A short while later, we arrived at the train station, it was a sight I shall never forget. The cold wind helped to pale the skin, eyes didn't smile, and the familiar lines of smiles, drooped. Nervous coughing and shuffling with the feet, the only noise heard. Many faces filled with sadness, dark babushkas worn by Grandmothers, including mine, along with dark clothing worn by most. Children like me, observing and looking to grownups for a sign of reassurance, but there was none.

Elderly women were quietly weeping, even some of the men had tears as they shook their heads in disbelief. Since most men and boys were in the army, this sea of people mostly women, children and grandparents. But most of all, for such a large crowd the silence became disturbing. No one knew exactly what was happening here. The unknown fate of their futures before them, gave their faces blank stares. What took hold at that very moment remained a vision in those only who experienced this abandonment. Staying alive was foremost in my family's mind.

We heard the train coming in the distance, as the soldiers stretched out their arms and told everyone to stand back, with us girls hanging on to our family. Our family stood silent, except for our Oma. Oma was wiping her tears as she said to my Mother, "I am going back. The dog needs to be fed and the chickens, too." Our Mother quickly took charge, for she didn't have much time. We could tell Mommi was upset, as she stopped Oma from leaving. "Okay Mother, okay if you go back, we'll all go and you know what will happen to all of us. What is it, yes or no?" Our eyes fixed on Oma as all of us waited for her answer. "Well, I have a hard time walking, I'll just hold you back," Oma said. "Please take the children, and go." "No, we will manage." Mommi replied. After a long pause Oma said, "Alright then," a sigh of relief as we waited our turn to board the train.

All the available trains in the area were used to carry us away from Jugoslavia and enemy lines. In our case, the train that was used to haul cattle before us became our wagon. One couldn't be choosy at a time like that. We didn't mind the wall to wall people as much as we minded the stench from the animals that were housed in this wagon before us. The smell of manure in the straw was so strong that I turned my head quickly to breath in fresh air as I climbed up the steep steps. A very offensive odour. We stood like cattle, only the elderly could stoop down and sit, the rest of us leaned against one another. Not one complaint was heard, we were startled as a jerk from the train meant the train was slowly moving.

Our eyes met in a sombre stare, as a feeling of unbelievable sadness filled the wagon. We listened to lonesome sounds of our usual city noises. In the distance dogs barked and farm animals made sorrowful sounds, as if they knew they had been abandoned. Without uttering a single word, expressions spoke volume. Before our very own eyes our city started to disappear. What had just taken place here was too much to comprehend for some. As the engines of the train moved slowly away from our city, yard by yard, a Nation of Donau Schwaben had been removed in a single day from their homes, their land, their country, their culture, their security and language. Swept away from every physical thing they possessed and worked so hard for, for generations. How could this happen to a nation of people who valued peace above all else and lived with human kindness on a daily basis?

I was only seven years old and my mother thirty-five.

Now that I am so much older, I still cannot imagine what this loss must have meant to our family. Can one comprehend being stripped of everything they held dear in everyday life, like baby pictures, a house, animals like our sweet dog, our goats, ducks and geese, the best of neighbours, our church, and the best fruit that grew in that region? Little every day happenings, like the open market, the linden trees all the way to the city square. The black locust trees, what a sweet uplifting fragrance when in full bloom, most of all, everyone and everything, a feeling of belonging and a place to call home.

Many hours later the train came to an abrupt stop. A loud

siren, unfamiliar sound to us was heard. Someone from the next car yelled run as fast as you can. The planes are coming to bomb the train. Oma didn't come for the stairs were too steep for her to climb. "Go!" she said, "it's in God's hands now, I am staying here." Reluctantly we ran as fast as we could. Hundreds of people were scrambling all around us running underneath trees and shrubs, as we lay on the ground. The engines of the planes became louder as they came closer. Our hearts pounding out of our chests, for all of a sudden out of nowhere the plane swooped down. The one man plane flew so low, that I actually saw the pilot. The noise piercing to the ears, it was that loud. The bullets flew all around us. Nearby the ground flew in the air and landed on the trees and parts of dirt on us as well. Miraculously, the train was not hit. We stood up, and cleaned ourselves of the dirt on our clothing. We started to turn around and headed back to the wagon, as the piercing sound of the plane returned. Mommi grabbed my hand and threw me on the ground.

"Get back!" someone yelled, "the planes are coming back." Instantly people threw themselves back on the ground. "Please God, please keep us safe," I heard someone praying next to me. Some held their hands together and just silently prayed. Reluctant to get up too early like the last time, people looking at each other in silence and just waiting. After some time, one by one, slowly we stood up. However, from the other side of the train a disturbing outburst of pain was heard. We knew someone was hurt. A little girl my age was hit. Apparently the plane flew so low that an electric wire was broken. The young girl died instantly. It took many people to carry the Mother forcefully back to the train, leaving her child behind. The cries of unbelievable pain from that Mother could be heard even over the loud horn, meaning the train was moving again. Then complete silence, as the wheels collected speed by the seconds. Again, hearts and minds stood still and so immersed in that moment of pain that we felt nothing. The only good news, that our Oma so happy to see us as she sat alone in the wagon crying as we opened the door.

When nightfall came, the train again came to a slow stop. No one moved. Finally the door opened. "We will stay here for the night," the soldier informed us. "Stay in your wagons, it is safer than moving." We questioned why? He replied, "Well, when we travel we need light and from the air we can be spotted easily. Staying here for the night is safer," was the explanation he gave. That evening we shared the bread and the crock of lard our Uncle brought from the cellar. Everyone in our wagon thanked us, for hunger pains were felt by all. However, the bread and lard had to be rationed, for none of us knew the length of time that would be spent on that train before we reach Hungary. The air was brisk and I am sure for many that night, sleep didn't come. But for me, I rested my head on Oma's lap and did sleep some.

That morning we didn't hear the horn, as the train started to move. Instead loud screams heard for the train to stop. "Please stop! Wait!" The train stopped for no one and kept right on moving. It was said that the elderly man was in the bushes nearby to relieve himself as the train started moving. He couldn't return fast enough and was left waving to his wife in the middle of the tracks. It didn't help that the wagon they were in was the last one. Also, the elderly couple didn't have any children and very devoted to each other.

Sometime that same day in the afternoon, another loud siren, which meant the train, was stopping and another raid. By now we knew exactly what to do and knew the drill well. We found ourselves in a fruit orchard. There was a God after all, food, for he must have known of our hunger. But, for now, our main concern, to stay alive. The planes came back in great numbers and the sound pierced in my ears so loud that I stuck my fingers in my ears, so I could stand it. Our luck, the trees, a blessing for we were scattered throughout the orchard and that is what saved us that afternoon. Some were not so lucky, with cuts and blood everywhere, no fatal injuries reported. My Mother put her hands together and thanked God. At one point I thought she scolded God as if He was there with us. "What are you doing to us?" she said, "We never did anything bad to anyone," as she held her hands up to heaven.

Our pockets were filled with delicious apples, as we waited underneath the trees some more until such time, that it was safe to return to our wagons. Oma unharmed, sat and waited for us to return. She was happy as we showed her the apples that we gathered, with Oma's concern foremost for our safety, as she gave us a squeeze of relief. It took two days to reach Hungary. Following the crowd, now that our load was a little lighter, for the crock of lard was eaten and left behind. Oma began to tire easily and could not walk fast anymore. We arrived in late afternoon and were stuffed into a large gymnasium. The town was called Segedin, Hungary this is where we stayed for a few days or so. Water was not plentiful, but we managed enough to clean up and wash our underwear. For our meal that night we stood in line for hours for a bowl of soup. The hot water, flavoured with onions and no noodles, they called soup. A piece of bread, oh it was so good. The first time in my young life I experienced hunger pains that lasted for many hours and turned into days. We slept on the floor that night, leaning against one another until finally morning came. When we complained, Mother didn't show much sympathy, "Be happy you are still alive," she said. She had no patience, or so we thought.

Susi and I made the best of it. We took each other's hand and walked all around the nearby town. We stopped at the Town Square and sat at a nearby wooden bench. Observing the town folk, it appeared as life was very normal. We looked at each other with questions about what happened to our city, with neither one of us old enough to understand. "I am hungry, Susi," I said. "Me, too," she answered. This little outing of ours made the afternoon hours pass by a little faster and helped somehow. We jumped off the bench, held hands and returned to the gymnasium. The following day, word came of very good news.

The elderly man that was left at the tracks a few days ago was reunited with his wife. The train that came after ours, which we of course didn't know anything about, picked the man up. The couple held hands all day long, like young lovers, refreshing to see since they celebrated forty years of marriage, we were told.

Being shipped to the gymnasium meant folks had some time to take in all that happened a few days ago in Jugoslavia. Young and old bonded and helped each other emotionally. Most of the conversations ended in shaking their heads in disbelief of the conditions we were left in. No toilets and definitely no privacy. We slept in the same clothes for almost a week. I especially remember how uncomfortable I felt to be without my underpants since Mommi insisted to wash them every 3 days or so. It seemed to take forever for the wash to dry in the cold. The hardwood floor was hard and cold, especially at night. Lying close to my Hans Onkel and feeling his arms tight around me helped to fall asleep.

Over a week passed when we received the news of our destination. A group of us were told to meet our leader at the train station at a certain time. We walked for quite some time till we reached the train station. People stood for hours, waiting and wondering what was coming next, I became sick. The cold we endured in the gymnasium gave me a fever and a cough. Holding on to my Mother's hand, I could barely walk. The train finally came and thank goodness, we could enjoy sitting with a little more leg room than the last wagon we were in. I don't remember much because I slept most of the time. Mother woke me just before we reached the town of Strengberg, Austria. This was our destination to get off the train, the man in charge advised us.

There we stood, the six of us in a row, with only the clothes on our backs, and the feather duvet in our possession. *Waiting.*

It was then we were given instructions by a man that carried the information in his briefcase. The man with many sheets of paper in his hand explained this to us. Some Austrian people from that region, mostly farmers, business people or anyone able, would take us refugees in for a short while in exchange for labour hours. We had no idea what was waiting for us. The train left quickly and left us standing there alongside with about ten other families. Before we knew it, the man started calling out names. In no time at all, one by one, families left with their designated sponsors. All names called, except for ours, Mother looked worried. The man tried to reassure us and said, "I don't know what's keeping Mr. Miller. He should be here. The man had to leave, and left us standing there, alone.

As we stood waiting, Mother said to Hans Onkel, "I am not surprised, with just you and me working, this is not a good deal for anyone. I don't blame anyone for six people to feed," Mother said. "What now?" Hans Onkel asked, as we looked around the area. With no one in sight, there was no choice except to start walking. In a confused state slowly we started to move. From the other side of the tracks, behind a train a man ran towards us with his arm waving, "Wait, wait, I am late." He reached us, out of breath, as he asked, "Are you the only family left?" Hans Onkel held out his hand, "Yes we are." Hans Onkel introduced himself and then the rest of us. The bearded man called himself the Miller. He scratched his head, "Six people hmm oh boy." Noticing this, our Mother quickly tried to reassure the Miller, and said, "I will work very hard and my brother, too. You won't be sorry." "Okay then, come on." He swung with his arm for us to follow him.

The Miller was a husky, strong looking man, with red bushy hair and a full moustache. We liked him right away; he possessed a charming way about him and smiling eyes. It turned out the husky man owned a small flour mill. A house near the mill just happened to be vacant at the moment and ready for us to move in. We walked to his wagon and jumped in. The ride to the house was anything but smooth. The dirt country roads took some skilled steering with the horses. Our Mother, Uncle and the Miller talked all the way and it was clear to see they liked each other. We girls along with Oma, just listened as we bounced up and down. After a long ride, the wagon stopped in front of a two storey building. We climbed off as the Miller in his deep voice said, "This is your place, there are a few rooms empty upstairs stay there as long as you want. The downstairs is used as a tool shop, but the upstairs is the living quarters," the Miller explained. We stood and looked around before we moved to the side of the building and looked up to the second floor. The stairs to the upper floor were narrow and steep and Oma struggled to climb to the top. I especially liked the balcony, which covered the length of the house. "This upstairs is vacant," the Miller explained. The house was furnished only in the bare necessities, but it had several small bedrooms, hopefully comfortable and clean. If by some chance that it wasn't clean, Mother would see to that. When Oma looked disappointed, Mommi tried to reassure her, "It's only for a short while."

Mother and Hans Onkel, to keep their promise, didn't waste any time and reported for work the next day. The mill was about one kilometer away from the house. Hans Onkel and Mommi walked through the field for a shortcut. They both left early in the morning, way before we woke up in our new place. Oma couldn't climb the stairs anymore, so it was up to us girls to bring the wood up for the stove. We became sharp with one another, much more so than before. But no matter what, by the end of the day, the chores were always done.

Since Mother and Hans Onkel made very little money and simply worked for food mostly, we felt the effects immediately. My hunger pains started in the morning even before I was totally awake and lasted all day. The only time I did not have hunger pains is one hour or so after I ate. Our diet was meatless, no salt and very little milk, most of our meals flour and water based. We considered ourselves so fortunate and grateful to have the Miller.

Top Row Left to Right: Sava Onkel, Susi
Tant, Grete, Mommi & Hans Onkel
Middle Row: Oma
Bottom Row Left to Right: Vera, Susi & myself.

A few months later word came, I don't remember how, that our Aunt Susi, Uncle Sava and Cousin Vera were looking for us. They had no place to stay and wanted to come and live with us. Mother without hesitation, with the Miller's permission, offered them one bedroom. Mother made us double up so one of the bedrooms would be available for our relatives. The sisters shared the kitchen, along with their Mother. This was good for Oma; she needed help by now and tired easily. Oma and our Aunt didn't get along as well as Mommi and Oma, but they managed. Apparently Oma did not like her son-in-law, Sava.

Well, we couldn't tell, for they didn't have words, at least not in front of us.

For my cousin Vera, an only child, I thought she must be spoiled. I made up my mind, I didn't like her for she had toys and I didn't. The first few days, we just looked at each other, and avoided speaking. It wasn't hard to figure out that she was my age, and my height exactly. Later, that afternoon on the balcony, as I sat by myself and overlooked the meadow, Vera appeared. Very confidently, she said, "Do you want to play with my doll?" Before I knew it, she handed the doll to me and left. Surprised at her generosity, I hopped off my chair and moved slowly toward the spot where she was playing with her toys. Not sure of myself, I sat near her. Vera looked up at me with her dark eyes and boney body.

"Do you want to play with me?" Not sure, I paused and quietly said, "If you want me too, I will." I moved closer to her, she looked me straight into the eyes, "You want my Doll. She is yours." "Why?" I questioned, "Don't you like your doll? She is so beautiful." After a second, with a pouty look on her face, she said, "I'd rather play with you and you can play with my doll anytime you want."

That afternoon Vera and I connected not just as cousins, but also as friends. Finally, I had someone my own age, not just my sisters, always older and smarter than I. Vera and I talked about everything. She told me of her Father being so strict and it wasn't long before I understood what Vera meant. Sava Onkel was a strict man, especially with Vera. When he was angry, and it was often, he'd take out his anger mostly on Vera. The prints of his strong hand imprinted on Vera's backside for days, that's how hard he hit her. Our new Aunt and Uncle argued often, something we were not used to, their disagreement mostly of his treatment of Vera. Their arguments ended with Sava Onkel slamming the door and leaving for the night. It was at this time that our family tried to console my aunt and give her advice that of course she never took. Our Oma became impatient with her oldest daughter and perhaps, it was this lack of respect that drove them apart. One thing for sure, I noticed that although our Mother was strict, most of the time our family settled their differences in a way that ended with a good tone.

Vera and I spent endless afternoons together. With our arms outstretched and gliding through the misty air in the meadow, as if we could fly. Running down the narrow brook with our worn out shoes in our hands, collecting shiny stones from the edge of the water, pretending it was money and that we were rich. Warm summer winds, that blew our hair softly around our heads, me with my dark hair and Vera blonde, singing our favourite songs at the top of our lungs, as we ran faster and faster through the meadow, laughing and giggling all the way as the day passed by. We lay on our backs with the grass in the meadow high enough so no one could see us. Far enough away from the house, so they couldn't hear our secrets. With our hands resting behind our necks, the sky above so blue, was so inviting for us to plan our whole life together in one single afternoon. We made promises to each other of always keeping in touch no matter where we end up. Promises we've kept to this day. With our arms around each other's shoulders, we walked slowly back to the house.

After our lean supper the chores were done, my duties to clear the table and dry the dishes. Just as we were ready to relax, someone knocked at the door. We all stopped, and fixed our eyes on the door. For it was unusual for anyone coming to visit for we had no friends at that time. Hans Onkel walked to the door and he reluctantly turned the knob. A young man stood in the doorway, out of breath. "Come in, come in," Hans Onkel said.

"I came to tell you the Russian Jeeps are coming this way. I am coming to warn you, they are doing terrible things to German speaking people, especially to women. You need to hide. I've been told of a farm house about 3km from here that is safe and helps people like you. Go there please," the young man, no more than sixteen years old said, with real concern. "I have to hurry back before I get in big trouble. If they knew I told you, I don't know what they would do to me." Mother made a small sandwich, pressed it into his hands and with a thank you, pushed him out the door. "Thank you again, and I hope you will be okay," Mommi added.

A lot of unrest in the house that evening as we girls listened to our family talking over their plan. Worried mostly, for we didn't know what to expect, before our family made the decision. Mommi thought we should hide Grete in the wood stove. What about the rest of us, we just didn't have enough places to hide. Then Oma and Hans Onkel came up with the solution. The two of them would remain in the house. Someone had to stay back. Oma had a hard time walking and Hans Onkel, a male, should stay. It seemed like a good plan. The rest of us waited till nightfall, when no one could see us and then headed for the farmhouse that the young man spoke about. That same familiar silence filled our house again. Just when we thought life was somewhat normal, it was not to be. In the meantime, we passed the word to other German speaking folks nearby, anyone interested in joining us to be at our house at sundown.

Nightfall came and the word spread fast for about twenty German speaking women and children came, one young woman among them, with a baby that was still nursing. In total darkness, quietly we made our way to the river, which we had to cross. In the background we heard voices from our building. The river was definitely too wide, and the current too strong for us to cross. The middle of the river was about four feet deep. Earlier in the day, Hans Onkel strung a rope from one tree to another on the opposite side, so we could hang on as we crossed because of the current. Guided by an adult, one by one, we made our way across. We could feel the current as soon as we hit waist deep, for it took all my strength to hang on to the rope and it was cold. We knew the Partisans were close, for we heard them talking to our Uncle. All of a sudden, the baby started to cry.

Panic stricken, we froze on the spot and we didn't move. The Mother franticly tried to calm the baby. Out of desperation she held the baby's mouth closed until she opened her blouse, to give the baby the breast. Then total silence. We waited holding our breath, so we could observe what was going on. It was so dark we could hardly see one another.

A light appeared at the house and it was moving towards us. We never moved an inch, stopped in our tracks. Terribly frightened, all we heard was our hearts beating so hard that we felt the movement in our throats not in our chests. Then the light disappeared, Russian words spoken, and the door slammed. "Hurry, hurry," whispered someone to the few women on the other side. All of us safely crossed over the river, now the long walk ahead of us. Oh, the wet clothing was so uncomfortable, but at a time like that, how could I complain. Oh, but my whole body wanted to cry, such misery and so cold. It was decided not to walk in the middle of the meadow, but rather by the edge of the trees, so we could not be seen as easily. Finally we reached what we thought was the safe farmhouse. We had to make sure, for with people so divided in this war it could be a disaster if we fell in the wrong hands. One of us had to go ahead, alone, to check it out. The Mother with the baby was the chosen one. Anxiously waiting, far enough away, so we could not be seen, we waited some more. All of a sudden, a middle aged man came running. "Come quickly, no noise please."

He guided our group to a trap door next to the house. This door was so well disguised we didn't notice it at all. It would be hard for anyone to find. The door needed the strength of several strong men to open, it was that heavy. We ran down the steep stairs quickly. The man said, I will bring some food later and the door dropped. Some of us took our outerwear off and hung it up to dry. That night we huddled together, with enough grownups for us children to lay our heads on their laps sleeping on the cement floor. In early morning, we heard the motors of the Jeeps. We stopped and no one moved as tension filled the room. People started to form a circle, holding on to each other, quietly praying.

From the shaded windows above, boots of all sizes kept walking, maybe about eight or ten of them. One by one they walked, as we could only watch. At one point a young girl was so distraught, not knowing her fate, a few of the grownups needed to do some fancy talking to calm her. Several hours went by, and still nothing. Still in total silence, we wondered what was going on, but too afraid to move. A few hours later, the door started to move a crack. A sigh of relief, as the farmer's voice called, "Help us open the door please." In sheer elation the door flung open, as we all helped to push.

"It's safe now," the farmer's wife reassured us when she noticed our reluctance, "They are gone for now. Here, come on, eat. We brought some breakfast, a meat sandwich and a crock full of warm milk." We passed the crock from person to person till every drop was gone. The farmer and his wife didn't linger to talk, just explained that we were not safe yet. They continued to tell us that from their past experience the soldiers do come back. "They go to the next farm," he said, "and then return, just to trick us. Don't worry I'll be back." He dropped the trap door.

We remained in the cellar for two days before the farmer opened the trap door again, and said, "We heard from the farmer next door that the soldiers moved on." There was absolutely nothing we could offer these generous souls, for we had nothing. Thank you, lingered on until we did not see them anymore. The Austrian people will forever have my gratitude, for without their kind hearts I would not be able to write this book.

We quickly walked to the edge of the trees, looking around constantly for fear of being seen or heard at any moment as we made our way back to the Miller's place. On many such trips people were caught and punished, but on this cold night, our prayers were answered. Hans Onkel anxiously waited for us, pacing the sidewalk by the house. He didn't know our fate, for there was no way to get word to him. When we reached the house, we noticed Hans Onkel had a bruise on his face. We sat around the table while Oma and Hans Onkel filled us in on what happened.

"They repeatedly asked me, where are the women in this house?" When Hans Onkel denied that any women lived in the house, the soldiers hit him, thinking he would confess, he told us. "My heart dropped when I heard the baby cry," Oma continued, "The soldiers immediately started walking towards the river. Just then, I called them and said I had food for them. They brought food with them and they ordered me to cook for them. Besides eating everything that they brought, they also ate the little bit of food we had in the kitchen. They ate everything I cooked and they drank the small bottle of whiskey we had, that we stored away for medicinal purposes." Oma was upset and shaking from the ordeal the entire time of her explanation. "It's okay Mother," our Mommi said to Oma, "I'll try to get some food from the Miller. We are not hurt. That is the main thing." our Mother reassured us.

It's been many months now since we left Kikinda and with the war still being felt, the thought of going back to our homeland, became a concern. But there was more to worry about. Food was scarce and never enough to eat just to keep alive was a struggle. Our stomachs shrunk by now, and the hunger pains became something we experienced every day. Once in a while, during midday, we surprised our Mother by walking to the mill to visit. Quite a walk, but we were used to walking and didn't mind. Mother, along with the Miller, welcomed our company. The Miller gave us a tour and explained the making of flour. Mother worked for the lady of the house, doing mostly housework, such as ironing, cooking and cleaning and of course our uncle worked with the Miller making flour. We chuckled for our uncle was sprinkled with flour dust all over, except the eyes and lips showed. The Miller of course wouldn't let us leave without a treat to enjoy on the way back.

In the spring of 1945, somehow word came that American

soldiers would be driving through our main streets and they were handing out candy and chocolates. I ran as fast as I could, so to be sure I wouldn't miss them. In the distance, I heard the soldiers screaming, we are going home, *God Bless America*, we are going home. With their fists full of chocolate bars throwing them to kids lined up on both sides of the street. I caught one chocolate bar and held the bar in my hand and I wondered "why are we not going home?" How lucky, the American soldiers were, I thought to myself. Yet our journey was just beginning.

The Miller was fond of our family, but after some months, he gave our Uncle the bad news. It was hard for him to let our Uncle go. "I held on as long as I could, but you know," he explained to our Mother with regret, "it's hard for everyone." He reassured us that Mother could stay for as long as he had work. Once more, Mommi was the sole provider for our family. Mommi received a few groceries for wages and whatever little money the Miller could afford to give by then. We considered ourselves lucky, for we had food, but extras of any kind was something we could only dream about in those days. From time to time, I asked Mommi, "When are we going home?" "Soon my child, soon, you'll see." she answered me.

More bad news came a few months later. The Miller could not help us out anymore and with his own family to feed, he let our Mother go. With sadness he gave our Mother the news. "You are such a good worker Kati, and your girls, I learned to care for them too. I feel terrible about this." After a long pause, Mother told us, she just stood there and said to the Miller, "When nobody wanted us you took us in. You gave us food from your own family's table. I have much to be grateful for," as they embraced. The Miller watched my Mother walk out the door from the place where they shared, many days and conversations together, for the last six months.

Not a month passed that our Miller did not pay us a visit, and of course, carrying a sack of flour a monthly gift. The Miller stayed in touch and he was a big reason that we had something to eat. He was a kind and generous human being. A few months passed when the Miller came with some wonderful news, we thought. "A friend of mine owns a small summer home and he needs someone to take care of the cows in exchange for free rent and some milk for the girls, hopefully," he came to inform us. "It's yours if you want it." It meant we had to relocate and move away. Only one problem, Vera and her family couldn't come with us for there was barely enough room for the six of us. Our family agreed and the decision to move was made. The only thing we owned at that time was the duvet, the rest belonged to the house, so there wasn't much to move. The Miller helped us and the same wagon that brought us there was used to take us away once again, and we left.

The modest small building we called home for the next six months was particularly lonely for me. Vera and family moved elsewhere, too far to visit, and I missed Vera very much. For the last few months, Vera and I spent all our time together, playing and laughing and just being kids, at a time when life for grownups was so different from ours. This so-called farm, isolated and no neighbours nearby made life hard not just for me, but our entire family. Mother walked for hours just to bring home enough food to eat for the day. They called it begging, but Mother always tried to work for a few hours for whatever food was available to give to her. It was lucky for us that it was spring time, for the dilapidated shed had thin walls and the size was unbelievably small. It was a good thing we only needed to burn the stove sparingly for wood was scarce and hard to find. One room, possibly the size of a bedroom, housed the six of us. I never heard a single complaint of our living quarters from my family, except frustration out of the unknown crept up on a regular basis.

My Mother had high cheek bones, beautiful hands, feet and teeth, a strong character, and a no nonsense personality. She had a soft side to her, that she often tried to hide from all of us, unsuccessfully I might add. But, the beautiful face is now showing signs of hardship. Mommi's face became drawn with black circles around her eyes from so much stress and lack of sleep. Her endurance and strong will brought us this far without a single complaint. She had no tolerance for complaining from us either. Most of all, seeing us children hungry all the time was very hard for my Mother.

More bad news as the land owner came to tell us of his own troubles. "I had to slaughter the cattle for the town offered me a good deal, and you know, money is, well you know," he said to Mommi. With a roof over our heads and so much unrest, my Mother merely said, "Don't worry about us, I understand, these are hard times for everyone." The land owner added, "You can stay here as long as you need to, that's the least I can do for you." This news was especially upsetting because this meant we didn't have any more milk nearby with the cows gone, the only nourishing food left for us kids.

Wondering, what was in store for us, kept the mind busy. We tried hard not to think of the worst. Standing by the barn, which was a fair distance from the house, I watched as friendly American planes flew by. The sky filled with bits of white paper like confetti slowly falling down. If lucky enough or close enough to retrieve canned goods that dropped once in a while, that made us happy. Running about the field, and searching everywhere in the high grass, became an exercise I liked, especially when at the end of it all I found a few cans of meat. I wasn't interested in the flyers, for I couldn't read them anyway.

By this time it became obvious to Susi and me that Grete, much taller than we were and strikingly beautiful, was our Mother's favourite. She seemed so much more grown up than Susi and I. Grete sat with the grownups and joined in on grown up conversations too. Susi and I had each other, and we didn't care, or so we thought. Past the barn down by the brook, a broken down Jeep with fire marks on the sides and the body, yet seats still intact, became our playground. This is where on long afternoons, Susi and I exchanged our feelings about our

Mother. The complaints were always the same, she is too strict and too critical of everything we do and say. The guilty feelings we experienced after our complaints, made us retreat and say, we shouldn't talk like that about our Mother. Susi and I made a pact, never to tell anyone of our feelings, and we didn't.

Every second day or so, the sirens blew over the meadow and without thinking, the drill for running for shelter underneath a tree somewhere, although a regular routine, far from ordinary. The attack by air usually lasted about 15 minutes or so. When noises from the plane engines could no longer be heard, the attack was over. We sighed with relief especially if no one was hurt. We simply stood up, wiped the dirt off our clothes, thanked God, and continued with our day. After these raids, many times word came from town folk of injuries, and in some cases death. Grenades, lying in places least expected, were my Mother's biggest fear. We were warned daily to never ever touch anything that remotely resembled a grenade.

In the next few months, on many days when the stomach was hurting from hunger and there was no food, I became weak. The playing turned into a nap instead; it helped to pass the time. But when the Miller came to visit, he came several times and brought flour and a little salt, it felt good to have some solid food for a change. Once a month, Mommi made us a simple noodle dish, with little divided portions handed to us in our porzelan dish. I savoured every centimetre of every noodle, so delicious. Any other time the soup, mostly hot water with a few onions for taste, with a thin slice of bread became one of our common suppers.

One morning a roaring sound came from behind the barn. Startled, we ran to the back of the shed to see what it was. All we could see was a cloud of dust coming closer in our direction. Hans Onkel noticed the motorcycle first. "Run! Run and hide in the barn!" he screamed. But it was no use, for the motorcycle too close, there was no choice than to run into the shed. Silently, our ears to the door, we heard talking in German, a big sigh of relief. A young man from the neighbouring farm, also a refugee, jumped off and came running to Hans Onkel. "A fleet of Russian soldiers with Jeeps are raiding all the neighbouring farms," he said. "I came to warn you." By this time we all stepped out of the house. "Oh, geez" when he noticed us girls, he said. "Listen, they are looking for refugees that speak German. They hurt women and especially young girls. Hide, they are heading this way." We thanked the young man as he rode off in his motorcycle.

Hans Onkel and Mother, without a word to us, walked together to the barn. We didn't play and we didn't talk. We sat on the long wooden bench in front of the house and waited, staring at the meadow in front of us, waiting for our Mother to return. We ran towards our Mother, as she stepped out of the barn. "Well, we arranged the bales of hay in such a way that we can hide the four of you," Hans Onkel said, meaning Mother and the three of us, girls. "Oma and I will stay here by the house. Now when we see and hear these Jeeps, you will have time to run to the barn," Hans Onkels lips quivering as his explanation ended in, "now remember, not a sound out of any one of you, please. It is important to be quiet. Do you understand?" he asked. We became frightened and just nodded yes.

It was a long afternoon, for every bit of noise we made we became fearful, that we wouldn't hear the motorcycles in time. So it was mostly silent. The time passed so slowly. Four hours passed, since we heard of these Russians, and nothing, not a sound. I heard my stomach growling and a sure sign that it was suppertime, but today that didn't matter. Not knowing what was in store for us kept the mind busy. The roaring sound was much louder than the motorcycle that came earlier. The four of us ran as fast as our legs could take us to the barn. One by one we climbed over the tightly packed bales of hay till totally hidden. I could barely catch my breath from the dust of the hay, but no time to complain.

The Jeeps came to a stop and the doors slammed. We heard

several soldiers talking at the same time. A language we couldn't understand. From their dialect a language we knew was Russian. Several of the uniformed men walked to the house, one of them in broken German stood in front of Hans Onkel and asked, "Where are the other people that live here?" "Only my Mother and I live here," Hans Onkel calmly replied, not letting them know how scared he really was. The soldiers turned away and said something in Russian. By now all six of the uniformed men stood together tall and were discussing our fate, we thought, for sure. Two of the men walked over to Oma and Hans Onkel again and repeated the same question. This time the soldier held a club in his hand and kept repeatedly hitting his boot, nervously. Hans Onkel gave the same answer as before.

We will search now. "You come," pointing to Hans Onkel. "Open the door," the soldier abruptly said to Hans Onkel, as they reached the door to our one room shed. All the while through the holes of the hay, we are observing. In despair holding our lips tightly together, so no noise could escape. Oma confidently waiting, for she knew there was nothing to be found in the shed. They stepped out of the shed. The soldiers again asked the same question, "Where are the other people that live here?" Oma this time answered, "Only my son and I live here."

After a pause the soldiers walked to the Jeeps to talk with the others standing there waiting for them. All of them gibbering at the same time, we didn't understand a word. Then two of them, approached my Uncle and pointed to the barn. We knew then, our fate was in their hands, as we could only watch, all seven of them, including our Uncle walking toward the barn. Mother just then made a shushing sound. Silence was so important we knew. I wanted to cry but I was too afraid, so I grabbed my Mother and held on tight to her hand. The door to the barn was removed long before we arrived here, as they walked right in through the large opening. At this point only leather boots were visible to us. A lot of talking between them in Russian was going on. One of them started walking around, took a long pitchfork, which hung on the wall and started poking. After poking around for a few minutes, he became angry, the pitchfork poked faster and harder, until the hay flew all around the barn. As they moved over to our area and started poking violently our Uncle could not take it anymore. With the pitchfork right over our heads for fear we would be hurt, Hans Onkel surrendered and yelled, "Stop, please stop, no more."

We stood up slowly and clung to our Mother. We started to cry, silently. "Please don't hurt us," Mother begged. There was a scuffle and one of the soldiers hit our Uncle, as he tried to come to our defence. "Let my Children go," our Mother pleaded, "do what you want to me, but let them go."

It was well into the night, before our Mother, Oma and Hans Onkel came back into the shed, as we heard the Jeeps leaving. When they returned to the shed, Oma and Mommi were crying, with Hans Onkel holding them up, trying to console them. I opened my eyes and saw Oma and Mommi walking listless and limp to their beds. Hans Onkel used words I never heard before and so upset a look of anger on his face that I never saw from my usual calm Uncle.

Austria at that time was split into four zones and occupied by America, Russia, England and Germany. All we wanted at that time to be in the regent of Upper Austria.Plans to flee to the democratic side of Austria (the American side) never changed. As long as we remained on the Russian side, Nieder Österreich, we would never be safe. This plan was the topic of every waking moment our family had. But it was not meant to be, not just yet.

The time to dream of returning to Kikinda was over. This reality set in for my Mother, while my Grandmother held to the hope of returning and wouldn't allow herself to believe what was happening to us. "Stop, Mother," Mommi said, as Oma cried and was homesick. "Please, stop. We will have food again, I promise," Mommi tried to reassure Oma. We've been through so much already and we will overcome this too. "We will."

Mother said. "Come on Mother, we are together. Isn't that the most important." she reminded her Mother and finally, a soft smile from them both, so as to reassure each other.

In the year since we left Kikinda, constantly living in fear for our safety was at times more than our family could bear. Not a day passed without hunger pains. No work and no money. The living quarters, indescribable, barely enough room to sleep. It seemed hopeless and bleak to say the least. Mother, especially, became more and more impatient with our meagre existence. Every day Mother walked for miles just to collect information for our escape plans to *Ober Österreich* (Democratic, Upper Austria). That was our destination and our goal to travel to. We needed to cross the River *Donau* (The Danube). A river too deep, and a current too strong to swim, that was our hardship. The bridges were controlled and passports needed to cross. How could we possibly do any of this, being refugees without any money or passports, it seemed hopeless, but, there was no time to give up.

Since Germany lost the war, the people like us in Jugoslavia of German descent lost all rights to our properties and returning was impossible. Mommi knew this fact, and kept it from us for she knew our status now, was homeless.

After weeks of walking, and every waking moment thinking of a plan, Mother came from the neighbouring town with some good news. "Rumours are," she said, "that several families have made it across the bridge safely. I don't know if they are true, but we have to try. We need passports and we need money." Our hopes shattered, for we had neither. Mother, however told us of the connection she made with a truck driver.

This is how it worked. Without a passport, you have only one choice. Truck drivers are allowed to cross the border to trade fruits and vegetables weekly. Mother explained that since this was a daily routine, there was little inspection for these trucks to cross. Crates that carried vegetables were the safest for hiding people. Our problem was that the truck drivers want money.

They were definitely taking a chance. If they were caught they would pay a big fine and in some cases even thrown in jail. Mother said to Hans Onkel, "This is my plan, what do you think?" The Miller listened to my Mother without a word. Finally, he said, "Let me see," and he reached in his pocket and gave whatever money he could. We had hope.

Mother explained more of her plan to Hans Onkel and Oma, "The two of us, (meaning Grete and Mommi) can try to cross, and if successful, rumour has it that once across, members of family can be sponsored and follow. Hopefully, my information is correct. A few families have been caught so far, well let's hope that we are not among them. What do you think?" Mother asked us. It was agreed to leave the life we have here is worth the risk. Hans Onkel said, "Let's do it" and we all agreed.

It was decided that Mother and Grete would make the first attempt. Somehow we received word that the truck my Mother arranged for was ready to cross the bridge in a few days. In the morning our day began as usual with a piece of dry bread, which was toasted on top of the stove. The milk heated in a large pot, with water added so the volume enough to reach for all of us. In white porzelan bowls, the milk divided into six portions. Hard old bread pulled in pieces then dropped into the warm milk. When the bread softened, we then ate. This was our daily breakfast, as well as on those days when nothing was left, it became our supper as well.

That afternoon, we bid our Mother and sister good bye. Oma handed the money, all our little savings which was wrapped in a piece of cloth to her. "Don't worry, one way or another we will see each other again soon." Mother explained one more thing before she left. "If we are caught," Oma stopped her daughter, "No Mother, listen to me. I have to say this. If we are caught there is a chance we could go to prison or they may let us come back, I am not sure. When we make it across we will get word to you, somehow, and then hopefully you can join us." Mommi put her hands together, looking up to the sky and started to make her case to God. "We have nothing to lose, please God, if there is a God please help us. I don't care what they do to us, this is no life. We have to do this."

We stood and watched our Mother and sister walk further away, with our arms waving, till they disappeared in the deep grasses in the meadow. Anxiously waiting, a few days passed and no news. We sat on the wooden bench in front of the house, and waited. Susi and I didn't play. It was midsummer and the afternoons were muggy and hot. Napping came easy, for the bench was big enough for the both of us. So we napped often. I was eight years old by now, and even at that age, one's mind wanders to the future and what it might bring. Will I be happy again? Will it ever be normal again? Will there be tasty meals again? I dreamt of my beautiful doll, that I left so neatly on my bed waiting for me to return. I dreamt of playing with our dog, I worried that Bengy was lonesome. I wanted to feel clean, with my beautiful pink dress on. Oh, those beautiful thoughts made life more bearable, before reality set in, always too soon.

Late that afternoon gazing across the meadow, two figures appeared far in the distance. Our necks stretched, so we could focus better. We waited for them to come closer. Almost instantly, we recognised it was indeed Mother and Grete. Susi and I ran as fast as we could through the high grass to meet them. Hand in hand we walked together to the house. Exhausted and hungry, they walked for hours. As a matter of fact they were so tired, that they fell asleep in the chair. It meant we had to wait to hear the rest, all of us a bit impatient.

Refreshed and on their feet again, we listened to their dilemma. The plan with the truck driver Mother said was well rehearsed. "A mile or so from the bridge we met. I gave the driver the money, but after counting it, he wasn't happy, but reluctantly agreed to take us. He felt the money wasn't nearly enough for his troubles. At the very front of the truck a few crates left half empty purposely for us to use. We climbed in, and the driver threw fruits and vegetables on top of us, and then closed the crate. The crates had holes on top for breathing.

"Now remember," the driver said. "No noise, please," "last week when I came through here, the line-up was long and the wait at least two hours. The Inspectors checked everything," the driver added. "Let's hope this week will be a little easier," as he slammed the large steel door. "Oh, please God, help us," we said to each other. "We drove for a little while, the road bumpy and dusty. The moving and stopping went on for a while. Finally, from the voices, we knew we reached the bridge." "What are you bringing across today?" the Inspector asked. "Fruits and vegetables," answered the Driver. "All right then, open the door." The inspector hopped on the truck, along with the driver. With a long thin stick, the inspector poked through the crack of every other crate. When he came close to ours, he ordered the driver to open the lid. At this point we were still safe, but we knew it was close."

Our hopes shattered as we could do little, but hopelessly stand up, or be hurt. So Mommi said, what could we do, we exchanged no words, and silently climbed out of the crate, all the while wiping off the stuck on fruit. It was strange Mother said. The inspector didn't say anything either. The expressions and the look of desperation in our eyes, standing motionless and begging, was possibly what saved us, and he took pity on. After a pause the inspector said, "I don't know why, I will let you go this time. But don't try this again." The truck driver was not released however. Mother didn't know what happened to him. We walked away as fast as we could, before they changed their minds and we would be called back.

The topic of every waking moment was to try again. This time would be different since information spread in our neighbourhood that passports could be attained easier than before. The Miller was a big help. Not only did he keep us from starvation, but he now offered to help with passports. He was known in the area and had connections. He entered our names without us knowing several months back. All he said was that there is a six months waiting list. The cold weather was slowly moving in and that was a concern. To spend a winter in this dilapidated shed, we called home for months now, seemed unbearable. But, again, what could we do?

One month passed and no news. But shortly after, good news did come. Mommi placed the passports in front of our very own eyes, a sight to behold. Is it possible, these passports could be our freedom from the life of misery we've been in for so long now? "We have not crossed the bridge yet," Hans Onkel said with caution. There was no guarantee we would make it, with passports because, so many forgeries at that time. I don't remember when and how we exactly left that rundown shed. But I do remember this, sitting next to the truck driver, shaking all the way driving to the bridge. With my passport in one hand and Hans Onkel holding my other hand, he tried to reassure me, "Don't worry, we will make it," he said.

And, so we did. We safely reached the democratic part of Austria, at least ten kilometers past the bridge the truck driver stopped and dropped us off. The trucks with the rest of our family took a long time and we wondered and worried until they joined us. "I wish you all the luck in the world for I heard of what you have been through. They built a *Flüchtlingslager* (refugee camp) just about a kilometer from here, go there," the truck driver said. "You will find shelter there." He closed the door and moved on.

We stood by the side of the road for a few hours, waiting, hoping and praying that the rest of our family made it through customs. After quite some time, we were reunited and started walking.

Forsaken In the Barracks

Our journey in Austria began in a small town called Ebelsberg. We stood at the edge of a small settlement, called Flüchtlingslager, a refugee camp, with just the clothes on our backs. What a sight we were, worn out, hungry, homeless, thoughts of despair, with a future uncertain, there was no time to cry or have regrets.

Flüchtlingslager was a settlement of barracks set in a large field about a kilometer away from Ebelsberg. These barracks were specifically built for refugees like us. They were built with cheap wood, such as pressboard and plywood, and unpainted. All lined up in one row like matchboxes, with every building exactly the same in shape and size. Each barrack housed eight families, one room, measuring 12 x 14 feet, per family, no matter how many. If a family was lucky, the room had a wooden door. For others, a cloth had to do. Privacy was a thing of the past that was for sure. There was one small window for every room.

Possibly, there will be better times ahead for us, we thought, as we searched hard to find one vacant room. The one we found was furnished with bunk beds with simple steel frames. The small mattresses were filled with pressed straw. The room didn't look too inviting. The walls covered with simple pressboard, one small cabinet, with a countertop and a few dishes. An old grey wood stove with a few coals lying around. Wooden planks with cracks everywhere, our floor. We stood by the door, just looking in for a moment, with a deep sigh.

"We will scrub the place from top to bottom tomorrow," Mother said. "I will try to get some soap. Well, I think this is better than the last place, don't you think Mother?" Mommi asked Oma. The first night in our new room, sleeping on straw was rough, but as it turned out not nearly as rough as the bed bugs. They crawled out of the straw mattresses as soon as we fell asleep. Grete was the first to wake with welts all over her body. One by one we woke to this horrible itch. By the time our Mother lit the candle, it was too late. We scratched our skin until it turned red. Being so tired when we arrived, considering the day we had, we fell fast asleep on the mattresses and it never occurred to us to check for these pesky little bugs.

The walls all around by the bed were crawling with them. We took our fingernails, and killed them. They made a clicking sound, for their shell was hard. In early morning, as the sunrise lit the room, I saw the walls full of spots of blood. It was horrible. But it was no use, there just too many of them to destroy with our fingernails. The bugs disappeared as soon as the sunlight came into the room, unbelievable, not one to be seen. It was barely light out when Mother came with a pump of some sort that filled the room with white powder. Mother made us strip and fumigated everything. I, particularly, complained and didn't like this odour and the fine powder made me cough. But, my mother had no patience and simply said, "Would you rather have the bed bugs?" "No." I said, pouting. Mother and Hans Onkel worked all day, and by the time nightfall came, the room not only looked clean, but it smelled clean. It didn't stop the bed bugs altogether, but it was a lot better. In the next few months to avoid more discomfort from disease and insects that ran rampant throughout the camp, soap and water became very important in our daily routine.

In the middle of a cube formed by nine barracks was a tap for water, called the community fountain. This was the only means of getting water, so hauling water in buckets had to be done for everything. The tap was high off the ground and when fully turned on filled our buckets to the top, very slowly. Sometimes we waited in line for our turn for hours. With so many people needing water, patience was needed. That chore became Susi's and my job daily. The fountain was at least a quarter of a kilometer away. The buckets so heavy, that I had to rest several times with every trip. Susi and I often made these trips together. It depended on what we did, for the number of trips that we had to make. The once a week family bath was especially tiring. When we took our weekly bath, in an old wine barrel, no one wanted to be last, for the water became cooler with each turn. The barrel was used for collecting rain water and used to do our weekly laundry. Usually, on a Monday, when the dirty clothes were collected and washed, it meant many trips to the fountain. It was a hard day, for with Mother's guidance we took turns scrubbing the clothes clean. The white wash soaked in hot soapy water, while the coloured clothes, in lukewarm water. In between all this, more water was needed and Susi and I continued with the buckets until everything was washed and hung on the line to dry. We had to work fast to be done by mid afternoon.

We cleaned our teeth the best we could, by gargling often and always at night. Twice a week, the fine grey ashes from the stove kept our teeth nice and clean. We simply stuck our wet finger in the ashes and used the finger like a toothbrush and rubbed all over the teeth, and then rinsed. I didn't like the gritty feeling in my mouth, so I rinsed well. A bucket of water, next to the water basin, a standard, with a ladle for drinking was always available. This was all good in the warm weather, but in the middle of the winter, when wood was rationed and there was no fire at night, the water had a thin layer of ice floating around like little pieces of mirror. I could actually see myself as I pushed the ice to the side so I could wash my face. I shivered just thinking about it and hated mornings.

At this time, food was scarce and I was hungry all the time. The three of us on many afternoons would end up in the high grass to play. With our arms outstretched on the cool ground, we discussed our feelings endlessly. On one of those afternoons, accidentally we started picking some grass within our reach and started chewing, for we were so hungry. The grass tasted pleasantly sweet and sour. We called it *Sauramble* (sour grass) and from then on many occasions it helped to curb our hunger pains, and we went back to the same spot often.

Those poor farmers that had fruit trees near our refugee camp didn't have a chance to harvest their crops that year. Being so hungry, we knew it was wrong to steal, but we did it anyway. I walked down the hill one morning and spotted an apple tree. I decided to pick only one apple, the farmer came running after me with a pitchfork and called me names. I ran so fast and I was scared, but I never let go of my beautiful apple. Eating that apple, I must admit, wasn't quite as enjoyable as it should have been. Hunger is painful and so hard to understand.

However, in the first year, our Mother went to a few farmers to ask for permission to take whatever leftovers they had in the fields, such as potatoes and corn. With a burlap bag on Mommi's shoulder, we combed that field to dig in the dirt to find cut up pieces of potatoes, that the farmer could not sell at the market. After about three days, we didn't want to be greedy, and felt we had enough potatoes to last for a few weeks.

During our second year in the Barracks, the aftermath of the war was beginning to show in many different ways. Every day, news came of suicides, mostly hangings from the nearby trees. One day as we walked to school, in the distance we saw a man hanging from a small tree. It was so disturbing to me all day that I could hardly pay attention in the classroom. Every time I passed this tree, I ran and didn't want to be reminded of that awful feeling. Folks received bad news of loved ones killed in the war. Every day folks walked to the community bulletin board to receive the latest news. Now that the war was declared over, waiting for any news about loved ones, for some became so difficult, that it drove them insane. Some people walked around the barracks aimlessly without any direction.

I was almost nine years old, the year I started school. The walk to school was long, but that didn't matter, for it was our time to enjoy our schoolmates. On one of those walks a man in front of us peeled an orange and dropped the peels. We picked them up and ate the peels, and that was the first time I experienced the taste of an orange. I was extremely shy at the beginning of school. The regimented routine in our classroom was very familiar to me. I conformed well to this routine and so, quickly became the teacher's pet. My new teacher, a woman with a humped back, a small frame, and middle-aged, brought out the best qualities in me, and working for her I was sure to succeed. I really liked my teacher, Miss Marta, and coming to school every day was a real joy. Grete was already well known in the school, being praised by every teacher for being so smart, probably helped me. I was proud to tell everyone that my sister was the smartest in her class, and she was pretty too.

Hans Onkel made a bench from pieces of old wood for the front of our humble home. With old flowered curtains on the only window, which our Mother managed to make out of an old sheet that was given to her by the generous town folk in the neighbouring village, it was starting to feel more and more like home. I don't know where our Mother found seeds to plant flowers. By the time summer came along, the outside of our only window was surrounded with sweet peas and morning glories climbing all over the window. Every day the dishwater had to be poured on the flowers. Since we had no inside plumbing it made sense.

Mother sat in front of our outside window every day after school, while she made us sit between her legs and she checked us for head lice. This was a daily routine and was done by everyone. Women of all ages from Grandmothers, Mothers and Aunts sat at the same time together after school and looked for lice. Everyone was checked, girls or boys, it didn't matter how old. I heard barrack gossip between Mommi and the other neighbours, listened of course without saying a word. It took about a year to control the lice problem. I remember when Mommi clicked her fingers together that meant she found one. To make this lice problem easier to control, Mommi cut all my hair off.

The only Photo of me when I was young

A small area behind our barrack was assigned to each family, room enough to plant a tiny vegetable garden. In between the rows of vegetables in the same area, two lines strung to hang our wash, every inch of space was needed for things of that sort. We children made the meadow with the high grass next door our playground. When the little flowers bloomed, called camomile, we combed the field. We picked the flower with white leaves and yellow middle, which we used for tea. Before that, on a clean sheet we laid these little flowers in the sun to dry. When dried, we stored the camomile in the pretty tins that our Uncle Pete in America sent us, our yearly fruitcake in. We drank this wonderful tasting tea all winter. It soothed our throats when we nursed a cold as well.

Mother found a new job by now, cleaning for a rich family, up on the hill nearby and was gone most of the day. The pay not much, but it put food on the table. A meal with meat was rare. Soups of any kind made mostly with any vegetable that we could find along with a slice of bread our daily diet. Once in a while, Mother made crepes. Spreading the crepes with a thin layer of apricot jam made it by far the most satisfying meal, but of course never enough. We called these meals mostly made with flour, salt and water, a poor man's meal. But it filled the belly and made the hunger pains go away. When Mother, on a rare occasion brought home a small piece of smoked bacon, it was a reminder of what we left behind a few years ago. This speck was not quite smoked the same as in Jugoslavia. Eating it with tomatoes, peppers and onions fresh picked from our garden and some crusty French bread was definitely a meal we savoured and it was enjoyed by all. Believe it or not, salt was hard to come by. By this time, everything of value, such as rings and gold necklaces, was traded for a little salt. In our house salt had to be rationed and used sparingly.

It was clear to see we were becoming more and more individual girls. Our opinions became stronger, and our voices louder, as we interacted with neighbouring children. When the outside world hurt my feelings and there was unkindness, it was comforting to know I could count on my sisters, always......

That summer, my cousin Vera came back into my life. I was overjoyed as they moved in next door. In spite of the few years we were apart, absolutely nothing had changed between us. Many afternoons, hand in hand, we walked everywhere together, and we could play. We collected all the fresh flowers in bloom, the blue cornflowers, the white daisies, the yellow dandelions so we could braid a tiara for our heads. She made one for me and I one for her. Vera had long hair with braids, just like me. We giggled as we placed the colourful tiara on each other's heads. In a circle we would hop, jump and fall, and all the time hanging on to the tiara, for whoever could keep the tiara from falling was the winner. It didn't matter who won, for we ended with our arms around each other, and walking, skipping and laughing all the way back home. I felt bad for Susi sometimes when I spent so much time with Vera. But Susi by this time made some good friends. She was always popular with the other girls. Besides that, our sisterly bond was so strong that no matter what, we were always there for each other.

One of the ways we could help the family to make some extra money was to pick berries, such as raspberries, blackberries and blueberries. When the berries ripened and they came in season, we walked and climbed the nearby hills, day in and day out. We girls and Mommi picked many baskets every day. We left mid morning when the dew had dried. We packed a lunch so we could stay for the day and sometimes until early evening, until every one of our baskets filled. On one of those mornings I encountered a snake between the bushes of the raspberries. I screamed so loud and ran to the area that was bare. Oh, it was so hard for me to return to berry picking. Mother tried hard to convince all of us that snakes won't hurt you. Although we continued to pick, I didn't enjoy it anymore. When the baskets sold on the market and we had a little extra food and especially a meal of meat, we felt it was worth the effort. Mother took some of the money and hid it, so no one knew of the hiding place. It was said, it will be there for a rainy day.

Summer was coming to an end and it was time to get ready to go back to school. The two changes of clothes I had needed to be clean and ironed which was my responsibility each day. Most of our clothes for winter contained some sort of wool, for they scratched my skin. My wardrobe consisted of one white blouse, a grey wool tweed sweater, a skirt and a dark grey wool

Pumphose (baggy pants). Mother made our underwear from any fabric that she could collect mostly from old sheets.

By this time, Oma could barely get around anymore. It was reassuring to know that when I opened the door my Oma was on the other side waiting for me. I sat on the edge of the bed often, with Oma telling me stories of her life. One story, I found amusing was about my Mother. "You know your Mommi was nursing till she was four years old?" "Oh, gross!" I said. Oma continued, "I came home from the market after selling apples one afternoon and there in the distance, I see your Mommi sitting on her little stool waiting for me. As I came closer, she looked upset and pouty. So I asked her, "What is the matter, my child?" She got up from her stool, and ordered me to sit down. "I am thirsty, I want to drink, give me some milk Mother, she ordered me." My Grandmother laughed as well as I did.

"So what did you do?" I asked. "Well, what could I do?" "Okay," I said, "but my child this is the last time." "Tell me more, Oma." "Your Uncle Peter, you know he was my first born," her eyes lit up as she said that. You know he left, oh a long time ago," with a sigh she said, as she looked up to the ceiling. Oma became sad and didn't want to talk anymore, "Go. Go outside and play."

The first day I returned to school, I wondered if everything would be the same. For many of us there was no connection and we didn't see each other all summer. As I entered my classroom, to my surprise Miss Marta stood by her desk waiting for her students. With a smile on her face, she assigned us to our desks for the year. She then welcomed the class and had a genuine interest in our summer vacation. At the end of the class, she greeted me personally.

"I've missed you this summer Käthe," she said with a big smile. I knew then that nothing had changed. I lingered in the courtyard after school, playing ball. Miss Marta on her way home spotted me and asked if I would walk home with her. On one of those walks, she invited me to come to her apartment. It was early, knowing that I wouldn't stay long anyway, Mother taught us not to overstay our welcome, so I said yes. The entrance to Miss Marta's upstairs apartment was filled with climbing flowers. Red and yellow flowers cascading down the brick wall and trailing ivy leaves winding around the iron gate, it was a vision of beauty and tranquility almost like a postcard. When she opened the door that same wonderful feeling I had with Nanna surfaced again. She placed the large key and the briefcase on a table near the entrance and asked me in. "Come, don't be shy and sit down," she said, as I slowly sat myself down on a wooden chair and said "okay." She walked into the kitchen and all the while telling me how much she enjoyed teaching, returned with a sandwich that was cut in half. "I hope this will not spoil your supper," she said with true compassion, pretending not to notice that I was hungry, each of us eating our half, mostly in silence, "Thank you," I said. "Your apartment is beautiful," I remarked. "Why, thank you so much. You like it?" she asked. It must have been my destiny to meet a woman again that was so much like Nanna. Miss Marta, also a spinster and who played the piano, was a woman with style and class, just like Nanna. I liked her personal quality. I was so tempted to ask her why she never married, but I didn't.

I had many invitations to Miss Marta's house and she helped to erase poverty from my mind, even if only for a few hours at a time. They were special times we spent together, singing, and talking about our feelings. For a tiny moment, thoughts of what we lost crept in and I felt guilty dwelling on all that I wished I had. Perhaps it was the luxury and fanciness that I craved so much. One of my fondest memories of my loving schoolteacher came one Christmas. It was the last day of school, when she handed me a small box to take home with me. She didn't know that I was not allowed to accept it and I certainly had nothing to give her, except to say thank you. I couldn't wait till I got home, so I found a little corner, so I could peek. I opened the little box, a pink satin ribbon for my hair perfectly rolled up inside. I don't know how long it was for I didn't take it out of the box, I loved the color, pink and it was beautiful. I didn't wear it for Christmas, for I didn't want my Mother or anyone to know that I accepted a gift. I opened the box every chance I had and visualized it in my hair.

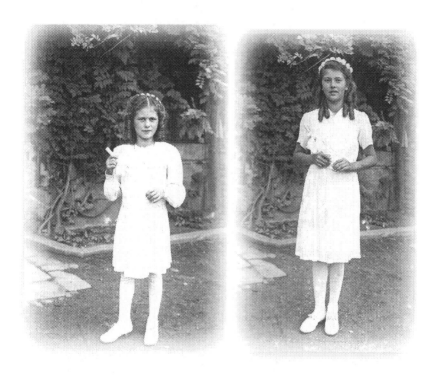

Grete (right) me (left)

The following spring, it was a very special occasion, to be able make our First Communion. Our First Communion was a big deal in our church. The complete white look, from head to toe, was not only symbolic, but beautiful as well. Hand-me-down dresses were passed down from one family to another. But there was nothing hand-me-down about our hair. It took hours with a thick curling iron to make large ringlets all over our heads. A neighbour lady brought steel curlers that were left on our heads all night, oh it was torture, but it was definitely worth it. In the morning our thick hair was full of ringlets and every one of them perfectly in place, we were happy. Mother didn't like all that fussing. She shook her head, but we knew she was proud deep down inside. When the little white flower tiara was placed on top of my head and the belt on my dress carefully folded and tied, we stood at attention for inspection. Hans Onkel, Oma and Mother stood nearby and made comments like, "Look at them, Grete and Käthe so pretty all in white." Vera and Susi took their communion some time after us. I cannot recall why. A picture of Susi proved to be unobtainable, as hard as I tried.

Hand in hand we walked together to our barrack church. Mother didn't come. She didn't think it was important to be there, besides she had housework to do. From our barrack church, where we all gathered, we continued walking in a group to the nearby large town church. We were careful not to wrinkle our dresses. The church looked like a dome, a baroque style and large. It took a long time to seat hundreds of kids in this enormous church. First Communion was celebrated yearly before the war. Several years passed without Communion, and so many children needed to receive the Holy Communion, so large churches, that held hundreds, were used by the Bishop so he could do many at the same time. This was done until such time as life could return to normal. I sat quietly between girls that looked just like me, rows and rows of them, my thoughts wandered to a time long ago. My face held a slight smile as I dreamed of the time of pink dresses, lovely Christmases, crispy white pinafores, the smell and beauty of cherry blossoms beside the porch. When my porzelan doll crept in, my heart became sad and quickly changed my mood. I couldn't understand the Latin mass, but for some reason unknown to me, the peaceful feeling surrounded my very being. I was certain, and felt confident that I was ready to receive the Holy Communion.

I stretched my neck a few times to take a glimpse of the many rows in front of me. Then came our turn to inch our way into the aisle where, in single file, we walked slowly behind one another up to the front of the altar, to receive our holy host. As I walked back to my seat, I spotted Grete, and we exchanged smiles. With the organ playing, and hundreds of boys and girls singing, we, in formation of twos, walked through the large double oak doors with our candles in our hands to the courtyard. The courtyard filled with cement flower pots, and intricate statues of holy figurines, made this occasion truly festive.

We were told a photograph was taken from the air, as we gathered in the courtyard. Although our family couldn't afford to buy one of those photographs, it was said to be a rare vision that looked like thousands of lily of the valleys all in white taken from above, for this memorable occasion. My favourite teacher was there and because of her kindness, I have in my possession a photograph of our class of that memorable day.

(Second Row from the Top - Miss Marta (my unforgettable teacher) First Communion, Früchtlingslager (Displaced Persons Camp)

In May 1949, our family moved once again and I saw my favourite teacher for the last time. As I turned and walked away from her, I looked back only once, as she stood in the same spot, waving. I remember this empty feeling in my stomach for the longest time afterwards. But the memories lasted, and as time moved on, I never forgot her kindness.

Our family made a financial decision to move to a larger city called Linz, Austria. Rumours surfaced of work in this industrial city and we not only needed work, but money as well. Food was rationed and our hunger pains less, but still a constant worry for our family from week to week. We moved into a much larger barracks called Lager 65. This refugee camp had an elected Mayor, a school and a church. It was definitely larger and more organized, but our living quarters no larger than our last place, still one room for the six of us.

That summer, I don't know what happened. I started to stutter and had funny feelings in my chest. It was disturbing to me and took up much of my time worrying. Deep in thought on many occasions, when Susi and Vera came and snapped me out of my shell, "Stop thinking, come on we have a game on the go and we need you." I don't remember why and when that happened I stopped stuttering and everything went back to normal.

That year my grades dropped in school and I wasn't interested in school anymore. The only subject that I was interested in was literature, something I was good in and somehow kept my interest. I loved sports, especially handball. Every free moment I had that year, I joined a game already in progress. Even the older girls didn't mind having me on their team. They liked the way I held on to the ball, without fumbling. When it came time to organize a game of handball, I was quickly a favourite pick. It gave me confidence in something I could do well. At certain times, I played so hard, till I ran out of air and bent over from pain. It was always too soon, when the eight o'clock village bell rang. I had strict orders to be home on time. If I wasn't home on time, I'd be grounded and that meant no sports. Often, I ran all the way home and at the end of it all, I'd end up at the doorstep, when the last dong rang on the bell. There would be my Mother standing by the door, smiling.

At Christmas, our village school put on a concert. Susi and I were waiting anxiously to be chosen for a part, maybe a part in the Nativity play. When neither one of us was chosen for the play, we still had a chance for the choir. They needed some angels as well. Susi came home with the wonderful news of being chosen to play an angel. I however lost hope. The next day, in the middle of the class, I was called to the Principal's office. My hands were sweaty and I was nervous as I walked down to his room at the far end of the barrack. I couldn't remember if I had done something wrong. I entered the Principal's office unsure, looking around the corner.

"Hallo Käthe," he said. "Hallo," I said. "Well, you are probably wondering why you are called to my office." I nodded my head, and said "Yes." "Well, your teacher tells me you have a beautiful voice." My confidence was starting to return, as he continued. "Käthe, do you think you could sing for me?" "Oh, yes!" "Please, let me hear Stille Nacht, Heilige Nacht." I don't know what came over me, but the melody just came pouring out. I wasn't nervous at all. After singing the first verse, the Principal put his hand up for me to stop. I became nervous and anxious again. The Principal said "Thank You, Käthe," and I walked back to my classroom.

In the afternoon, just as the literature class began, our teacher excused herself and left. Before she left, she made us open a book so we could read while she was gone. So consumed in my thoughts, I didn't notice that our teacher had returned. "Käthe Krämer," she called out. "Käthe, please stand up." My face started to turn red, I was so embarrassed. "Käthe, you have the part in the concert to sing solo, Silent Night Holy Night. The Principal was pleased with your singing." she said. I was so happy, I almost started to cry, but I didn't.

Our teacher wasted no time and immediately started our first practice that afternoon. "The class will hum, while Käthe sings," she informed us. She blew into a little tube, and then motioned for the humming to begin then it was my turn. After several practices our teacher in amazement said, "I can't believe, Käthe, how good you sound." She praised me many times in those few weeks, which meant so much. That day, I ran all the way home, only to find the room empty. Even Oma, who was usually home, was gone. She must have gone to the neighbours, not a regular habit of my Oma.

I lay my books on the table, which was placed in the middle of the room. On the wall next to the window, a single bed, with a board above for storage. The bunk beds, made with steel frames of brown on the opposite wall. Another set of bunk beds on the third wall. The walls were mostly bare, with one coat of cheap paint that Mother applied shortly after we moved in. The beds covered with a dark wool blanket. All the beds had matching pillow cases of flowered fabric that Mommi handmade from old fabric. The pillows rested on one end to make it look as if we had a headboard. Our extra clothes hung on the bedrails the only available space left. The small countertop under the window had a hot plate, ready for cooking. Underneath the counter several shelves that stored the dishes and silverware, and a few pots and pans. A definite must to wash dishes after every meal so dishes would be ready for the next meal.

I looked around the room, as if I had seen it for the first time. In a space no larger than an average sized bedroom, for the six of us to live in, made me wonder what happened to us and what forced us to flee so abruptly. On quiet moments like that so many memories of the past returned and it never failed to take away the happiness I should have felt at that time.

As the concert was quickly approaching, I reminded my Mother every day of the time and the date. "It is at 7pm sharp," I'd say, "and on a Thursday. Mommi you will come, won't you?" I asked Mommi from time to time. Mommi seemed preoccupied and passive about my request. On the day of the concert we had one more practice in the afternoon, just to be sure. When my

Teacher nodded her head, with the approval of my singing, I felt secure and happy. The concert was held in a barrack that was usually used for a dance hall, so large that it held and seated 200 people for sure. The stage was raised high enough to make the audience comfortable to view the performance.

I stood behind the curtain, I heard voices in the audience, shuffling about to find their seats. From time to time, I'd peek around the curtain to find my family. The hall filled up quickly, as the clock showed five more minutes before seven. The Nativity scene was in place with everyone ready as the curtain opened. The applause from the audience made us feel proud. I noticed Susi nearby, in her angel costume, as I moved my way over to her. She looked truly angelic, all in white with wings. With my hand next to my mouth, I whispered. "Did you see Mother in the audience?" "No, I didn't," she answered. "Did you?" "No, I didn't either. Oh well," I said, "maybe she is just late."

The choir, the last performance of the night, marched up to the stage in our matching robes. The three tiered choir got in place, with my spot in the middle of the second row. I felt secure not being singled out. The audience clapped and we began. My eyes gave the audience a quick glance from side to side as I saw our Teacher's hands go up. It was our cue to begin. Just as we practised, the humming started with the first few lines of *Silent Night*. My childlike voice bellowed out, while the humming continued in the background. I was so proud of myself, every tune I carried was crisp and clear. As we marched off the stage, we heard the clapping of the audience. Our reward, a small basket filled with sour candies, walnuts, one chocolate bar and one orange. But my best reward came from my Teacher.

"Good job, Käthe. Very well done," she said with her hand on my shoulder. I smiled from ear to ear. Anxiously, I looked over the crowd of people around me, families grouping together and embracing each other, as I was still searching for mine. When I caught up with one of our neighbours, she gave me a big hug, "I didn't know you can sing, Käthe." "Danke schön," and then nervously I asked, "Did you see my Mother?" "No," she shook her head, "no I didn't." My face fell and my lips quivered. I just wanted to cry. I knew Mother didn't seem interested, but never did I think she wouldn't come. I quickly worked my way through the crowd because I surely didn't want anyone to see me crying. When I reached the edge of the barrack it was dark out. I put my hands on my whole face and cried bitterly all the way home. I felt so forgotten and so full of emptiness.

Susi caught up to me, and she said, "Why does Mommi do that?" Susi didn't cry, but her words were anything but kind about our Mother. With strong conviction and a crackling voice I said to Susi, "I will never do this to my children that's, for sure." As we approached our barrack, I saw around the corner through the open door, Mommi talking to Grete. I wiped my tears off my face with my sleeve and straightened my hair. Just as I thought I was ready the tears started flowing again, I said to Susi, "I can't go in, I can't face her." "Yes you can." Susi replied. Come on.

We took a moment, I wiped my face again and straightened my dress and followed Susi into the door. My eyes looked down to the floor the entire time. I was so relieved when the lighting in the room was dimmed and no one could see my puffy eyes. Mother made a comment about the concert, but I looked the other way. "Oh, Käthe is mad," Mother said. At that very moment, painful tears turned into anger, but I said nothing out loud. My thoughts were disappointed and my Mother lost a part of me that evening. Just one word is all it would have taken. Just one word would have made so much difference. I longed for that word, as sleep did not come easily that night.

The next day, Hans Onkel and Mother had words. Hans Onkel told Mother what she had missed not coming to the concert. Hans Onkel came to the concert and looked for me, but I disappeared too quickly and he couldn't find me. Mother became defensive and said, "Oh, that concert stuff, who needs it anyway." "Your girls do, Kati," he yelled at her. I saw my Uncle mad only a few times before. Oma agreed, as Mother threw her arms up in the air, "You two," stop it! You think I have nothing to do. Who will do the work? You know what I mean," and the conversation was over.

The feeling of distance from my Mother had a profound effect on me. I can't explain it, but somehow my small world suddenly became bigger for I needed to depend more on myself, and more than that, the nagging question, "Why me?" came to mind way too often.

That fall I experienced for the first time feelings for a boy. I was eleven years old. Susi and a group of our barrack children gathered in the nearby field every night to play tag. The air brisk and the weather turning colder meant playing handball was over, playing tag, every night now our new evening sport. Every time Karli was tagged, he'd chase after me. At first, I thought it was the challenge for him, for I ran so fast, and it took some time for him to tag me. It was noticeable, a certain move, a special touch, and a certain smile he gave, that, he liked me. Although we didn't acknowledge these mutual feelings, instead we acted them out in laughing a lot, and walking together whenever possible.

I experienced another feeling that fall, jealousy. I didn't like that one at all, and didn't know how to handle it, except to pretend I didn't care. One afternoon I was skipping down the path that led to our so-called park, hoping I would run into Karli. When I turned suddenly by the clump of the mulberry bushes, there behind the bush, I saw Karli with a girl. They were clearly arguing, but I stayed long enough to see them making up by holding hands. I turned away quickly, so he wouldn't see me and ran home. It felt terrible, this new feeling, and I didn't understand. I felt helpless. As it turned out, Karli and this girl liked each other. They had a fight about the time I met him. After seeing him with that girl, I didn't like him anymore, or so, I told myself.

The following summer, the Red Cross offered families of

refugees to send one child per family for a summer vacation to recuperate with a wealthy family, somewhere in Austria or Switzerland. It was actually more a place to go for undernourished children. Since I was the most undernourished and the youngest, and the thinnest of the three of us, I was chosen to go away for July and August.

The morning when I left and said good bye to my family, I had mixed feelings and didn't know what to expect. A group of kids were placed in train cars according to our destinations. In every car, an adult was there to guide us and informed us of our new families for the two months. It felt strange to be without my sisters and made me feel lonesome, and I barely left. I rested a little, but most of the time I found myself looking out the window. We travelled through several long dark tunnels and I wasn't even scared. I stepped off the train with my little rucksack on my back and my sweater hanging on my arm. I was greeted by a couple with great big smiles. The woman immediately put her hands together in a praying form, turned to the man, and said, "Stefan," looking up to her husband, "it's a girl. Isn't she pretty? Can I take your hand Käthe, and we will walk to our wagon together, ok?" Before we started walking to the wagon, the man politely slipped the rucksack off my shoulders. "I'll carry it, okay Käthe?"

It didn't take long as we arrived what they called their farmhouse. Large double wooden doors, with huge black hinges, squeaked when opened. The doors were wide enough to drive the wagon through. Once inside the house the woman, called Rosi, said to me. "You must be hungry, you are so thin. Let me make you something. Okay, Käthe? " "Yes, thank you," I said. I was so hungry. She turned and walked into the kitchen and returned with a plate full of food. I couldn't believe this, for I hadn't seen this much food in one plate in years. She must have noticed the surprised look on my face, "Eat it all. I made it for you, Sweetie." "Thank you," I said, and of course, as hard as I tried, I couldn't finish everything.

"Now, let me show you. Come Käthe, I'll take you upstairs to your bedroom." She took my bag and kept turning around, as if she was uncomfortable walking in front of me. We made our way up three flights of stairs. The beautiful bedroom looked so cosy, but plain. At first glance it reminded me of my bedroom in Kikinda, simple, but friendly. Frau Rosi, as she asked me to call her, explained about Mitzi, the maid, who will be sharing the room with you when she gets back. That explained the two single beds. "Mitzi, she is a good soul, just a little slow at times. Listen to me talking away, you must be tired," Frau Rosi said, "I will go now. Käthe when you are ready come on down and later you will meet the rest of the family." She gave me a kiss on the forehead and squeezed my hand. "Thank you," I said, as she closed the door.

Slowly, I started to unpack, then noticed the narrow window between the two beds and walked over. For the longest time, I stood and admired the scenery. Rows of wheat, or perhaps barley or oats, as far as the eye could see, with the mountains in the distance, a warm feeling I felt at that moment. I took my shoes off and lay on my back, looking up at the ceiling. The sunshine streaming through the narrow window made an art formation on the ceiling with the large tree nearby. For some time I lay in silence watching the leaves move gracefully back and forth.

After some time, I opened the door, and started climbing down the stairs. I heard voices getting louder with every step I took until I came to a landing, and I stopped. Frau Rosi spotted me. With her hands on her apron she quickly came to me. She grabbed my hand. "Come, I want you to meet my boys. Hansi, come and meet Käthe," she said. A blonde curly haired young man, maybe seventeen or so, came out of the kitchen with that same smile as his Mother to greet me. "Grüss Gott, Käthe," he said. "Mother has been looking forward for you coming for weeks now, but me," he continued with a devilish smile and a huge dimple on his chin, "a girl in the house, I'm not so sure." "Hansi, don't tease her," his mother scolded him.

That afternoon I also met Michael and Rolf. The ages of the boys ranged from thirteen, fifteen and seventeen years old. Michael, the middle child, was reserved, tall and handsome with brown eyes and hair. He looked very different than Hansi. I visualized Herr Stefan looking like Michael when he was young. Rolf, carefree with the same charming looks and personality as his older brother, only his hair was longer. It made sense to me why Frau Rosi was so happy that I was a girl. In my family, all I ever knew was girls, except for Hans Onkel.

In the following weeks the teasing the boys exposed me to was very good for me. When we roughhoused a little too roughly Frau Rosi reminded her boys to go easy on me. Her constant worry was that I might get hurt. The boys often urged me to hit them harder, don't be so gentle, come on be tough, but as hard as I tried I remained in their eyes, always a girl. They had charming ways, Hansi already looking like a grown man, strong, tanned face with those unforgettable blue eyes and strong lips. He made me feel safe and he was funny too. Michael the quiet one with a deep character, he paid total attention to me when I had something to say. Although his brothers teased him about his seriousness, I could tell they also looked up to him the most. Michael was thin and tall with straight, dark brown hair small nose and very attractive. I bonded with Michael the most for he understood my shyness right away. I also felt safe and comfortable with Michael. Rolf, the youngest of the three, only thirteen and I, eleven at the time, didn't feel at ease with one another right away. Rolf looked exactly like his older brother Hansi, but at times seemed uncoordinated. Rolf made me feel strange every time he came near me, so for awhile we avoided each other. The feeling passed in a few weeks and the teasing started. These three boys introduced a boy's world to me with their roughness, combined with their gentle nature. It was something I quickly adapted to and enjoyed.

During the week the boys and Herr Stefan worked hard in the fields and with the cattle. Most of the work was done by hand, such as cutting the high grass with a sickle and then piling the straw when dry in bundles. Thrashing the wheat, barley and oats and making the necessary delivery to a holding barn was heavy work. Milking the cows daily, cleaning the stalls and leading the cows to pasture every day, endless work for the family. Frau Rosi and I made many meals together and she complimented me often and praised my Mother for teaching me such good working skills. Many evenings Frau Rosi and I took food out to the men in the fields. Because rain was in the forecast, they worked until way into the morning. Strong winds were also a problem, especially when the hay was dry. The boys introduced me to a drink that was called *Moscht* (apple cider) one evening. This drink was made yearly from left over apples in the orchard nearby. The boys showed me the wooden press; the press was large and interesting. They also extended an invitation for me to come back in the fall when this drink was made fresh.

However on Sundays, they didn't work out in the field, only tended to the cattle. It was a day of rest. After a hardy breakfast, bacon and eggs, homemade thick bread, jam and butter, we all went to church together as a family. What a quaint church. With the bells ringing and the singing, it was something special. Everyone sang, including the boys, with Hansi looking over to me, giving me a grin from time to time. I could tell the boys were proud to introduce me to their friends. It was not hard to figure out that this family was well liked in the community.

After Church, it was time for the four of us to go hiking up to the mountains nearby. That afternoon, Michael and Rolf were endlessly teasing Hansi because he had a girlfriend. I was looking forward to meeting her. When we reached the edge of the mountain, there she was. A beautiful brunette called Ingrid. Hansi greeted her with a hug and a kiss, and introduced her to me. Ingrid was very nice and perhaps a bit younger than Hansi. They held hands all afternoon.

Rolf was not too tactful at times about asking questions. "Ingrid what do see in Hansi anyway?" Rolf questioned Ingrid. Michael tried hard not to laugh, but he couldn't help himself, as he shoved Rolf over a rock, pretending to show Hansi that he minded. Besides being devilish at times, all the brothers treated me and Ingrid very nicely. Michael took my hand and helped me climb over big rocks. When Hansi spotted an Edelweiss, considered the Austrian national flower we gathered around and enjoyed this rare white velvety flower. The Edelweiss we could only admire and not pick, for we were told it was actually against the law. They grew mostly in the mountains, in the rocks, and liked the cool nights. Rolf offered his hand when I was tired, and jokingly pulled and pushed me around in a teasing way. Halfway up the mountain we stopped for a well earned rest and enjoyed our lunch which was neatly stored in Hansi's rucksack.

We sat in a circle, with the brothers handing Ingrid and me a sandwich and the teasing started. Ingrid, a good sport, blushed only a few times when Rolf made fun of Ingrid's and Hansi's affection for one another. Hansi quickly returned the teasing by saying, "You Rolf, we noticed you looking at someone a certain way lately." "Be quiet," Rolf said, as he gave his brother a certain look that only they knew what it meant. Hansi was easy going, and said, "I'll let you off easy this time Rolf," and they laughed.

The weeks with this wonderful family, were an absolute joy for me, so much so, that a few times I didn't even think of my family. The balance of this family, between hard work and still knowing how to take time to have fun, was perfect. In the second week of my stay, is when I met Mitzi. I had mixed feelings about my first impression of Mitzi. I thought she was boring and uninteresting. She had thick, red, kinky hair that she wore tied back in a way that showed off her large nose. But, spending every evening together before sleep came endlessly exchanging our feelings I learned that she was anything but passive. I found out she went home to see her family, in the neighbouring village, that's why she wasn't here when I arrived. She returned to the farm with a bad feeling about her family. She often spoke of her dysfunctional family, and said, "I am not going back there anymore. This is my family now."

The boys teased Mitzi with caution, not at all like they teased me. The attention I received from those boys, a combination of flattery underneath and self worth all rolled into one, was exactly what I needed at that time in my youth. Our affection for one another showed in the way our eyes lit up with joy every time we met. Frau Rosi had a good figure, blonde, naturally curly hair, with small features, a small nose and mouth, along with a kind heart, it is her soft voice I remember the most. Her gentle manner towards me was entirely different than her treatment to her husband and her boys. Although, I missed my family, to my surprise I wasn't lonesome.

Mitzi talked about her feelings for Michael which was a secret only I knew. She made me swear not to tell the rest of the family, and of course I didn't. She started to tell me about the family, "A few years ago, Frau Rosi lost a baby, it was a girl, and oh, the depression that followed when she was told she couldn't have any more children. Herr Stefan was very worried and the boys, too. The family took me in when I was only fourteen and I knew I was here to work. I do the work gladly," she said with a grin and a mischievous look in her eyes. "They treat me as if I was their own," she quickly turned her head, and asked me this question. "Käthe, do you like me?"

She startled me, but I quickly answered, "Of course I do." When I didn't say anything else, she started to cry. She cried quietly and I knew she was sad. I felt sorry for her, real sorry, and I became sad, too. Words started to come out of my mouth and I told her that my confirmation was coming up soon and that I didn't have a sponsor yet. "Wow," she said, "what a special occasion. Käthe," she asked awkwardly, "I would like to be your sponsor. I've never been asked for such a special occasion before." I wanted to make her feel better, so without thinking anymore, I replied, "Sure you can be my sponsor." It restored her happy smile as she grabbed both my hands, and kept repeating, "Thank you, Käthe. Thank you so much." She made me promise to keep my word. "I'll give you my address," she said and we both fell asleep.

In those two months I developed a very pleasant habit. Every morning I made time for daydreaming. It was my time to stay in bed and think about the day that past or plan the day coming. With my hands folded under my face, many pleasant dreams lingered on and on. Frau Rosie's longing for a girl was obvious when the day came for our goodbyes. My rucksack much thicker now than when I came, with the blue dress, new shoes and the matching ribbon for my hair, all stuffed in there. Mitzi handed me the sweater she knitted for me, I thanked her and told her I loved the sweater as I laid it over my arm.

When the time came, Frau Rosi stood in the kitchen along with the rest of her family. "It's time," Herr Stefan said. "Käthe, I will take you to the train station." "Okay," I nodded. Hansi, with his devilish smile, was the first one to tease his way out of a very emotional moment. He picked me up by the waist, "Oh wow, Käthe you are a bit heavier now than when you came, watch it now," and he gave me a kiss on the cheek.

Michael gave me a long hug and he looked so serious and sad. Perhaps I connected the most in friendship with Michael because we were similar in personalities and I had a different feeling for Michael than the others. Michael and I found ourselves many times in the two months drawn to each other by nonstop conversations. Even his Mother commented that my being there has brought Michael out of his shyness.

Towards Rolf, however, I had an uncomfortable feeling. I knew, even before Mitzi told me that I had a crush on Rolf, and that he felt the same for me. We never acted on these feelings, it was enough just to be near him, I told myself. Rolf, the most carefree of the boys, hugged me, waved, and said quietly, "I will miss you, Käthe."

Frau Rosi kissed me many times through the summer, but this was hard for her. I reminded her of what she was missing not having a girl. For me, I was so happy to be with boys for a change. My last vision of this lovely woman was, as I turned around to wave once more, made me feel sad to see her crying. Seeing her boys there supporting their Mother, with their arms around her, I felt better.

Back on the train, I stared out of window, daydreaming of the past two months. Among many flashbacks, I seemed to be plagued by the promise I made to Mitzi and it lingered on all the way home. Grete and Susi came to meet me at the train station. Oh, it was so good to see them. Grete looked so grown up and beautiful, her shiny hair perfectly groomed and styled. Susi looked just like always, just like me.

Susi let it slip that Grete was now allowed to go to the Saturday night dances in the barrack dance hall. Grete immediately corrected Susi and told us it was the Sunday afternoon dance that she was allowed to go to. That sure made sense to me with Mother's strict rules. Going out alone in the evening was not an option. We talked all the way home about my summer. "You know they had three boys," I said. "Wow, you were alone with three boys. Oh, if Mommi only knew," devilishly I said to my sisters. "No big deal," I added, "they were lots of fun."

Mother wasn't home as I opened the door to our modest room. For a short while, I forgot of our meagre existence. For me, life was as it should be for the past two months, a home, a bed to sleep in and enough food. But, back to reality now that I am back, that's for sure. Hans Onkel and Oma were so happy to see me. "Käthe, you look so healthy and so tanned, and I think you are taller as well." Hans Onkel said. By this time, I was all of five feet three inches tall, and turned eleven over the summer. The door opened and Mother walked in. "Oh, you're home," she said. "How was your stay with the Austrian family?" Before I answered I walked over to my Mother and gave her a hug. Something had changed in me. It's hard to say exactly what, except that my heart felt full from my experience with this other family and I was able to show affection to my Mother, even if she didn't give it back.

To make a better future for us was still an every evening topic. Still, without a country and without a home of our own, and very little money, something needed to be done. Many families started to move to France and America to begin a new life. Susi, Vera and I were together all the time and became quite settled in our barrack village. We attended church every Sunday, even joined a youth group, and of course our school. I was hoping that we would not move again, but it was not meant to be.

Before school started in September, Vera's family and mine successfully qualified to immigrate to France. We were disheartened when we heard the news, but Mother dismissed our feelings, and said, "What have we to lose, if we don't like it, we'll just come back." So once again, in search of a better life we moved to France. The Village of Toul in north-western France is where we ended up. Vera and family only stayed long enough until they found work elsewhere and left. I missed Vera so much that I became lonely and depressed.

Mother and Hans Onkel found themselves doing farm work. Hard work with little pay, not at all what they hoped for. With the winter coming, the future didn't look too promising for us. Hans Onkel became sick with a hernia and couldn't work anymore. Mother was struggling, not only with the work, but also the language barrier. It was not a happy household. Once a week, Mommi made us go to the nearby village to the butcher shop to buy lunchmeat and other necessary food. We walked into the butcher shop. Not knowing the language, we were so embarrassed that instead of staying in line and taking our turn, we'd go to the end of the line. This went on for some time, when the man behind the counter finally asked for us to step forward. He realized we didn't understand or speak the language, "Oh, no problem," he said, as he motioned with his hand to the scale. "Come, push," he motioned for us to show him how much by pushing down on the scale. So once a week we enjoyed this outing. From then on every week, the butcher taught us to speak French, with a little humour thrown in there, it made this trip fun.

We lasted all of six months, before we packed up and moved back to Linz. We moved back into the same Refugee camp, Lager 65. These camps still housed immigrants like us that came from countries such as ours. Our homeland was now occupied and taken over by the Serbs and Russians. The hope of ever returning was never going to happen. This hardship had taken its toll, for Mommi in particular, her face drawn, her eyes sunken, and her body thin and tired.

The barracks became more and more vacant as families immigrated to other places. Some families stayed in Austria or Germany, if lucky enough to find good paying jobs. Our Mother's brother Peter lived in America. Moving that far for my Grandmother was impossible, and our Mother wouldn't hear of leaving our Oma behind. So it was dropped for awhile.

The winter was hard, with wood for the stove now scarce. We managed somehow, by only having the fire on for cooking. Many mornings I pushed away the thin layer of ice in the basin that built up overnight, with the edges as sharp as a knife. I washed my face and hands and oh, it was so uncomfortable that getting up from under the warm covers. It made mornings unpleasant.

Although food was rationed, what we grew in the summer was put in jars and canned. Usually by Christmas Mother started to worry that it might not last until the summer when a new crop was planted. Our Christmas that year was like any other day of the week. The Christmas tree was mostly bare with only a few foil-wrapped candies, a few for each of us. However,

I was allowed for the first time to attend Midnight Mass. It was held in the city, about a three kilometers walk. I felt so grown up, walking alongside the older kids that belonged to the youth group. Mother gave orders for me to stay with the group of about twenty of us. Grete, Susi and I stayed close together the entire time. From a fair distance near the city limits, I heard the church bells ringing. It was more like a symphony of music in the air. The cold brisk air in my face, I loved the feeling of belonging and celebrating.

Once inside the church, the elegance of intricate statues and paintings of a baroque style, and that spicy smell, somehow gave me a feeling of peace and serenity. The mass ended with a lit candle in everyone's hand, as *Silent Night* echoed through the entire church. This beautiful song has been a sad reminder that lingered throughout the years for me, no matter how hard I tried.

A few days after Christmas, a package came from America. Our Uncle Peter's lovely wife, whom we didn't even know, sent us a package. The package contained woollen socks, hats, sweaters, mittens and chocolate. Among them was a hat made of wool, and beige in color. I wore every day. I loved it. A fruitcake in a beautiful tin, made with nuts, raisins and fruit, was displayed on our Christmas table. The tin boxes were kept from year to year for storage of such things like dried beans and peas, things of that sort.

In the central area of the barrack village stood the community hall, which employed a Mayor that supervised all these barracks. Every year **UNICEF** supplied enough used clothing for the people, especially winter coats. The community hall was filled with clothes for the winter months. The flyers were handed out to every barrack, turns taken by the alphabet. Finally our turn came and Mother made sure to remind us. "Take only what you need," she said. That winter I needed a coat, for mine was too small. After trying several coats on, I decided on a brown wool mid-length coat with a large collar. All of us girls walked home hand in hand proudly with our warm clothing for the winter.

In the winter months besides homework, we passed the time playing board games. *Mensch ärger Dich nicht* was played for hours, up to four people could play at the same time and it was fun. However, it was then that I became competitive and losing more than two games made me mad. On one of those evenings my frustration took over and my sisters started teasing me. I didn't like that feeling of being teased and left the game. But, the next day I wanted to play again and hoping of course for a better outcome.

As autumn set in, I became interested in writing. I scribbled for hours, and at the end of it all, a short story, or a poem. When anyone asked what I was doing, I became embarrassed and said quickly, "Oh, nothing." That winter, I thought about Vera often. We kept in touch, but it wasn't the same. Vera's family found work in France and decided to stay for the winter.

In the summer of 1949, our Mother arranged for Susi and me to join a working camp for girls. These camps gave us an opportunity to learn the domestic skills we couldn't learn in the barracks. Not only could we use the money, the pay minimal, but much more important we learned new working skills and also how to discipline ourselves. The camp accepted a few young girls from our barracks, we felt privileged to be chosen. Besides, being gone from the house meant two less mouths to feed. It would definitely help. Grete already had a job in the city looking after two elderly people, for the summer.

The first day at our summer camp, it didn't take long for us to figure out that this was a strict and orderly place. We had to make a two month commitment and not return home for the months of July and August. Our work began the first day we arrived. Our names for our assignments for our weekly duties were posted on a blackboard by the entrance. The jobs consisted of four categories. For each category five girls were assigned, to do four different jobs which worked out evenly and well.

- *Kitchen*
- *Cleaning*
- *Dining Room*
- *Sewing*

My first job was dining room duties. All together, the camp held twenty girls ranging from twelve to eighteen years of age. We quickly divided into two groups, the younger and the older group. Susi joined the older group and she had a pretty good time of it. I, however, being shy and naive, didn't really fit in with either group at the beginning. It took awhile for me feel comfortable.

We wore white uniforms as well as white hats that tied in the back of our head, quite flattering. I learned to cook several dishes that summer. One dish, a cream of wheat casserole, browned on the bottom, with a crusty top, and real raspberry syrup poured over the casserole, was everyone's favourite. Most of us girls liked this meal because no matter how much we made, there were never any leftovers. We took alternate turns weekly with these assigned chores. I was definitely familiar with the cleaning and kitchen duties. My sewing week, which was coming up, gave me some concern.

"Käthe, just do what they tell you and you will be all right," Susi tried to reassure me when I ran into her in the hallway. The sewing machine was large and felt awkward, as I placed a cloth underneath the needle that was already threaded. But in no time at all, I finished an apron. Miss Ilse came along to inspect my work. After turning the piece back and forth, "Not bad, Käthe" she said. Not only did I learn how to sew, but also how to thread and work the machine. By the time the week ended, I was confident making sheets, pillow cases, aprons and enjoyed this work the most.

At the end of the month, parents were allowed to visit. The girls that had no visitors, like Susi and me organized a game of handball in the courtyard. It was a well earned day off, and our team won. Some of the older girls brushed my head as they went past me and smiled. "It was a very nice Sunday, even if Mommi didn't come," Susi and I said to each other.

Our beds were arranged in rows of five. As I looked down the middle of the room, it was plain and large. Every bed the same, steel frame and dark brown in color, the duvet and pillow, a crisp white. Head Madam came to inspect every morning. God forbid, if our bed looked sloppy, we knew our duties would be reduced to scrubbing floors. Within one day, the room looked neat and clean. We learned fast, for no one wanted to scrub floors all day.

In the evening hours, with our nightgowns on, Miss Ilse opened a book and she read us a story out loud. We formed a circle with Miss Ilse in the middle. When it came to the most interesting part of the story, Miss Ilse closed the book and said, "tomorrow night, I'll continue." We were disappointed, but the lights went out and it was time to sleep, for tomorrow came early, seven to be exact.

It was an educational summer. We learned the value of routine and there is a word that I learned, called *Ordnung* (being organized) that I totally understood and needed in my life. Besides taking some wonderful memories home with us, we especially liked Miss Ilse. She was young and beautiful, and had a way that expressed warmth, very likeable. A group picture with our uniforms on was taken out in the Courtyard before it was time to say good bye. It was not easy to leave this orderly house without a tear or two, but seeing our Mother outside the gate definitely helped.

The walk all the way home was filled with conversation of our experiences and our pride for our accomplishments. Susi and I took turns telling our Mother about our new recipes that we couldn't wait to try out when we got home. "I know how to sew, Mommi." I said, "I made aprons, pillowcases and sheets." Mommi could barely keep up with our new energy and enthusiasm. Finally, she had a chance to tell us, that Oma was now bedridden and was having a hard time getting around. "Is Oma all right?" we asked. "She will be happy to see you both." Mommi replied. Susi and I left Mother behind, as we ran to our barracks which came into view. Racing to the door was fun. Outrunning my sisters most of the time was my only leverage. My athletic body was just the advantage I had over my sisters that I needed so desperately to feel that I fit in somehow, being the youngest and the smallest.

The door flung open, and Oma looked scared. Oma was sleeping and we woke her so abruptly. She quickly recovered, stretched out her chubby arms and held us together with much emotion. Hans Onkel, however, was not home yet. The two of us sat by Oma's bed the whole afternoon as it passed away with comfortable conversation. Sometime late afternoon, Hans Onkel came home. Susi and I jumped up for we knew it was him. We hugged each other tightly. He held his hands out and grabbed ours, "Look at them, Mother. My goodness, in just a few months they've grown up and so pretty too." With a teasing smile he said to our Mother, "Boy, Kati, I think you will have to watch the boys soon." We smiled from ear to ear, but our Mother quickly responded to her brother's comment, "Boys, what boys? Not if I have something to say about it."

I didn't really know what it would feel like to have a Father in my life. My Mother very much the disciplinarian, but my Hans Onkel was always there for me. I grew up feeling men were gentle, kind and easy going. My Hans Onkel was the youngest of six boys. I heard this story many times. When Hans Onkel was just a baby, apparently, he slept in one of those swing cribs. Somehow, the crib swung so high that he was thrown from the crib. From the trauma of this fall he developed epilepsy. His medication worked so well that I didn't see him having a seizure, ever. Oma was protective of him, for getting upset apparently triggered an attack. But to me, he was so gentle, warm and caring. My Hans Onkel and I talked about our feelings often.

Hans Onkel

On our arrival home, someone was missing, it was Grete. She worked in the city through the week and returned home late Friday night. I was happy when at last the weekend came, we were all together again in our little room. Susi and I took the next few days to reacquaint ourselves with our neighbours and friends. It didn't take any time at all for everything we left two months ago to be exactly the same. We joined right in with our play of tag. There was one change however, every so often one of us needed to run home and check on Oma, since she needed help now and couldn't get out of bed on her own. Our curfew was the same as always, 8 o'clock sharp. Mother was as strict as ever, we knew our rules well.

Every evening a group of us girls made a habit of walking together to the common toilets. We were upset, and not amused, that in our common toilets privacy was only a piece of plywood away. Boys, being boys, somehow made holes in the thin walls as pranks, and were caught by several of us girls, watching us through these tiny holes. We chased them and called them names, but couldn't catch them. They were lucky that we spared them and didn't tell our Mothers, for there would have been hell to pay.

However, one thing had changed about our Mother. A few times through the week, she didn't return home at her usual time, which was always suppertime. We didn't know where she was and that was different for our Mother to stay out late into the night. Grete was growing up so fast, and she looked so mature and tall. She had curves. It seemed as if she was transformed into ladyhood in two months. She was definitely not a girl anymore, although she was only fifteen years old. Perhaps, it was the hardship that we endured for so many years that made us all mature way beyond our years. Perhaps being robbed of our childhood was the reason. Our mature ways were beginning to show in our serious attitudes and responsibilities.

Everything was normal again at the home front when September came. Grete started high school that fall. It was a big deal to start high school, for in some ways she was now considered an adult. Grete's responsibilities in the house became different than Susi's and mine. We didn't think that was fair. Our chores stayed the same. Hauling water from the common fountain meant a lot of trips in a day, doing dishes, scrubbing the floor, sweeping, etc. Susi's and my chores, and Grete's chores, we were told, would be selective. Like Mother put it, "We need

Grete to fill out important papers, pay bills and she needs to study more." Well, Susi and I had a laugh about the studying part. She had a photographic memory and never did she study before. She ended up at the top of her class, not like us, studying every night and lucky to get a B once in a while.

Susi and I complained to each other, but we had no solutions. When we mentioned our concerns to Oma, she did not disagree. Oma had changed and lost her spunkiness, for years back she would have raised her voice and expressed her feelings towards our Mother. Hans Onkel however did speak up. It was only a few times I heard them use strong words and loud voices with one another. It was also the third time in our childhood that I recall Hans Onkel accusing Mother of favouritism. "You should remember you have three children," Hans Onkel said. Mother was quick to defend herself. She reminded her brother of the hardship and responsibility she felt taking care of all of us and the issue of favouritism was cast aside, for now.

Susi, more gutsy than I, took charge one suppertime. Our supper was as usual, our plates empty, and I mean empty, the bread made one more swipe around the plate to make sure that every bit of food was eaten. That evening, it was Susi's turn to wash dishes, and I to dry. Ordinarily, Grete would have to do the pots and pans, but not anymore. Susi did the dishes all right, and walked away. Mommi, noticing this, said, "Susi, finish the pots," and I knew from her tone that Susi was in trouble. "No," Susi bluntly said. Mother again asked the same question. "No, I am not," Susi said again. By this time, knowing what was coming, Grete and I, were willing to do them and headed for the sink. "No," Mother said, and pushed us aside. Again Mother said, "Susi, do these pots." "No, I won't," and at that moment, Mother grabbed one of the pots and hit Susi on the head. Susi immediately said, "Go ahead Mother, hit me again. I am not going to do them." Grete and I, crying by this time, made our Mother soften. Mother threw her arms up in the air and said to Oma, "What am I going to do with her?" Clearly, very frustrated and breathing heavy from anger, our Mother could not change Susi's mind. I don't remember how this all played out or the length of the punishment Susi endured. I don't know who actually won this battle. All I know, it never happened again.

My sister *Grete* was three years older than me. Being the oldest she grew up fast and had most of the responsibilities way too young. She had a photographic memory and was very loyal to family and friends. I didn't play with her because of the age difference, but I knew I could always count on her. She was poised, private and a forgiving personality. Skin perfectly tanned even in the winter, with dark eyes, shiny dark hair and a voice distinctively her own, strong and soft mixed together, which I recognised instantly no matter where I was.

My sister *Susi*, she had a heart of gold and a very likeable personality. As a child she was secure, personable and outgoing, and a bit stubborn and gutsy. Susi's complexion was fair and her hair much lighter than mine. She had a turned up nose that was fun to tease her about. In our teens, we were inseparable. She lost her twin way too soon, but she got me instead.

As a child *I* was shy, sensitive, pouty, with deep feelings, and I kept to myself a lot. Honesty and loyalty were very important to me.

In many ways our house was normal again, as I heard my Uncle, Oma and Mommi talking when they thought I was asleep. They worried about our future. Mommi's concern mostly, now that we were older and more exposed to the outside world, that we would be influenced by others and especially boys. "I'll kill them if they come home pregnant." "Wow, Kati, pretty strong words," Hans Onkel answered, a bit disgusted. "No, I mean it," Mother replied. "You know there are bad people out there," she said, as Oma nodded her head in agreement. I however didn't know what she was talking about, for none of us would ever listen to anyone but our Mother. We were so afraid of our Mother that the fear outweighed our desire to listen to anyone else, for we knew the consequences. It was not in our favour to go against our Mother's wishes.

It was 1949 and another Christmas had come and gone. Aside from a small tree with pieces of foil wrapped candy hung all over, no presents or any bulbs or decorations. Making the move to France had taken all our savings. Except for a meal with meat, Christmas was like any other day. Even so, there was hope. There will be festive Christmases again, we were certain of that.

A flyer was passed all over in our village, telling of a Sunday afternoon dance, with a live Polka band, too. Grete was already going, so maybe Susi and I could join and go along. Mother wouldn't budge. She said, "You are just too young to go." Mommi softened when Oma gave her that look, and she then offered, "You can go and watch, but no dancing with boys, do you hear me? And only if you behave yourselves," she said as we walked out the door. So off we went with our mixed feelings. Hearing the peppy music from a distance changed our mood instantly, and put an extra step in our feet, as we skipped all the way to the nearest window at the dance hall. We parked ourselves on one of the many deep window ledges, where we rested our arms. Oh, the dance floor filled with lovers, gazing in each other's eyes the whole time dancing beautifully to the beat of the music. I visualised myself being one of those couples, they felt warm, these pleasant thoughts.

Our heads bobbing through the open window gave us a chance to practice with our feet below, so no one could see us. Susi and I bumped into one another from time to time for the space was not meant for dancing, but we didn't care. We burst into laughter, ending up with swaying our hips back and forth. The afternoon passed quickly, even if just looking from the outside in. When the last dance played *Auf Wiedersehn,* we noticed couples holding each other just a little tighter and some even kissing. Oh, someday we will feel these things too, we thought to ourselves, someday.

Our sister Grete danced past our window with her flared skirt and her beautiful hair flying away from her head. She looked gorgeous, definitely outstanding, dancing with a good looking young man, made us proud to be sisters. She, however, seemed bothered by our childish behaviour. She had that certain look with the corner of her lips raised. We knew that silent look well, her look of disapproval, but she didn't get anywhere, not this time. We carried on, and giggled even more, for we thought the look on her face was so comical. On the way home Grete tried to explain to us how to behave like a lady and act properly. Susi and I just continued laughing and found the whole thing amusing. Lecturing us was pointless since our Mother did plenty of that sort of thing. Grete was upset as she ended up by saying, "If you behave like that again I'll tell Mother." We stepped it up a bit and pulled away from our sister so she couldn't hear us talking. We learned many points of etiquette from our older sister, although we never outrightly told her, or ever admitted to her how much we looked up to her. And so, our sisterly growing pains never stopped. No matter what, we felt secure to know we had each other through good times and bad. We knew each others deepest feelings without having to say a word.

Barrack's School
First row, second from left me with my favourite Male Teacher Herr Quass

My grades in school started to improve somewhat. I was now in grade four. For the first time since I went to school, I had a male teacher. Herr Quass, our new teacher, was young and no question he was fair. He possessed a flare for making school hours fun and interesting. When he picked my story called "My Sister's Funeral" to read in our literature class in front of all my schoolmates, I was so proud. It was a turning point for me to work harder for my grades. Mr. Quass also encouraged my story writing. He recognized that my writing was good which was hard for me to believe. My self confidence had not yet begun to grow. He didn't dismiss my attitude easily and persisted to reassure me to keep on writing stories. Little did I know then what he saw in me. He tried very hard to make me understand and he definitely helped, especially with my self-image, for I became more secure about myself. When I put my nose up in the air and practiced my newly felt security, one of my family members quickly brought me down to normal. As the days and months passed, little by little, girlhood turned into young ladyhood without my even noticing.

The following summer when school was finished, it was time again to find work outside the home. Any little bit of money that we could make, for no one made good money at that time, was put in a jar. I guess it was important for our family to know there were a few schillings for emergencies handy at all times. Mother hid the jar, only Oma knew where it was. Oma was, by this time, totally bedridden and could barely walk anymore. But, there was no problem with Oma moving enough for hygiene purposes. That was a relief for all of us, especially our Mother. It took two of us to help our Oma, so she could stand on her feet before slowly moving about with her wooden stick.

Oma was near death several times that year. We thought for sure we lost her when she had what they called the death rattle. Oma, all of a sudden, turned pale and started to rattle her teeth. I was so scared. It just so happened to be my turn to check on Oma that afternoon. The Priest came and gave her the last rites. When the Doctor came, he made an incision in my Oma's arm and I couldn't believe it, the blood was gushing out, in a stream as thick as a pencil. In a few days, Oma made a turn for the better, and in several weeks, was herself, again.

Our after-school duties depended strictly on time. Whoever came home first started the meal and stoked the fire. One by one, us, girls pitched in with the necessary chores. With Oma's experience and telling us what to do next, it was a good system and worked well for our family. Applications for undernourished children had been passed out once again. I was so thin, like I had been last year. Mother thought I should go. I was reluctant, but Mommi's mind was made up. "It's only for six weeks this time," she tried to reassure me. As I stood at the train station and said good bye to my Mother, I don't know why, I started to cry. "Oh, come on. You'll be back before you know it. Behave," she said, as I stepped up to grab the rail and reached to my Mother for her to hand me my cloth traveling bag. I turned away and climbed the stairs up to my designated seat. My destination this time was Switzerland.

The train ride was long and I mostly stayed by myself. My lady guide was nearby and gave me all the information about the new family that I would be staying with for the next six weeks. After hours of travelling, I was picked up by a beautiful carriage, all painted in shiny black. I knew by this carriage that this was no ordinary family, that they were rich. A middle aged man picked me up, dressed in a uniform all in black, introduced himself as Otto and took my bag. "Follow me, Käthe," he helped me step up the steep steps to the carriage seat, while all the time hanging on to my hand. We drove through narrow streets of cobblestones. I took in as much of the scenery as I could of this old well-groomed village. The flowers were in full bloom, with various colors streaming from every window, crawling on walls and windows, a heavenly scent in the air, a welcoming place to visit. Otto slowed down and then came to a stop. A wrought iron fence enclosed the entire property. I was in awe that I would live here. Otto stepped out of the carriage and came around to open my door.

"Come, Käthe," he said and he took my hand. Otto opened the large gate just enough for the both of us to walk through. The flowers covered every inch of the sidewalk's edge, right up to the door that opened as soon as we approached. "Grüss Gott,

Käthe," a charming middle aged lady said as she held her hand out to me. I stood in the doorway, I moved my hand a little as she gently grabbed it and pulled me into the room. "Danke, Otto," she said as he handed her my bag. She turned again to me, still holding on to my one hand, and said, "You can call me Frau Herta, Ja." I nodded and said, "Yes." We walked hand in hand through the kitchen as Frau Herta introduced me to the cook, Miss Ilse. We continued through a large hallway till we reached an open door. Frau Herta walked right through, with me behind her. She turned to me and said, "You must be so tired, my dear. So long on that train, are you hungry?" Little did she know that I, in fact was starving. I said, quietly, "*Bitte schön* (yes, please)." "Well, I thought you might be, so I had Ilse bring you a snack. See, it's here on your dresser," she continued, pointing to the plate. "I will leave you to rest for awhile. In case you fall asleep, dinner is at six o'clock and don't worry, someone will wake you." She reached for my hand again, squeezed it and said, "Welcome. We are so happy you are here," as she walked to the door and closed it behind her.

I stood in the room for a moment and stayed in the same spot, as a lonely feeling came over me, and I was sad. My eyes started to move all around the room. The room, surrounded in pastel colors of yellow, green and white, had a soothing effect on me. The two single beds were covered with fine fabric of pink roses. I walked to the dresser and started eating the delicious snack. I must have dozed off for awhile. The knock at the door made me jump from the bed. "Come in," I said, as I straightened my skirt. A pretty uniformed young woman stepped in and offered to help me unpack my bag. I politely declined and said there is not much to unpack that I could do it myself. "My name is Mona and I am the housekeeper. I am here from Monday to Friday and I am your roommate, for this is where I sleep too." "Oh, you do," I said surprisingly. My mood changed, and I was pleased to have someone at night with me.

"Well," she said, "did you see the bathroom?" "No," I

answered. She opened the door to which I thought was a closet. "It's our bathroom alone, we don't have to share it with anyone," she explained. "I have to go now and set the table. Frau Herta gave strict orders for the cook to make a special dinner for you." "Oh, really," I said. "Nice meeting you Käthe," she said. I followed Mona, said, "Danke schön," and closed the door. I unpacked and then slowly started to walk down the hall. I heard voices from around the corner, but too shy to walk further, I stopped. How would I fit in? The more I thought about it, the more nervous I became. I turned around to go back, as I heard Frau Herta call my name.

"Käthe, come and let me introduce you to the family. Come, Sweetie," she said, as she reached for my hand. "Here is my husband, his name is Rudy. You can call him Herr Rudy." Herr Rudy was perfectly groomed. His almost white hair and short beard perfectly cut. His belly jiggled as he put his wine glass in his other hand and laughed as he shook my hand. "Käthe, I hope you're hungry. I am starved," he laughed as he said that. Mrs. Herta poked him and said, "Oh you, you're always hungry and thinking about your stomach." "*Aber komm, meine liebe frau,* (come, my lovely wife)," Herr Rudy said, as he bowed. He took Frau Herta's arm, laid it into his and they started walking into the dining room. "Come, Käthe. Follow us," as I walked behind them.

It was in the dining room where I met their beautiful grownup daughters. Brigitte and Erika had an elegance and gracefulness about them that only a lifetime of living in luxury could one possess. They didn't talk much, but their tone was gentle and quiet when they spoke with their parents. Even though servants, maids, silver and crystal was not an everyday occurrence in our house, my manners never wavered. I fit right in and felt sure of myself in this stylish home. Mommi would have been proud, if she were here, I thought to myself. All those times she taught me good manners, how to hold silverware properly, never reach over someone and most of all always be polite, paid off. If only

I would feel more comfortable to talk to grownups. I agonized over this shyness.

At night with Mona, I'd make a game of imitating Brigitte, the oldest. I'd talk like her, walk like her and when Mona caught me, she laughed and said, "You're good Käthe, maybe you are more like them than you think." Brigitte was the one that took me for a walk and gave me a tour of the gardens. As the wind was softly blowing and moved her pink chiffon dress around her slender legs, it made me think of another time long ago. For a moment I didn't hear Brigitte talking to me, for my mind wandered back to a time when I had a beautiful pink dress. Brigitte noticed my distraction and simply repeated her offer, "Käthe, would you like to go to the village with me on Sunday for ice cream?" "Oh, yes. I would love to go," I said. By this time we reached the back yard, where a large cherry tree stood loaded with red ripened cherries, ready to be picked. Brigitte had no way of knowing that cherries were my favourite fruit. She was observant enough that when we approached, she immediately extended an invitation for me to pick cherries any time I wanted.

I wasted no time and the next afternoon I circled the branches within my reach and picked every one of the plump cherries with one hand and ate them with the other, as fast as I could, the juices flowing through my teeth, and the sweetness, so delicious. Knowing when to stop eating them came too late. I ran to my room and felt relieved when no one was around. I washed my face and hands and lay on my bed. After some time lying perfectly still, I heard my stomach making noises and my face felt warm. Minutes later, my stomach heaved and the toilet filled with cherries. What a relief to rid myself of this awful feeling. I avoided the cherry tree for a few days. I ate moderately after that, remembering that awful feeling from before.

On Sunday, Brigitte and I had a fun time walking around in the village square. Of course going to church came first before our afternoon began. Otto took us as far as the edge of the city square and dropped us off. Brigitte made all the arrangements for the time when Otto could pick us up. "Käthe, take my hand," Brigitte said, as she reached for mine, swinging them back and forth, we headed slightly down hill between two large buildings to the village square. Our first stop, the water fountain in the middle of the town square, with water shooting out from four sides. This fountain inviting enough to jump in, but instead Brigitte handed me a Pfennig, a coin. We turned our backs to the fountain, paused, and simultaneously threw the coins in the water. We laughed as we faced each other and walked to the nearby bench. "Did you make a wish?" Brigitte asked. "I did, but I am not going to tell you," teasingly I answered. "Did you?" I asked her. "Yes, me too," she answered.

We sat and talked for a while. We exchanged information about our families. Brigitte was interested in my family, especially my sisters. She confided in me and told me she had a crush on a boy, but he didn't know it yet. "Will I see him today?" I asked. "Well maybe," she answered, as she, blushed, a little. The ice cream store filled with people and they all seemed to know each other. I could tell that Brigitte was well liked, for everyone stopped and talked to her. The ladies with their pastel organza dresses on, and hats to match, made me feel as if I were in a movie. Such an elegant and pleasant Sunday outing. Finally, it was our turn with me ordering raspberry flavour ice and Brigitte orange. At one point, Brigitte socialized so much that our ice ran down our fingers and started to melt. However, the ice, as they called it was too good to waste. Our slurps were not too ladylike, but we didn't care. We just giggled the afternoon away.

The clock struck five in the nearby church and that meant Otto was waiting. We hurried back to our spot, where Otto stood at command waiting for us. At bedtime, I was tired, for I had quite a busy day. Mona was a real talker. The moment I walked in the door she started to tell me of her day. I was wise enough to know that some of her opinions were somewhat exaggerated, but I just nodded, and every once in awhile, said "yes." When I changed into my nightgown, Mona turned her head to the wall. I was so pleased, for privacy was important to me. I also returned the favour when she changed into her gown.

Herr Rolf ran a men's store, adjacent to the house. I was given the tour and Herr Rolf offered to make me a new dress. "Tell Frau Herta what color that you like," he advised me, "Okay, Käthe?" he said. I was so excited and couldn't wait. In this elegant household, Frau Herta was definitely the boss, but Herr Rolf the master in the store. Frau Herta, a friendly, warm and easy woman to be with. Her gentle voice complimented her gentle nature, not at all like her husband. She had fine features, but it was her slightly droopy eyelids that I remember. Her middle age face made up with soft red rouge, and lipstick to match, gave her a well groomed appearence of wealth. Frau Herta wasn't overly friendly to me, but was definitely kind and generous. Her giving nature was obvious, for she offered food to me all day long. Doing social functions in the community kept Frau Herta busy. Our afternoon teas in the garden with Frau Herta, elegantly served with fine china cups and as much desserts, small petit rounds with creamy feelings of vanilla and chocolate so rich and so delicious, were special times for me. Oh, but no matter how hard I tried I couldn't indulge, for I didn't crave sweets much. Once in awhile Brigitte and Erika joined us, I loved listening to them. It made me feel grown up, especially when they included me in their conversations and described Erika's upcoming wedding to me.

I befriended Erika in a different way than her sister. Erika was the younger of the two, only twenty four years old and engaged to a Frenchman. His name was Jacques, and I'd get a chance to meet him this weekend. Erika told me that Jacques was making the trip from Paris to finalize their wedding plans. Erika's long blonde well groomed hair and her slender figure gave her athletic body a spring in her step and a beautiful tomboy appeal. Erika had small features, like her Mother, except for her lips. I particularly liked her flawless skin and mischievous smile.

Erika and I played ball in the courtyard for hours, and when she discovered my love of sports, we bonded quickly. She challenged me with her skills of handling the ball and made it tough for me sometimes. I challenged back, and even beat her once. Both out of breath, she'd pat me on the head, and jokingly said, "You're almost as good as I." We both laughed as we walked in the house together for a snack.

That weekend, Erika came down the stairs with that spring in her walk. She looked gorgeous. Her long hair wavy and her lips ruby red to match her red full skirt dress. As she passed me in the foyer, she reminded me, that Jacques was coming from Paris today. "Otto is picking him up as we speak," she said. I could tell she was excited, for she had trouble putting her bracelet on. When she became impatient, I offered to help. "You know," she said, "we will be busy because Jacques will only be here for the weekend," she said, apologetically.

Jacques walked into the room and in seconds they flew in each other's arms. They kissed on the lips and held each other so tightly, they looked like one. After a pause, from the corner of his eye, he looked my way, as their bodies parted. "Bonjour, Käthe," and he walked over to me. His dark hair and one wave partly hanging over his forehead, strong features and dark eyes, yes, he looked just like I thought a Frenchman would look. The dark blue suit and matching tie, made me stare. He must have noticed and quickly said, "I heard much about you, Käthe. You come from Austria, yes?" "Yes, I do," I answered. "Erika is so disappointed because you won't be here for our Wedding," he said, as they walked holding hands out into the gardens. Oh, they made a beautiful couple. Every moment that weekend they spent together.

Brigitte gave me a special tour of the rest of the house, meaning the upstairs, which seemed off limits to me and the rest of the staff. I was in awe as I stepped into Brigitte's room. It seemed like a fantasy. Every inch of the walls covered with pink georgette fabric gathered fully up to the ceiling. The bed was fluffy with many pillows, also in pink and white. Brigitte noticed my surprise and extended an invitation for me to hop on the bed. "Come on, try it out, come on." "Really? Okay," I said, as I jumped on this luxurious bed. Brigitte lay next to me, and she asked, "Käthe, tell me how can you be so nice when you have been thru so much in your young life. I can't imagine being poor. Do you think I am terrible for saying that?" "No," I quickly replied, "you are really nice too" "I am sorry, I shouldn't have asked you about the war." "That's okay." I replied.

It happened the third week that I stayed with this wonderful family. One morning as I came out of my room and walked to the kitchen, I noticed only Ute, the cook, was in the house. Ute offered to make me breakfast. While she was working by the stove making my eggs, she offered to make me lunch as well. She told me she was taking the afternoon off and maybe even the next day. "There is a family crisis and I am needed," she explained, as I listened to her while I was eating my breakfast. In the morning I went outside for awhile. The gardens, so full of color and relaxing, just sitting on the bench made me feel comfortable. After awhile I got bored and walked back into the house. I walked through the whole house and no one seemed to be home. I walked to my room and started writing a letter to my family. I must have dozed off for a while, for when I woke, I heard the clock strike one. After washing my face, I walked to the kitchen to eat my sandwich that Ute made for me earlier.

As I past Herr Rolf's office, the door was wide open. I walked slowly and quietly so I wouldn't disturb Herr Rolf who was sitting behind his large desk. "Come in here Käthe," Herr Rolf said, sounding somewhat like an order. My body felt uneasy. "Ok," I said. I slowly walked up to the desk and stopped. "Come here a little closer Käthe," he said, as he guided me with his hand stretched over the desk. Moments later, he started to explain different objects on his desk. I felt his fingers slowly moving up between my legs. "That feels good, doesn't it Käthe," he said. My feet seemed to be stuck on the floor, I didn't move. I didn't know if I should cry or scream, all I knew, that I wanted to run and was extremely uncomfortable. "Don't be scared, Käthe, I won't hurt you," looking at me as he said that. When he reached all the way up to my panties, I jumped away.

He stopped, and took his hand and placed it on his desk. "Can I go now?" I asked, barely getting the words out of my mouth. He didn't look at me as he said. "Now Käthe, you won't tell Frau Herta, Will you?" "No, no," I shook my head. "You have to swear you won't tell," as he looked me in the eyes then, waiting for my answer. I promised and ran all the way to my room. I closed the door behind me and just leaned against the door for the longest time. It was then I started to cry and could hardly keep my body from shaking. I didn't understand what just happened here. I don't know how long I leaned against the door, but when I heard voices from someone other than Herr Rolf, I was relieved. It was then that I lay on the bed in a doubled up position for what seemed, forever.

The next three weeks passed slowly for me. The anticipation of being alone in the house with Herr Rolf terrified me. Although Herr Rolf never did anything like that again, it didn't matter, for my carefree daily joy now was consumed in worry. Frau Herta seemed confused by my change of personality. She often asked, "Käthe, what is the matter, are you not happy here?" That lovely woman, how could I ever tell her such a thing? There were times I was tempted, when Herr Rolf openly treated her as if she was the only woman for him. Of course, I remained silent and just answered, "Frau Herta, I miss my family." "Oh, I understand, Darling," she said, with affection. I wondered how someone could live with such a lie, and I was deeply bothered by his action. However, a few days before I left, Herr Rolf told me so no one could hear that he was sorry for what he did. I didn't answer him. His apology helped, but it didn't change my mind about him, for he violated my trust and spoiled three remaining weeks of joy with this wonderful family.

Sitting on my seat on the train with my head resting on the window, I relived the last six weeks of my summer. Erika and Brigitte had a profound effect on me, their gentle and charming ways about them, something to hold dear. Frau Herta, a classy, respected lady in the community. For me, I felt sorry for her. With every experience in life we learn something. I learned about mistrust and deceit that day in Herr Rolf's office. I trusted Herr Rolf. "Why did he do that? How can I make these thoughts go away?" I asked myself over and over again. Finally, I stopped my train of thought when I remembered what was waiting for me at the end of this trip. I smiled as I thought of my family. I was so excited and couldn't wait to be reunited with my sisters.

I jumped off the train and not far away, I saw my Mother arm in arm with a man. He had an unshaven face and greasy hair. After our greeting, Mother said, "This is Karl." "Say hello, Käthe," "Hello," I said. The feeling in my stomach was not good and the ants in my chest even worst. I pulled away from my Mother as I spotted Grete and Susi coming to meet me. I was so happy to see them, and the feelings mutual, I was sure. We purposely slowed down our pace in walking until far enough from Mother so they couldn't hear us talking. "Who is this man?" I asked. Both Grete and Susi talked so fast I couldn't keep up or understand what they tried to tell me. My sisters concerns about Karl made me feel uneasy. Finally I said, "Stop, you're scaring me." I learned that Mother and Karl had seen each other for the last six months. That explains where Mother has been late at night. Oma and Hans Onkel did not approve of Karl either, they told me. There was talk because of money reasons, or so Mommi said, of a possibility that Karl might move in with us. This was a grim thought. For I could tell by Hans Onkels and Oma's reaction, that Karl did not fit in our family.

Mommi and Oma had many differences in those winter

months. Oma voiced her opinions openly of her disapproval, his manners especially. "How can you tell your girls one thing and then do something else yourself. With his morals, are you sure your girls are safe? He has no manners, oh yai, yai!" Oma said disgustedly. Mother replied the same way everytime, "I am tired of working and the responsibilities of everyone and not getting anywhere." "Kati, but we don't need him," my Oma pleaded. This unrest in our house is something we experienced rarely between Oma, Hans Onkel and Mother before Karl's arrival. The constant bickering made us feel happy to be outside the house and we stayed away every chance we had. Playing turned into Susi and me walking together and talking of our unhappy family. We tried to find solutions, but like always we didn't have any. All we could say, selfishly thinking only of ourselves, was, "How could our Mother do this to us?"

Mother found a way out of poverty, for Karl worked for the city, rebuilding roads and pouring asphalt, a job that paid well at that time. Our Mother, only forty one years old, needed a life outside our family. Karl flashed his money around every chance he had. He paid for groceries here and there, making sure that our Grandmother knew of every penny that he spent. It was insulting to stoop to his tactics and Oma told him so. "Don't bring us anything," she told him one day. There was a major blow-up. Their voices so loud the whole neighbourhood could hear. They argued so fiercely that Karl lost his temper. When Mother told him to leave, he hit our Mother in the face. All of us especially us, girls, absolutely stunned by Karl's barbaric actions. First of all, this kind of arguing felt disturbing to us, only once before we experienced such an outburst with Vera's parents. Second of all, hitting our Mother was more than we could bear. We could do nothing more than run to our Mother, trying to console her, held on to her, and cried. "Please stop, please stop," we pleaded. Karl slammed the door and left.

When the house calmed down and was normal again, Oma and Mommi talked for the longest time. It turned into days of

Mother trying to fit Karl into our family. Oma wouldn't budge and couldn't excuse his bad manners, and she didn't trust him either. I remember so well, she referred to him as **The Bear.** "Here he comes again, **That Bear.**" That's what she called him, not by his name.

It happened one afternoon when I understood what my sisters and Oma meant when they said they didn't trust him. I sat at the edge of the barracks by the meadow, I don't know why, maybe just picking sauramble, when Karl came walking towards me. He sat next to me as he greeted me. After a pause, he said, "I hear you like sports." "Oh, yes I do," I answered. "Well how would you like for me to show you a trick." "Sure," I said. He lay on his back and instructed me to step on his hands, which he had stretched on the ground. "Come on, step on my hands," he said. I was starting to feel something was wrong here. He lifted me slowly up over his head, slowly in a balancing act as he started to spread my legs apart. As he spread my legs further and further apart, disgustingly, I jumped off quickly, excused myself, not to make it too obvious that I was uneasy.

"I'll go now. My girlfriends are waiting for me," I said and left. I became angry and thought to myself, does he really think I am so stupid that I didn't know what he was trying to do. Then on the other hand, I couldn't tell Mother. I knew what would happen if I did, so I told my sisters instead. With this, our feelings of mistrust grew, and he kept giving us more reasons not to change our minds. When Susi and Grete heard of this, we made a pact to stick together and never ever be alone with Karl. We agreed not to talk to our Mother for so many reasons. Mother was determined and it was a sad day when Karl moved into our small living quarters. Our household and our harmonious family was never the same again. Our lives changed, it seemed, overnight. The tension in the house began almost the moment he moved in.

It started that first night. All tucked in our beds, me sleeping with Hans Onkel, Grete used to sleep with Mother and now slept with Susi, Oma alone, and of course Mother with Karl. Karl waited only ten minutes or so before we heard our Mother fighting him off. "Karl, my Mother and the kids are here. Wait till later, Karl, please," our Mother pleaded. The squeaking of the bed that followed was so offensive to us, that I in particular didn't know what to do. I didn't know what they were doing; I just knew it was uncomfortable and strange. Hans Onkel handed me the pillow to cover my ears, but the noise didn't go away. After a long silence, we finally fell asleep.

The next morning, Oma confronted Mother, "Do you have any idea of how uncomfortable last night was for us, especially your girls? Can't you tell him to leave? Please Kati, please. Get rid of him," Oma pleaded. Mother was uncomfortable too. "Well, what can I do, with no privacy?" Oma had no way of knowing that Karl returned and was listening on the other side of the door. Karl stormed in. "What is this I hear, you don't appreciate me helping out?" His voice was so loud, all could hear. Can one imagine the embarrassment we endured? We had always lived with strong values, and now all our neighbours knew of our dysfunctional family.

Oma quickly told Karl of her disappointment concerning his actions the previous night. "Well, that's too bad," he said, "get used to it." Oma was so disgusted, she was lost for words. "You can't talk to this man," she said as she threw her hands up in the air. Karl wanted, all of our Mother's free time. He was jealous when Mother spent any time with us. Because of this, they argued about everything. When we needed money, mostly for school functions and lunches, Mommi decided it was best for us to ask Karl, so he would feel included. That was hard for us. We didn't want to, but we had no choice.

"We don't want to ask him, Mommi," we pleaded. "Why do we have to?" "Well, he makes the money and he feels better," she answered. In the end, we swallowed our pride and put our beliefs aside. We asked, held out our hands and in silence, accepted the money. Mother also gave Karl the freedom to discipline us. Our personalities now formed through our past upbringing, we had deep rooted morals and manners by this time and very aware of right from wrong. We needed guidance and fairness more than anything else. Karl, a single man all these years, had no experience with children. His discipline was unfair and caused many fights.

After Karl moved in, the first Sunday meal that we were able to afford with meat, our enjoyment now turned to a big disappointment for us girls. The meat, usually a cheap cut of beef with plenty of fat, was made into a big pot of soup cooked with carrots, parsnips, onions and potatoes. When ready to eat, the large piece of meat was divided in seven pieces. We were never forced to eat the fatty bits, which we hated, that part of the meat went to the grownups before. Karl divided the portions and gave all of us fatty pieces. When we left the pieces of fat in our plate the arguing started. "Eat it," Karl ordered. "Eat it or you are grounded for one week." Mother was visibly upset and angry, "Stop it Karl, they can't eat it," Mother came to our defence. "Be quiet," he lashed out at Mother. "I am the boss," he said. I tried so hard, but it was no use, I gagged and could not swallow. All three of us girls were grounded. We gave in and simple said, "Go ahead ground us. We can't eat it," trying to stop the argument.

My sisters and I learned quickly to survive in this new house. We needed to agree or be passive—either one—a feeling so disturbing and we never did get used to it. The outside world, believe it or not, was even crueller than our new home life. Some neighbours distanced themselves from us. They stood around and talked openly about us, as if we were some low life. However, some were kind, felt bad for us and understood our dilemma. The cruellest of all, when the gossip reached our school, some of my friends whispered to each other so I could hear them. When I came near, they turned away from me, laughing. It was awful. I withdrew from everyone, and walked with my head up high, pretending it didn't matter, that I didn't care, but all the while my heart was screaming with pain. My sisters, in the same place as me and one sure thing that I could count on, made this awful time bearable.

I learned many things that year in 1950. With the war behind us, still homeless and practically nothing to our name, our future was still uncertain. My so-called childhood almost coming to the end, now thirteen years old, with our family divided and much conflict. Our small room, barely enough room for the six of us, now held one more. It seemed impossible. For privacy, a blanket held and spread by two of us, so we could change, only if we were nude. The rest of the time, we just respected each other's privacy and looked away.

So then the unthinkable happened. Oma and Hans Onkel must have talked about finding a new place to live for some time now. Their decision to move elsewhere was possibly the worst feeling we girls endured so far. They had been with us all our lives. No matter what we always had each other. Oma and Hans Onkel found a farmhouse to rent in Innsbruck in the hope that by leaving, our lives would improve. Reluctantly the decision was made to move. "It is for the best," Oma explained. "With two less people in our small room, perhaps the arguing will stop." She noticed our disappointment, as she said, "Don't worry it will be all right, my child. I promise. Don't be sad. You can come. Hop on the bus anytime." Oh, we knew that was much easier said than done.

It was a sad day as we watched Oma, with her cane, she could barely walk anymore, and Hans Onkel, with one small suitcase between them, walking down the long barrack until they turned the corner and we couldn't see them anymore. At least, with Mother's and Oma's relationship strained, they parted on good terms, but not until our Oma had the last word. "I am telling you Kati," with Oma's finger pointing in my Mother's face, she said, "You are making a big mistake. **That Bear**, he is mean, you'll see."

Feeling *verloren* (lost), we tried to make some sense of it all.

Susi and I aimlessly walked without direction till we ended up in the nearby meadow, our spot, and we had privacy. Hoping and waiting for this emptiness to pass. Selfish thoughts we shared, that afternoon, as we tried to pick each other up out of this terrible emptiness we felt. Who will be there to rescue us now, who will be waiting for us when we come home from school, and who will be there to hear our concerns? These were some of the questions that went unanswered. We remained in the meadow for most of the afternoon. Susi and I felt helpless, and became troubled as conversations of our home life totally consumed our waking hours. For the first time in our young lives we couldn't depend on anyone. Was it growing up, or did we fear the unknown future, we asked ourselves. In any case we trusted only each other, and silently hoped that Mother would come back to us. But, it never happened.

Mother was so consumed with her life with Karl that it changed not only our everyday routine, but us girls, too. The days turned into months, uncertain feelings put a shield around our hearts, and so the strength we developed from our past carried us through this time. Susi and I became inseparable. Grete tried hard to talk to our Mother on our behalf, but in the end of it all, it fell on deaf ears.

Being hungry continued to be a constant struggle. We could deal with the hunger pains, but now just when there was a slight hope of better things to come, Karl came into our house. We still considered ourselves lucky, for news came, everyday of relatives left behind. We wondered what happened to Nanna. Was she spared? We knew she was of Serbian descent and stayed in Kikinda because of that reason. Donau Schwaben people, like us, that stayed behind in Jugoslavia ended up in concentration camps. Some starved to death; news of torture came every day. Some were sent to the Russian coal mines for years without word from them. Some survived and the really lucky ones even ended up being able to go back home.

The first week that Oma was gone it happened.

One evening every week, on a Wednesday, Susi and I attended a youth group at our Catholic church. The highlight of our entire week, we played board games, ping pong, and had a sit down conversation hour. The local Priest organised these few hours of fun for teenagers, like Susi and me. We knew something was brewing when Karl found out that boys also attended. Mother tried to explain to us that Karl doesn't like us going out in the evening. We immediately defied our Mother and asked, "What do you think Mother? You know we are not doing anything wrong and we are going." "Yes, I know. I told Karl that." That Wednesday, we went to our youth group fun evening, knowing full well that we are safe. Karl worked nights and he was long gone before we left. Toward the end of our evening, we sat in a circle and just talked, each one of us exchanging our concerns and feelings. A loud knock at the door interrupted our talks. Every one, of us kids looked toward that door at the same time.

There he stood, Karl, with that look of rage on his face that we had seen a few times before. Without saying a word, he turned and left the door wide open. Susi and I rushed home, fearful of what laid ahead for us. In the distance we heard arguing, so loud that our neighbours one by one opened their doors. Our fears overshadowed the embarrassment we might have felt any other time. The door flung open before we even touched the knob. Karl was red in his face and full of rage when he screamed, "What do you think you are doing, going out when I said no!" Susi answered, "We've gone every week, Karl." "Well, no more," Karl said. Mother tried to reason with him and said, "Don't be ridiculous, Karl." "They are not going anymore," he repeated. "Yes they are," Mommi answered. Karl was so outraged that once again he hit our Mother. Susi and I ran over to our Mother and started to cry. Their arguing was unbearable for us and we gave in, "Stop, please stop. We won't go anymore." Karl, without a word, slammed the door and went back to work.

The following day, after school the kindness flowed out of his mouth. He offered us money for ice cream. There was so much sadness inside our hearts. We put our hand out and accepted the money so there would be peace. As always, in the following days Karl and Mother made up. For us, however, these bad feelings lingered on and we wondered how long before the next episode.

A month passed before we could get enough money together for the bus to visit Oma and Hans Onkel. It was an all day trip. The bus took us only to the edge of the dirt road and the rest of the way we walked. A farm house that we passed along the way raised ducks and geese, these geese chased us and we were afraid of them, for they nipped the back of our legs and it hurt. Hans Onkel and Oma couldn't be happier to see us. We had so much to tell them. Oma wanted to hear all about the home front and Karl's behaviour toward us. Reluctantly, we told them that Karl hit our Mother again. Oma, obviously upset, said with disgust under her breath, "I knew this was going to happen. I told her, she just doesn't listen. Well, come on let's enjoy the potato soup I made. I know you love it so much." A thick slice of homemade bread to dunk in, it tasted so good. We said our Aufwiedersehn and left. Oma shook her head, "Oh dear, those poor girls," she said as she waved to us. Just being with Oma and Hans Onkel for a few hours made us feel like it was old times, peaceful and safe. Visiting them often was a luxury we couldn't afford.

Many things changed that year, possibly our lifestyle changed forever. In school, our classmates realized quickly that Karl coming into our family didn't change who we were and they started to treat us as before. We, however, didn't feel the same. I felt resentful to those that were so heartless to me at a time when I needed them the most. I wanted to hold a grudge and I didn't understand that kind of cruelty. In time, as we played our usual games together in the school yard, my heart softened. I tried so hard to forget, but the heart takes time to heal.

For my thirteenth birthday, Mother took me to Linz for a haircut. For so long I pestered my Mother to cut my long hair. "Are you sure, Käthe? You want to cut your hair off?" Mother kept asking me. I was sure. Maria, a popular girl at school got her hair cut and everyone was envious, including me. I was convinced I knew my mind. I sat in the barber's chair with a cloth draped around me. For the first time ever I had a professional, instead of my Mother, cut my hair. The man didn't cut little strands; he took one big handful and cut. My face said it all. I wanted him to stop, but it was too late. He cut my hair just below my ears in a blunt cut. I cried all the way home, as Mother tried to tell me, "Don't worry, they will grow back." Every chance I had I wore a scarf tied behind my ears while I waited for my hair to grow back. My family had so much fun with me with this unfortunate haircut. Every so often one of them chuckled as they passed by me. "Oh you, stop it," my answer always with a smile.

I was beginning to notice my body changing and like usual, I let my sisters lead the way and I followed. That Summer I realized how precious life can be. Being the youngest in my family gave me the ability to give in easier than my sisters. I was always too young to do this, or too small to do that. One hot summer afternoon, our neighbouring friends, my sisters' age mostly, decided to go swimming as a group to a nearby lake. Well, as usual, I wasn't allowed to go. This one time I persisted until my Mother gave in. As we reached the lake somehow I separated from the group. I had my bathing suit on so I decided to go in the water. When I realized I swam too far, and I couldn't reach bottom, I panicked. I turned around, but I wasn't moving. I was so scared I could hardly catch my breath. A young man close by told me to calm down and helped me to shore. Sitting by the edge of the lake for some time made me realize what Mommi meant by sticking together. I joined my sisters and never said anything. I was cautious and it definitely spoiled part of my afternoon.

At the home front everything was different. The peaceful days, with Karl in the house, was a thing of the past. Those days of our childhood now replaced with tension and mistrust. Mother and Karl argued often. Our evenings were somewhat normal with Karl working nights and leaving about six in the evening. We didn't see much of Mother for in the evening after supper when the chores were done it was our time to play with friends. We still had our eight o'clock curfew which always came too soon.

By now Grete started to see a man much older than she was. The first time I saw Franzi is when I ran into them walking arm in arm on the street. Grete introduced Susi and I and I liked Franzi right away. He had a kind way with children. On a Sunday afternoon, they let me and my friend Magda tag along as we climbed the hills and enjoyed a Sunday outing. Mother and Karl didn't approve of the age difference. There was really nothing to worry about, because Grete was responsible and mature for her age. Threats surfaced from Karl, like, "I better not see them together, or else." A few days later, word came of a fight on the street. Karl and Franzi indeed had a confrontation and when Franzi didn't back down, Karl threw the first punch. For such a classy, intelligent man like Franzi this was a disappointment and a disgrace.

When Karl returned home and Mother heard of a fight from neighbours earlier, she was furious. Another blow up and Mother again got the brunt of it. Karl lashed out and hit her again. We were not home this time but heard the loud voices as we turned the corner to our barrack. I must say, not being there physically when the fight began, felt different. Not being so totally involved with the heart and soul made me realize that it was easier. I could distance myself from the pain and fright, which I had always experienced before now. The anticipation of what was coming or when, was a constant fear.

Mother was so angry. "I won't take him back," she said. But it never happened. The next day, they acted like nothing happened. I for one, and I am sure my sisters too, became disillusioned with our Mother. We wanted to bring friends home so badly, but not knowing what to expect when we opened that door, it wasn't to our favour, that's for sure. Karl, in broad daylight, walked around the room with his boxer shorts on, the fly open enough I could see the pubic hair. I didn't know where to look, downright uncomfortable for us girls and especially my friends.

I missed my Grandmother. Only twice Susi and I made the trip. Our poor Grandmother, so torn between feeling guilty of leaving us and trying to please her daughter, she was in a no win situation. She listened to us and tried so hard to reassure us that life will get better. Hans Onkel felt bad too. "Karl better not hurt you, or else," our Uncle reassured us, always.

In early spring our outside games began. Hopscotch was a game I played every day with my friend Magda. We smoothed the ground the best we could, then with a stick we made equal squares. Beginning with three exact squares in a row, then two squares across, till we reached the number ten. Somewhere we found a flat stone and the game began. Jumping into squares without landing on a line was the trick. I played this fun game with all my friends.

Around the same time handball started as well, for me much to look forward to. These games usually consisted of groups as small as ten or as large as twenty of us. Two captains assigned one for each team. The game began as soon as the teams were picked. One long and one short stick thrown in the air made the decision which one of us started first. The wide string or rope, made of anything we could find from underwear to bed sheets, were tied together to divide the teams. The rope was stretched tightly about four feet off the ground and tied from one tree to another and the field ready to play. Each team lined up in rows waiting for their turn, the object of the game simple and competitive. The ball, the size of a basketball, was thrown back and forth to everyone once. If you dropped the ball, you had to leave the game. When the number of players reached six, the cheering began. I learned quickly if I kept my body in a blocking position, I had a better chance to catch the ball. Some of those girls, much older and bigger than I, gave me a real workout until the last ball was thrown. My red chest was proof of that afterwards. Equal in handling the catch, it was now a matter of luck. I won a few of those battles and it made me look forward in hopes to repeat the same outcome the following night. These games started in early spring and lasted into the late fall. It was fun and exercise too.

In June 1951, Grete and Franzi became husband and wife. Grete was a radiant bride, with an elegant groom beside her. Together they walked down the aisle, a fairytale ending to their courtship. The wedding was all beauty and class even though on a shoestring budget. The satin white dress with long sleeves, a small round collar, slightly flared skirt draped all the way to the floor. The dress was homemade but strikingly beautiful. Grete and our new brother-in-law moved to another barrack two blocks away from us. It felt strange to have our sister living elsewhere. But in no time at all, visiting them often, we felt welcome and comfortable in their little quarters.

Shortly after, news of work for students somehow spread through our barracks. Susi and I had come to the conclusion that making money was a good thing, and being away from home even better. We signed up for a job with a large farmer, picking tomatoes and peppers. Our Mother woke us at 5a.m. on Monday morning. We walked to board the train at 5:45a.m. It took us approximately one hour on the train. Walking for awhile, we reached a brick building that stood alone at the edge of a vegetable field with nothing but miles and miles of ripe vegetables in every direction. The building was used for the sole purpose of storing vegetables. At the far end of the building stood a large woodstove, with two large tables for us to eat our meals on. The farmer supplied the meals for the workers. A mature woman was hired, to cook for the group of twenty of us workers. That morning, we had bacon and eggs and a thick slice of bread, delicious.

The long wagon came to pick us up, at seven o'clock on the dot. Twenty of us children, ranging from fourteen to twenty years, hopped on. The tractor stopped at the end of a long row of tomatoes and dropped us off. Susi and I grabbed a few baskets, as the young man said. "When you fill these baskets, bring them to the end of the row. Okay?" In no time at all, the basket was full of juicy tomatoes. The baskets were so heavy that Susi and I could barely lift them, let alone carry them to the end of the row. As the day wore on the baskets became so heavy that I couldn't move them. Susi encouraged me to keep on going. If we didn't fill the baskets, we'd surely get fired. We had too much pride for that to happen, and Mother would be so disappointed in us, we thought. By the time the lunch bell rang, I was so tired, and couldn't move. Susi reassured me she would cover for me. So I stayed behind and thought resting during the time for lunch might help. "Don't worry," Susi said, "I'll bring you something to eat."

I opened my eyes and realized that I fell asleep, when I heard voices, among them Susi's. She brought me a ham sandwich which I ate as I worked between the rows. I drank water from the community bucket that a porzelan white ladle was attached to. One such bucket filled with water was dropped off at the end of every row. I felt refreshed and much better for awhile, but six o'clock couldn't come soon enough for me. I slept all the way home on the train. Six of us took the train together from the barracks and that night we all slept on the way home. Our work week was Monday through Saturday. I, the youngest in the group, wondered if I could last, with Sunday the only day off for the months of July and August.

On the second day I barely made it to the building for a hot lunch. The cook, a hefty woman, actually made some tasty meals. Such good food, like stuffed peppers, cabbage rolls, real meat and rice. What a change. It had been almost seven years since I tasted food this good. Just for the food alone I had to make this work. As Susi and I walked back to our rows, with our scarves tied behind our heads to shield us from the sun, we smiled at each other with pride. After a few hours of bending down, my back ached and I wanted to lie down. Just then, I heard the tractor behind us. Johann, a blonde, young man, maybe sixteen or so, jumped off and started walking towards me. "Are you ok?" he asked. "Yes, I am," I said. "This is your first job, huh?" he said with a smile. "Well, yes." "Oh don't worry, I won't tell the boss that you are having a hard time. I'll see ya," and with that, he hopped on the tractor and drove off.

All the girls wore headscarves, and some were in housedresses, mostly light weight fabric and pastel colors. Some of us wore baggy pants that came just below the knee with elastic on the waist and knees. My pants had to be held up with a belt, for they were so loose and baggy by the waist. Susi's and my blouses were cotton and white, to help us feel cool. For the first week Susi covered for me and encouraged me not to give up. I was so tired and my back hurt and I felt weak at times. Johann stopped often and helped with the baskets, so much so that everyone teased us about favouritism. But, it helped a lot for those first few weeks. Without Susi and Johann's help I, for sure, would have not lasted. On the train home most of us slept. We made many friends that summer being together so many hours in a day. Since I was the youngest and so naive, the teasing continued all day long, especially when I didn't get a joke. The older girls thought the look on my face was so comical, especially when I pretended to get a joke and it was clear to see, I didn't. I wasn't used to it because in my family we teased each other only once in awhile. I learned to laugh a lot that summer.

After a few weeks, our Boss came early one Friday afternoon and picked us up with the tractor, which we thought, was for a well, earned lemonade and an extra break. "Wash up," the Boss

Man said, "and go home and don't come back till Monday."
I remember all of us dancing around in a circle displaying
sheer joy of this wonderful news and appreciating the Boss's
recognition of our weeks of hard work.

That Sunday, I stood in front of our small mirror that hung
above the wash basin. My hair was long, all the way down to
my waist again, and with the dark tan, I looked so healthy. I
usually wore skirts for church but this dress was waiting for
me to grow into, and it finally fit. A white dress with tiny, red
polka dots with spaghetti straps and a bolero jacket with red
trim to match. It fit perfectly. As I stood in front of the mirror
fussing with my hair, my sister appeared with a used tube of
lipstick. "Susi," I said, "What are you doing with this lipstick?
Where did you get it?" I questioned. "Not here, Käthe. This
afternoon when we go to the mountains hiking, we'll put it on,"
she informed me. "Oh, Susi, but Mommi said only floozies look
like that," "Oh my gosh," Susi said, as she gave me a hip check
and we both laughed.

I couldn't relax all afternoon. I expected my Mother to show
up at anytime and at every corner and see me with lipstick on. It
just would be my luck I'd be caught. Susi and I had quite a time
trying to remove every trace of lipstick on the way home. The
harder we rubbed the redder our lips became. Luck was with us
however. When we opened the door we spotted a note on the
table. Mother and Karl went to the movies and so, we knew we
were safe. Home at eight, the note read. What a relief.

Back at the vegetable field, the work was hard and the hours
long in those two months, but we made the best of it. We had
a lot of good times and good food, and the unending teasing
about everybody. I was teased a lot about Johann's feelings for
me. I knew that already the first time he came to help, because
I liked him, too. Johann looked rugged, with muscles bulging
on his arms from the hard work on the farm. His blue eyes and
white teeth stood out more because of the dark tan, definitely
attractive, although we never acted on these feelings but we

sure smiled a lot. All I knew that whenever I needed any help he was always there. I was glad that he was so kind and never tried anything with me.

The last day at work fell on a Thursday. The acres and acres stripped of everything ripe enough to pick, now bade us farewell. I was glad it was over, but sad to know I wouldn't see some of my friends again. Some started to cry, as we exchanged hugs. Johann kissed me on the cheek as I thanked him for bailing me out so many times. I learned something for sure that summer, that farm work would not be my choice of work for my life. On the ride home that day no one slept. We talked all the way home about the good times we had. But most of us agreed, because of the hard work, we definitely would not do this next year.

In our hands the envelopes of money for the hard work we did all of July and August remained sealed.

We handed the envelopes to our Mother with pride that evening. Before we started this job our wish was to buy a watch and the rest would go into the family fund.

In the next few weeks of free time before school, our every day chores continued as if we never left. I caught up with my good friend Magda and within hours, I heard all the news in our little community. That fall, school had a whole new meaning for me. My grades picked up again and I made a few new friends besides always being with my sister. At times, I was envious and jealous when after the summer holidays the rich kids wore their beautiful new skirts, blouses and shoes. Some of the girls knew I was a refugee and they felt uncomfortable talking in front of me, others didn't care. It was the first time I remember feeling self conscious about my clothes. I longed to look like them, but I pretended not to care.

The winter of 1951, a lot of snow fell and winter sports, like tobogganing down the long hill, became our every evening fun. These Austrian toboggans were long and about a foot off the ground. At least six of us could hop on at one time. We couldn't afford a toboggan, so between many of us kids in the barracks, we had to share one. You could say it was a community toboggan. Needless to say, the older kids had first choice and sometimes arguing and fighting, by us younger kids about the unfairness, became heated. All the complaining didn't seem to do any good. Mother's answer was always the same. "Don't bother me with stuff like that, just get along." It was frustrating, but we kept going back for more.

On one of those outings, for some reason that I cannot recall, everyone left without the toboggan. It seemed the hill was too icy even for the big girls. Finding myself finally alone with a toboggan, I couldn't pass up the opportunity. I walked to the edge of the hill, holding onto the rope wondering if this was a good idea. I slipped and fell on the toboggan sideways and didn't notice the glare ice underneath my feet. The toboggan started to slide, me bouncing up and down over several moguls, holding on with the most helpless feeling as we picked up speed all the way down. On the bottom of the hill I laid on the toboggan on my back for I couldn't move. Everything hurt. Slowly I started to move the toboggan with pushing my legs in the back and steering with my arms. I had to take another route home, for I knew I couldn't make it up that steep hill. Instead of twenty minutes, my way home took two hours. I managed to stand up and walk, so Mother wouldn't notice and quickly lay down in my bed and said I didn't feel well.

Susi and I started to go to the Sunday afternoon dances in the barrack dance hall that winter, with our Mother as a chaperone. A bit young, I was only fourteen, especially when there was no shortage of boys to dance with. When Martin, a seventeen year old, took special interest in me, my Mother became nervous. Her concerns, I could have told her were unnecessary for I didn't like him. Nevertheless, dancing is what I enjoyed most. Besides, we could only stay for the afternoon from one until four. Susi and I mainly enjoyed the dancing, for being so naive and shy, we had no trouble attracting boys. Most of the time the boys we danced with, were just like us, young, inexperienced and from the same culture. Only one time, I was nervous when a twenty year old tried to lure me outside during the intermission. As always, I used my sister as an excuse and said, "My sister is waiting for me," Besides that, Mother being close by, kept a pretty good eye on both of us. That spring, Susi and I not only learned how to dance, but also listen to some peppy music. In no time at all, we learned the words to songs like *Lily Marlen, Schwartzer Zigeuner* and hummed a lot. But most of all, we had fun.

Susi and I didn't always get along. At the time we started going to the Sunday afternoon dances, our Mother acquired second-hand nylons and she gave each of us a pair. I carefully put mine in a little box, I wore mine only for dancing and Church. On Sunday, when I took my nylons out, one of them had a runner. Without hesitation, I knew Susi had worn my nylons during the week, for I knew she went out without me. I was so mad, that Susi and I started to pull each other's braids from anger. This went on for awhile pulling harder each time. I wanted to stop and said to Susi, "I'll stop, if you stop." Susi was so determined to have the last pull. Being so frustrated, I didn't want to give in, but I didn't have a choice. My head was starting to hurt. Of course, I gave in.

Another time we didn't get along revolved around milk stamps. Every month our family received a certain amount of milk stamps. Twice a month, we walked about a kilometer to the store to bring our bucket of milk home. Mother gave strict orders for us to share the carrying of the bucket. One particular run, Susi carried the bucket first, but only a quarter of the way, set it down and said to me, "okay, Käthe, your turn." "But Susi," I said, "Mother told us halfway each." "Nope, it's your turn." I tried to reason with her, as I kept walking away from the bucket. Clearly, I was so upset that I screamed at her, "I'll tell Mother." "I don't care, I'm not going back," she said. I walked back to the bucket and managed to bring the milk home without telling Mother, but held it against Susi for a few days.

Before school started, our Mother had some important news to tell us. Karl left for work and we wondered what was so important for us to miss our nightly handball for. "Come and sit down," Mother said. "We are moving again," she announced. "Oh, no not again, not to France" I said. "No, not to France," she quietly said, "to America, that's where we are going," "What!?" Grete said, "so far!" as we sat stunned. Mother added, "Oh and one more thing. Karl and I married this summer." When no one said anything, Mother continued. "Oh, I don't know how to say this," she paused, "but Oma and Hans Onkel are staying behind." She started to cry and continued the best she could. "I feel so bad, but we need a better life. People all around us are moving on. Besides your Uncle Peter lives in America and this is the way it works," Mother explained "your Uncle Pete pays a fee and is our sponsor. He signs a paper and takes full responsibility for us. We sign a paper also, to promise to pay Uncle Peter back. This spring when I applied, they told me that Karl could not come with us unless we are married. So that's the reason. It came up so fast there was no time to waste. The papers are signed and sent, it's only a matter of months before a designated date and time for us to make this journey."

With this latest news, something happened to me and I didn't understand. I couldn't concentrate on anything. I cried about everything. Susi wasn't happy either, and we often cried together. Our school grades dropped and we lost interest. Oma cried when she heard the news, but quickly tried to convince us that our lives needed to improve. "You know," she said, "if I was twenty years younger, I'd go too." This decision to move to America became the lowest point in our lives so far, knowing that only a short time remained to be with our Oma and Hans Onkel. Mother knew deep down inside this separation from her Mother to be the final one. The war and its aftermath divided many families. Although I never spoke of, my thoughts occasionally wandered to my Father and who he was, where he might be and was he still alive. The one thing that remained constant through it all was that the six of us stayed alive and together.

Our last day, November 15th, 1951, we boarded the train in Linz, Austria. The hardest moment of all, for all of us, was our Grandmother. When it came time to say goodbye my Oma tried so hard to be brave, the tough woman she was, holding her emotions in. The tears started to fall like raindrops as we clung to each other, until a final call to board. It was horrible leaving our loved ones behind. I remember waving and the look in my Oma's eyes will be imprinted in my memory always. Her hand gently waving and her full face drained of life and her eyes full of pain, staring at each other as the train moved us farther and farther apart. Once again our family, in an instant, was changed forever.

Innocent Love

I was fourteen and a half years old when we boarded the ship to America, December 1951. By this time my skinny body had grown to almost five feet, five inches tall. Everyone told me, from time to time, that I was changing, possibly meaning growing up in mind and body. My hair, mostly in braids, reached down to my waist and the way it was naturally wavy around my forehead, made me feel especially attractive. I would have preferred blonde hair, for mine was dark brown and I thought it was so ordinary. It must have happened for some time that I was beginning to care about the look of my figure. When I was lucky enough to pass by a full length mirror, I'd look at myself from every angle, back and forth, side to side, just to fling my arms up in the air and silently speaking to myself, dismissing the whole adventure of young ladyhood. I remembered conversations between my Mother and my Uncle expressing concern of our shyness and us girls, growing up so fast, it especially bothered Hans Onkel. "You should help them, Kati, there is a cruel world out there, they need you," Hans Onkel advised our Mother. Mother, like usual said, "Oh they are fine, don't you worry about them."

The train arrived in Bremer Hafen, Germany where we boarded a bus. My Mother carried a large brown suitcase. Two leather belts for strength and to keep the suitcase from opening were strapped around it. Karl carried the identical suitcase as our Mother only his was beige in color. Susi and I carried nothing. The bus stopped at the edge of a holding barracks and dropped us off, along with refugees from other cities. The complex was totally enclosed with a high chain link fence. The entry gate was an opening just large enough to drive a bus through and was patrolled around the clock by a man in a grey uniform. This is where we stayed for two weeks before actually boarding the ship to America. We were to be immunized, briefed for citizenship and to learn the English language.

Every morning nine o'clock sharp, our English lesson began. The Instructor slowly pronounced a word, like please, thank you, good morning, and we altogether repeated the word. At the same time, we learned songs and sang *I've been Working on the Railroad, Good Night Irene, and God Bless America*. The hours for our meals were assigned and strict; the food was good and served cafeteria style. Together as a family we walked to the dining hall, as they called it, with breakfast at eight, lunch at twelve noon and dinner at six. In the afternoon there was some time for play, relaxing or even a nap.

That first afternoon, I walked by myself around the grounds and I noticed in the distance some swings. When I reached the playground, I sat on one of the swings and pushed myself slowly back and forth, my feet just dangling. For so long now I hadn't thought of Kikinda and what used to be. My daydreams seemed so far away, the beauty of it all and the life we left behind. My doll, my comfortable window sill, who is dreaming there now, I wondered. Totally consumed in the moment, I wasn't aware of a young man standing by the post. As I looked up I saw his devilish smile on his slightly crooked lips. He kept looking at me with an extreme easiness about him. Finally, he said. "Did you arrive today?" I just nodded my head. "Me, too," he said. He then walked over and sat on the other swing next to mine. "What are you thinking about?" he asked. "Nothing," I answered quickly. After a pause he continued, "I watched you for awhile and you didn't even know I was here." My eyes met his for a moment, as I heard Susi calling me, "Käthe, it's time to come home." I let go of my ropes, as I slid off the wooden seat and said, "Adieu." I turned just enough to notice his eyes following my walk. The flushing of my cheeks and the strange pounding in my chest were incredibly uncomfortable and exciting all at the same time. Anyway, I walked slightly uphill until I caught up with Susi. She was smiling as I came closer. "What?" I asked when I saw the funny look on her face, but she didn't say anything. She just put her arm around my shoulder and looking at each other we walked home.

That night, I had a dream. I dreamt I fell in love with a singing American Cowboy. The feelings so real and pure, and intense especially when he kissed me, it wasn't ringing bells, instead I felt mellow and limp surrounded with a feeling that could melt away like the snow in the sun.

The next morning, the same routine as the day before, but my mind was not on the English lesson. A few times that morning, my thoughts wandered to the swings. I was fighting this feeling, but I couldn't stop thinking of him. The afternoon finally came. Susi wanted to play a game with me, but, I said, "No, maybe later." She gave me that strange look, but reluctantly said, "Okay then. See you later." When Susi turned the corner and couldn't see me anymore, I slowly started to walk to the playground. It was a little embarrassing to notice from the corner of my eye, he was sitting on my swing. I took a guess that his age was about sixteen, maybe six feet tall and slender dark wavy hair and blue eyes. He wore a dark brown woollen cap and brown corduroy pants. He looked handsome and self assured. I said nothing as I walked passed him, and sat on the other swing.

"So you came," he said after a pause. "I like your name, Käthe." Startled, I thought how does he know my name? I looked straight ahead and said, "How do you know my name?" "I heard, yesterday. It must have been your sister calling you," he answered. "What else do you know?" I asked with a grin. "Nothing else, except that your name is beautiful," he answered me back with a grin. The blood seemed to rush all at once to my face, as I smiled at him a little. My name is Franz, but you can call me Frank, that's American," and he laughed. We silently swayed back and forth in total sync for a while. "Where are you going to in America?" he asked. "My Uncle lives near Detroit, Michigan, that's where my family is going," I answered politely. After a pause, "Where are you going?" I asked. "New York. Also a relative of my Mother's is sponsoring us. That's our destination." My eyes focused on the sand below my feet, the air brisk and cold. My mitts all wool, but I was starting to feel my fingers getting numb, as I turned my head towards his swing, his head already positioned towards my direction. With both of our eyes meeting it felt peaceful and warm. I noticed the dimple in his cheek as he smiled at me. I returned the smile. With a flirty move, I jumped off my swing, "Good bye, Frank," and I left.

My mood was so pleasant through the day and I felt so

joyful. I was afraid my Mother would notice. Oh boy, if she knew I was talking to a boy. I must act normal, so no one will notice. Is this what love feels like, I asked myself. I really didn't know, except that I couldn't wait for the afternoon when Mother dismissed me and I could see Frank again. Every moment of the day I thought of him. We saw each other every afternoon for two weeks. We talked about our families. We exchanged our feelings about war and hard times. Our backgrounds were similar, for he came from Jugoslavia too. Conversations came so easily and we felt a sense of freedom talking about our past as well as our future dreams. We also exchanged our American addresses, so we could stay in touch.

The time came when there was only one more day with Frank. Both of us sat quietly on the swings that afternoon and then Frank asked, "Do you think you could possibly, slip away in the evening, to meet me one more time by the swings?" "Oh, Frank, with my Mother so strict, I am not sure." "Please try. Seven pm", he said. "I'll try." I said, as he let go of my hand. I'd been dreaming of what it would be like to be kissed by Frank. That evening, Susi and Mother were busy packing and talking to the family in the next room. I saw the clock on the wall and it read five minutes before seven. Oh, they are occupied, now would be the time to ask. Finally, I got the courage, my eyes still on the clock as it moved closer to seven. Do it now, I told myself, finally I asked. "Mother can I go to say goodbye to Sophie?" "Who is Sophie?" Mother said, looking over to Susi as she shrugged her shoulders. Susi looked at me, changed her mind, "Oh, just a girl we know," she said. "Okay, you be back in one hour."

I grabbed my coat and started down the path to the park. It was a lovely December evening, but real cold and dark out. I didn't walk too far, when Frank walked towards me. He had his hands in his pockets. Our eyes fixed on one another as he held his left hand out to me and said, "I came to meet you. With the darkness, I thought you might be scared." Gently hand in hand, we walked to our special place. Both of us quietly sitting on the swings, when he finally said, "Käthe, I am so glad I met you. When I came here I thought it would be the longest two weeks of my life. It turned out so different." I fought back my tears. It was hard and I kept blinking.

"I will never forget you." He reached for my rope on the swing and gently pulled it close to his. By this time we are face to face. In a crackling voice he whispered, "I've been so happy since we met, and you're so beautiful, too." I returned the feelings by saying,"Yes Frank, I will never forget you either." I couldn't stop the longing look on my face, as he leaned over and kissed me on the lips. Every part of my body awakened with a feeling so helpless and warm. It felt as if heaven opened its gates and we floated all over the clouds. His arms surrounded my slender body, as mine surrounded his, clutching each other. It seemed we could be locked in this position forever, it felt so warm and comforting. We wanted this feeling to last, and go on forever, but it was not in our power. For a very short time, I experienced a feeling of innocent love, that lingered, and played in my daydreams over and over again, as I whispered, "It's time to go back."

"I know" he said. He never let go of my hand as we jumped off our swings. We both stopped and looked around the park, as if to say thank you for this wonderful experience. He walked me back almost to our door, as I turned around once more to face him. "I will write every chance I get," I said. "Me too," he answered. He touched my face with his colds hands, as he said, "You're so special, Käthe," and kissed my face three times, and placed one more kiss on my lips. I started walking and looked back only once, as he disappeared in the darkness. I tried to collect myself outside our door for the longest time, before entering our quarters.

The following morning we boarded our ship to America at nine in the morning. I couldn't concentrate when Mother kept giving me orders. I couldn't think and I didn't hear anything.

All I could think about was Frank, and since his ship was directly across from ours, maybe I could get one more glimpse of him. His ship departed at eleven, one hour after ours.

I could hear the engines roar. Little did I know that I had experienced being in love for the first time in my life. The thought of never seeing Frank again, gave me a pain in my heart that just wouldn't go away. The ship departed shortly after 10 am. I stood on the deck with hundreds of other people leaning on the side. My tears streaming down my face, I certainly didn't look out of place for many people cried, including my family. As the ship slowly left the harbour, relatives left behind, they started singing the German National Anthem. People wept, leaning over the rail as if to hang on a little longer, as far as possible, a sad sight. Besides the loud horn of the ship, it was silent.

Most of us left relatives behind. Who knows if, or when, we would ever see each other again, much uncertainty for many. Most of our parents had no idea what the future would bring in this new country called the United States of America. The hope of starting a better life, was foremost in the minds of most.

For me, no one knew the wonderful weeks of innocent love I would take with me. When we passed the last part of Frank's ship, there in the corner I saw Frank waving his arm as high as he could. "Aufwiedersehn, Käthe," he called my name. I quickly walked away from my family and all I could do was say goodbye, and wave as the ship disappeared in the crowded harbour. That was the last time I saw Frank.

The water was rough as we left the channel and reached the open section of the ocean. People on deck, women, children, men young and old, became sick everywhere. The smell of vomit was terrible throughout the ship. Susi and I climbed down steel stairs to our assigned beds. This was no luxury ship, for the large room we entered had as many as fifty cots with one pillow and one blanket placed on each cot, with just enough room between the cots to walk. We found our number, and decided to try to get some rest. But it was no use, chains rattling nearby, and so much noise from the engines it was impossible to sleep. So we climbed back up to the deck to get some fresh air. We found a spot on the deck that we claimed for our own and decided to stay the night. It was then that I got sea sick.

In the evening Mother took us to the dining room for something to eat. We stood in line with a tray. I pointed to the black man, who stood behind the counter of the food that I wanted. In the meantime the ship was rocking back and forth. I could not eat, especially when I put my tray down, it slid all the way over to the other side of the table which had a raised edge to prevent trays from falling to the floor. I ran back upstairs to the deck and sat down quickly so the heaving would stop. After some time, Mommi came with a blanket and a piece of bread.

Susi, Mother and Karl agreed to work so we could afford the journey, with their assigned duties Mother and Susi in the kitchen on opposite shifts, Karl by himself in the bakery. Mother worked full time and Susi only part time. I, of course was too young to work. Besides, every waking moment I had, I relived my dreams, of the time spent with Frank. Mother talked to me and every so often I'd nod my head to let her know I was listening. Although, I never heard a word she said. With Susi's shift over now, I couldn't wait for her to replace Mother. When Susi came she brought bread and oranges, the only food I could keep down. It became my thirteen day diet. Susi was tired, for bouncing around in that kitchen doing odd jobs was tiring. The first night out on the cool deck, Susi and I leaned back to back against one another to keep warm, and fell asleep. When I woke up early in the morning it was still dark out. The ship stopped rocking, and the water bright blue and green and calm. The ocean smelled fresh, the splashing of the waves, a lonesome sound, I thought to myself. I sat for quite some time, daydreaming of Frank. After a while, I poked Susi and said, "Are you awake?"

"Leave me alone," she said, "I'm tired." Susi fell onto her

side and continued her sleep. When I stood up, I felt something moist. Confused at first, I thought maybe I was sweating. Well, one way to find out quickly is to go to the public toilets. In the middle of the ship the public toilets, they consisted of two large rooms, one for ladies, and one for men, and totally open, with one stall after another. Adjacent to the toilets, one large room, a community shower, with water spraying from all directions. We pressed a button and the water sprayed.

As I reached the toilet stall, I looked down to my panties and I saw a red spot. I was so scared, "Oh my God," confused and worried, I didn't know what to do. I took my clothes off and took a shower and let the water run all over me. When I stepped out of the shower a trickle of blood ran down my leg again. I immediately returned to the shower. By this time, I was crying and hoping no one would come in and see me this way. The kiss, when Frank kissed me I had this strange feeling that must be it. I am going to have a baby. Susi will know what to do. Finally it stopped. I picked up my panties from the floor, and rubbed and washed the spot. I could barely see, I was crying so hard. When I returned Susi looked really worried.

"Where have you been? I've been looking all over for you," she said. By this time I sat down. My hands on my face, I started to cry. I cried so hard I could barely talk. "What's wrong, Käthe," in a worried tone, she asked. I didn't answer, she said, "You look sick, you should see the ship doctor." "No," I said firmly. "What's the matter?" and she knelt next to me, "What is it, tell me? You know Mother's shift is over soon." "I am going to have a baby," I blurted out. "What?" her voice fearful. "Yes," I said. "Did you and Frank do it?" "Well, yes." "Where, Käthe? I don't believe it," she said. "What did you do?" Susi asked again. "Well he kissed me on the lips, and I had this funny feeling." "Well, what else?" she urged me to tell her." "He kissed me three more times." Susi started to smile. "What?" I said, "What are you smiling about?" "You're not having a baby, Käthe," and she started to laugh out loud, but she stopped when she looked at my worried face. She shook her head, "You're so dumb, Käthe, oh, my gosh, you're so funny." Knowing she was serious, I started to laugh, too. The both of us laughed until we cried and our stomachs hurt.

That was the first time I heard how babies were made. Susi and I talked about everything. We truly liked each other as sisters. Mother never talked about these things so how was I to know? Susi had a carefree nature and was able to make light of our sisterly adventures, much more so than Grete or I. It wasn't just her disposition, but she looked different than we did, too. Her hair was lighter, she had a little, turned up nose and in the last year, I surpassed Susi in height by several inches. As adults, our heights were: Susi 5ft.3in., Grete 5ft.9in., and I 5ft.6in. Although Susi's bone structure was the smallest, her weight was normal, not like Grete and I who were extremely thin.

The Americanization of Käthe

After two weeks on the ocean, land was finally in sight. They called it Ellis Island. Mother had all the instructions and passports ready for inspection. Like cattle we stood in line in between ropes and steel railings to hold us in place. We stood for hours, for this ship was large and carried thousands of refugees to America. We worked our way slowly through the gates. The suitcases were heavy and dragged on the floor most of the time. For most of the afternoon we waited in a huge warehouse, for our turn to board a bus. No one paid any attention to us, for the workers went about their business, driving little wagons all around the place. The motion of the ship, back and forth was still with us, but every bit of sea sickness gone. I lost weight while crossing the ocean and my stomach made loud noises, which was embarrassing. We noticed a coffee booth in the middle of the warehouse. Susi and I walked near the booth, but stopped walking when we noticed the man behind the booth looking at us. We were embarrassed and shy, and we didn't have any money. The man in the booth had shiny black skin and pearly white teeth and a very pleasant smile. He left the booth and came over. He must have noticed our shyness for he motioned with his hand for us to come to the booth. We shook our heads, but his pleasant smile made us change our minds.

"Come come on, free donuts and coffee." We slowly approached the counter as he poured two cups of coffee. "Cream and sugar?" he asked. We nodded. He then pointed to donuts, "Sugar coated or plain?" Susi and I moved over and pointed to the sugar ones. He passed them to us over the counter as we showed our appreciation and said "Thank you" in English. He chuckled as he offered us another coffee and donuts, before we even finished. He must have sensed how hungry we were. He was a nice and generous man. We exchanged warm glances at each other all afternoon. The word *thank you* we learned in Bremer Hafen, a word we liked and used often.

A uniformed man called our number finally and we immediately grabbed our belongings and followed the man out to the street. A large bus stood in front waiting to take us to the train station. Sitting in the bus, I had my first glance to see this large city called New York. Frank's city, I thought to myself. The sound of car horns and so many lanes of traffic made me wonder how anyone ever crossed the street. The buildings so high, I couldn't see the top and there were so many people. Wow, what a place.

We were dropped off at the train station and told to follow the uniformed man. Many people, many stairs. I stumbled at one point and stayed behind, but keeping my family in sight, I hurried till I caught up. Finally we reached our train that took us to our destination, Detroit, Michigan. Our suitcases neatly tucked into place, it was now time to find seats. Mother and Karl sat in front of Susi and me somewhere in the middle of the car. I sat back in my seat and being so tired it didn't take long to doze off. In between naps, I repeated my daydreams of Frank. Between every little town or field Frank crept into my thoughts all the way to Detroit, and I never tired of the same thoughts. My mind drifted to another time when we boarded the train, oh so long ago. I wondered what this move all across the ocean had in store for us. Uncle Pete, our sponsor, was the oldest of my Grandmother's sixteen children. Three sets of twins that died at birth. Eight of the sixteen children made it to adulthood, six boys and two girls. Uncle Pete was the oldest and our Mother the youngest, with nineteen years separating them. After the First World War, four of my Uncles boarded a ship just like we did, and they came to North America. Only Uncle Pete stayed in North America, the others moved on to South America, with intentions to make enough money, so they could return home. Unfortunately for my Grandmother that never happened. The boys never returned home and Oma didn't see her boys again.

Mother and Uncle Pete have not seen each other in thirty five years. I wondered and had doubts if I could like this Uncle as much as I loved my Hans Onkel. Oh, well, soon we will find out. I became excited.

I looked out the window, and saw a bit of snow on the ground. One more hour, someone said, before we reach Detroit. Susi and I walked around a little and stretched our legs before we freshened up. The train travelled slowly for a long time before coming to a screeching halt. Mother tapped us on the shoulders and said, "Wait and follow Karl and me, okay?" We walked through a long room when suddenly Mother dropped her suitcase. I looked up and there was a middle aged man running towards my Mother. They embraced and kissed, so much joy, unbelievable happiness between them. Mother had tears in her eyes. I didn't see my Mother cry very often, but it was clear to see how happy they both were. Uncle Pete knew all our names and we didn't need an introduction. Just one look at my Uncle and I knew I would like him. He took my Mother's suitcase and we followed him out to his auto. One by one, we piled into his black auto. Mother and Karl sat in the front seat with our Uncle, Susi and I in the back, just listening to them talking nonstop till we reached the farm in Deckerville, about two hours driving north.

Uncle Pete's wife, also named Katy, stood by the aluminum

back door as we pulled around the corner of the farmhouse. I peeked through the car window and saw a well groomed, silver haired woman extending her arms, smiling at us. The same as our Uncle, no introductions necessary, for Mother sent our names and ages to them before we came. After the embraces we hurried into the house. It was December after all and very cold. "Come, welcome," Aunt Katy said, "I made chicken soup," and looking at us a little closer, added "you are so thin. Oh, but I will fatten you up, you'll see." The sisters-in-law exchanged a laugh and a pleasant feeling filled the air. Four steps led to the small kitchen. As I entered this room of cupboards that reached all the way to the ceiling, it became clear, just with one glance, that this kitchen housed all the necessary gadgets and tools it took to make good meals. The aromatic smell of the pork roast in the oven filled our nostrils with a strong yearning for meat. Undeniably, a taste we could not wait to enjoy again after so many years. This charming kitchen of light blue and white did however only seat two people, with a tiny table in the middle of the room.

"Come," as we walked through the kitchen, following our Aunt and Uncle to the dining room. The table was already set with porcelain china and a crisp white tablecloth with six wooden chairs tucked underneath. The chicken soup with lots of thin homemade noodles, so tasty and hot, we ate every drop. As a matter of fact, we ate everything Aunt Katy served. Our Aunt again said in a much softer tone, "You are so thin," as she shook her head. "My goodness, what you've been through." Our Aunt didn't weep, but a tear or two ran down her face. Our Uncle Pete cut in, and said, "I am so glad you are here," after a deep sigh, he added, "you will never go hungry again. I promise you that, Sister," with a serious look on his face. "We have so much canned fruits and vegetables in the cellar that has to be eaten before it goes bad." After the delicious sponge cake with fruit and whipped cream, that Aunt Katy made, we just sat around the table and talked. Our Mother and Uncle, after so many years, reuniting was truly overwhelming to both of them. They had so much to talk about, as Susi and I in silence watched all these wonderful feelings unfold.

After dinner Mother and Uncle Pete brought our few belongings in and took them upstairs. It was then that Aunt Katy addressed Susi and me personally. "Well girls," she said, "let me take you upstairs and show you where you will sleep tonight. Okay." She waited for a response as we nodded our heads. Once upstairs, we followed our Aunt to a small room. We first walked through what she explained was our Mother's bedroom. She opened the door and a beautiful, shiny brass bed sat against the large wall. On the white duvet, I noticed two nightgowns with embroidery around the neckline. Aunt Katy whispered, "I bought them for you because I wanted you to have something nice and new." "Thank you," was the only thing I could think of to say.

Susi and our new Aunt had an immediate connection with each other, unlike me, being younger and so uncomfortable talking to grownups. I watched the two of them walking downstairs, so consumed in the moment they didn't even notice that I stayed behind. Alone in the room, my eyes took a good look at the quaint but small room. A far cry from our one room in the barracks that we had lived in for seven years. I walked over to the bed and sat on the edge. The mirror was directly in front of me as I looked up, my face drawn, with dark circles around my eyes. A strange feeling in my chest surfaced. My body felt tired and worn, my clothes old and smelly. I hung my head, in deep thought, as a lonely feeling so painful came over me that my only relief was to cry. I thought of everyone we left behind, of days gone by, and so many memories I wanted to leave behind, but for some reason just couldn't. The adjustments to what happened to us, in the last few weeks were hard for me and I had to grow up fast.

Susi called me from the bottom of the stairs. "Käthe, what are you doing up there, come on down," she said. "Okay, in a minute." I wiped my tears and headed down the stairs to join the family. My Uncle took one look at me and he must have sensed my loneliness, he never said anything to me directly, we just knew, when he gave me that certain look. Actually, as I said before, I liked him the moment we met at the train station.

Susi (on right) and me - Our First Christmas in America 1951

Aunt Katy didn't waste any time and enrolled us in a nearby country school. Christmas was right around the corner as we arrived two weeks before the holidays. Our Aunt and Uncle owned one car, Aunt Katy didn't drive and our Uncle left early every morning for his construction job many miles away. So that meant we needed to walk the two mile stretch to school, every morning and night. Not knowing what to expect that first day of school made us uncomfortable. Down the road a ways, Aunt Katy informed the children that we would join them, knowing all about us, they would lead the way. We didn't speak English, but surprisingly didn't have too much trouble understanding one another. From every house along the way, one more child joined our group until the children totalled six. Four girls and two boys, all different ages, Susi and I of course the oldest. When we turned the corner and walked down a snow covered trail, the white steeple with a bell peaking through could be seen. I knew with the smoke coming out of the chimney we were not the first to arrive. Our new teacher stood by a small wooden desk as we walked into the room. She looked up and greeted all of us with a smile and a good morning. Of course, I just saw her lips moving, as she motioned for Susi and me to come closer. She placed her hand on the desk that I guessed she wanted us to sit in.

Left to Right: Susi, Mrs. Josephine Hancock & Me

"Come," she said. We followed and she pointed to large hooks where the coats hung. It wasn't hard to figure out what to do, for being orderly was natural to us. Our new teacher seemed pleased with us. She said something to one of the boy students and he left. Moments later the most beautiful sound of bells ringing filled our classroom. The boy returned and took his seat, and school began, with a prayer first, and then the Pledge of Allegiance to America. The teacher looking at us pointed to herself, and said. "I am Josephine Hancock." Then the most embarrassing moment of all came. Mrs. Hancock called Susi and me to join her at the front of the class. With her most charming way, she introduced us. Each one of the students stood up individually and greeted us by saying their first names. We were so shy, and to be singled out like that was sheer agony. It didn't take long for us to feel at ease and comfortable in this little schoolhouse.

I wrote to Frank every week. Every day I ran to the mailbox, hoping a letter would be there for me. Finally, the second week, Aunt Katy, with a smile on her face, handed me the letter. "I believe this is addressed to you Katie," she said as she handed it to me, for it came while I was at school. I ran upstairs as fast as I could, tore the envelope open and started reading.

> *December 18th, 1951*
> *Dear Käthe,*
> *I hope you arrived at your new home all right. My new family is very nice, and I am eating them poor. Oh, but I am so lonely, and I miss you. Are you learning English yet? I go to school every day, and my Uncle is an engineer and is already planning for me to be one too. Well, I don't know, we'll see. I can't wait to get your letter, please write. I can still see your face, and I really enjoyed that kiss. I wish you were here.*
> *I'll write soon, Love Frank*

After I finished reading the letter, I started all over again. I laid the letter in my underwear drawer. When no one was around, I'd read it over and over again, every chance I had.

Back at school, what a pleasure it was indeed to have been

fortunate to be part of this small schoolhouse with such a big heart. Mrs. Hancock possessed warm, personal qualities. It became the most relaxed place I had been in, in a long time. Every morning, words were not spoken, who would do what, but rather everyone pitched in to do their part. The wood had to be in for the day, the classroom swept, the dishes washed and the snow shovelled. Someone to ring the bell, and oh yes, the kettle filled with water, which was taken from a hand pump outside, for our afternoon tea.

Mrs. Hancock stopped everything in the afternoon for at least thirty minutes to enjoy a cup of tea which was steeping on top of the stove for awhile, with our assigned cups in our hands it gave us a chance to relax. On many of those afternoons cookies in a tin were handed to us for a treat. My fondest memories of this neat, tall and proud lady, was her sitting on my desk while telling a story and at the same time doing my fingernails. She herself had the most beautiful long, manicured fingernails I ever saw. I loved the attention and also my finished lacquered nails, so elegant, made me feel grownup.

Our teacher taught from grade one to eight so it was easy for Susi and me to learn English. We simply sat in on every grade, from beginning to end of the day. With everyone's help, it took no time at all before the English language became almost as fluent as our German. With Christmas so close, a concert was already planned before we arrived, so that meant lots of practice for some. Mrs. Hancock pleaded for Susi and me to perform something in German. We were so shy and didn't want to do it, but with a lot of urging from our classmates, we reluctantly agreed to sing a few songs. After the first rehearsal of singing, *Leise Riselt der Schnee* and *Stille Nacht, Heilige Nacht,* Mrs Hancock was full of praise and we felt more comfortable. For our school it was such a novelty for two refugee girls to be in their class, speaking another language with a different culture. But for us, it was normal and we didn't understand all the fuss.

Aunt Katy heard about the concert and offered to take us shopping in a nearby town called Sandusky to buy a new dress. Once in the store, we saw the racks of clothing hanging all around us, a sight to behold. I stopped and glanced around the store in awe of the various colors and styles. Aunt Katy and Susi walked ahead and stopped at one of the round revolving racks. "Well, Susi, I believe this rack is your size," she said. "Pick out whatever you like so you can try it on, okay?" Then she turned to me, and pointed to the rack for my size. After trying several dresses on, I picked out a teal blue, crepe dress. The dress was mid length, with a slightly flared skirt and a small peek-a-boo hole above my bust. Susi and I both stood and modeled for Aunt Katy's approval and we got it, as she said, "Oh you look great, well even if I say so myself." I was so excited, a new dress, and all mine. I couldn't wait to get home, so I could try it on again and again.

Susi and I couldn't sing along with our fellow students, for we didn't know the words, there just wasn't time to learn them all. The Christmas concert was a real success. Every one of us buzzing around setting up props, the Nativity Play was a lot of work for all of us, but worth it. The schoolhouse filled with family members, and so supportive, clapped loudly after every scene. Oh, boy, it was time. Our teacher gave a short introduction of our past and then it was our turn to sing. Susi and I sang our two German songs and by the second song, we were not so nervous anymore. I am sure Mrs. Hancock had a lot to do with that. Knowing she was right there with us made all the difference. One by one Mrs. Hancock handed us a red collared bag full of goodies and a hug and a kiss. Merry Christmas exchanged by everyone as we departed into the cold brisk air on our way for a few weeks off to enjoy our Christmas break, as they called it.

Susi and I graduated in June 1952 from grade school. The experiences, the loving care, the classmates in that little schoolhouse, and most of all our kind and loving teacher, I will cherish always. Upon graduation that June we brought memories with us that Susi and I will never forget. Back at the farm, our Aunt, like I said before liked Susi right off. Aunt Katy and Susi milked the cows together and did the necessary chores in the barn. Farm work was not something I enjoyed doing. Feeding the chickens every day was my chore. The smell of the chicken coop, the moment I walked in I threw my head back for the strong odour of ammonia, was so potent that it took my breath away. I held my breath as long as I could, or on some occasions, pinched my nose. However collecting the eggs every day I liked. The chickens actually became familiar with my voice, and I could swear, they talked to me. I felt good after cleaning the eggs, putting them in my basket and bringing them into the house after school.

Susi and I spent every free moment we had together. After the cows were fed and milked, chickens attended to, kitchen cleaned after supper, homework done and our lunches in our lunchboxes, it was our time. We'd go upstairs for a well earned evening of rest and to be alone. We listened to country music on the old red radio and listened to lonely songs. For hours we put ourselves through this lonely feeling. In those winter months Hank Snow, Hank Williams, Patsy Kline and many more filled our hearts with the lonesome blues.

When spring came and the trees were full of leaves and a beautiful shade of green, we had a new attitude, it seemed overnight. On a thick branch high up on the old apple tree, Susi and I sat for hours and discussed our life. Our concerns always shifted to Karl and his barbaric treatment of us. Although Karl seemed different around our Uncle, for now at least we felt safe. Our concerns and conversations much more opinionated and personal, we not only started to change physically but mentally as well. We felt positive about our new life and enjoyed these peaceful evenings while they lasted. Oh well with a sigh, we climbed down the apple tree, one step at a time, to the lush grass underneath. With our arms around each other, and swaying our hips back and forth, we walked back to the house to help Aunt Katy with supper. Aunt Katy was an excellent cook. After so many years of hunger, we ate everything she put in front of us.

"I haven't enjoyed cooking like this for years," I heard her say to our Mother, as they stood together by the sink peeling potatoes. "It is a pleasure," Aunt Katy said, "to watch the four of you enjoying my food like you do." Aunt Katy continued, "Kati tell me, how bad was it?" Mommi didn't want to talk about it, and answered, "I never imagined that our life would turn out like this. You know in an instant, they stole our house. Never did I dream that I would live my life out without my Mother. You know, Katy, the Russians and partisans, oh boy they did horrible things to us," she stopped, with her head down paused before continuing, "We are here now and a chance for a new life, thanks to you and Pete." Aunt Katy put her hand on Mommi's shoulder and together they joined their husbands in the parlour.

Meal times, for me, were the most comfortable time of the day, especially the one they called supper. It all began with whoever came home first. The potatoes and carrots were peeled and dropped in a pot with cold water, ready for cooking. A salad, for some reason was my job. Aunt Katy along with Mommi taught me to totally dry the leaves of the lettuce after washing or the salad did not taste good. They made sure I knew this procedure well for they mentioned it to me more than once. It took no time at all for the kitchen to be filled with inviting smells of garlic and onions. It made us hungry and we looked forward to gathering in the dining room for a good hearty German meal. Susi and I set the table the same way every evening. Coffee, which we were allowed to drink and Aunt Katy's weekly sponge cake with fruit, finished our meal. And, just like the olden days conversation followed about everyone's day. I loved that half an hour, but as usual Susi and I just listened in silence.

Aunt Katy tried to educate our Mother, by pointing out some

of the American culture. I remember one of these conversations in particular. "You know Kati, people here, they don't like garlic smell on your breath, remember not to eat garlic when you go out in public." Aunt Katy tried to explain to her sister-in-law, "Hmm, really? Okay," Mother answered, not quite sure of what she just heard. "They avoid you," Aunt Katy whispered, as she moved closer to Mother. Listening to all this, we continued with the dishes while our Aunt stored the leftovers in small glass containers ready for the next day. Mother swept the floor. Uncle Pete and Karl continued speaking in Hungarian and moved into the living room, which was an extension of the dining room to roll a cigarette and have a smoke.

Back in the living room for the evening, Susi and I stayed long enough just to be polite, but we didn't join in the conversations. Aunt Katy noticing this, asked curiously of our Mother, "What have you done with these kids? They are so shy!" My Mother was startled by her sister-in-law's comment and answered, a little annoyed, "They talk when they are asked a question and besides, children should be seen and not heard." Our Aunt immediately looked at our Uncle and said, "How about we invite friends over for these girls?" "I think that's a good idea," our Uncle answered. Our Mother and Aunt truly liked each other, so Mother reluctantly agreed that might be a good idea. But this was easier said than done.

The first time visitors came, I hid underneath the bed. Aunt Katy came and made me crawl out. Rather than to meet anyone, I started to cry. "My goodness, I had no idea this is so hard for you Katie," she said. "I am sorry, I won't make you. Why don't you come when you are ready, okay?" and she left. As usual it wasn't as uncomfortable as I thought. All our lives we lived in the barracks where neighbours, a stone throw away. Everyone knew each other their whole lives. It was hard to be around total strangers. How was I to know what would happen? I slowly walked down the stairs and stood by the bottom of the stairs, listening to grownups talking. Susi, however, a bit braver than I, walked down a few minutes before me. The strangers were German speaking and Susi already down there, gave me courage. I walked to the living room, but stopped when I reached the dining room wall. I was spotted quickly and stepped forward.

"Oh, Kati," the lady said to my Mother, "your two girls are so beautiful," as she stepped towards me. A girl the same age as Susi introduced herself to me as Diana. Mother reminded me a few times to talk, and before I knew it, the ordeal was over and Susi, Diana and I moved to another room to talk.

Diana had skin as smooth as a china doll and lips that were large and ruby red. She wore her hair with a deep wave over part of her face. Wow, she could pass as a movie star, so gorgeous. Susi and I, with our long braids all way down to our waist, we suddenly felt so childlike. Oh, but Diana, much older in her desires for boys, taught Susi and me a few forbidden tricks. Oh, if Mother only knew. "Come on," Diana said. "I'll show you how to French kiss." She grabbed Susi and actually kissed her on the lips. "Oh, gross!" I said. "Uh, that looks disgusting." Diana's father was a sophisticated man and our Uncle's boss. His wife, Diana and him came on Saturday morning and left late that evening, I mean late, like three or four in the morning. The four of them played pinochle all that time and stopped just long enough for something to eat. Our Uncle periodically asked us girls to bring them drinks. The men drank only a few beers, mostly strong coffee, for the percolator was on the entire time they played this interesting game. The two men possessed competitive natures that made this activity every weekend truly enjoyable. Of course the wives found this passion of their husbands amusing.

In the six months that we stayed with our new relatives we learned a new way of life, a new culture and most of all, we felt safe. My shyness was not totally gone, but to talk to grownup people became much more comfortable. Uncle Pete and I talked together often and these are some of stories he told me. Uncle

Pete with his authoritive voice said, "Katie, when I was young about your age, you know we owned a *Salas* (farm) in Topola at that time. My brothers and I were bored and decided to walk to the village just for something to do. As a prank we decided to steal some honey from the local store, you know, just for fun," he said jokingly. "The storekeeper, a stern man, made this kind of a prank even more fun. A small wooden barrel filled with honey, and another filled with pickles, stood side by side in front of the store, waiting to be sold to customers who brought their own containers. So, me being the instigator," Uncle Pete said with a grin, "here is how this prank worked." I said to my brothers, "I'll keep the storekeeper busy." Seppi, the youngest of the three stuck his arm in the honey all the way up to his elbow. It was an important part of the prank to make this worth it. When his arm was full of honey the fun began. Martin's job was to whistle to let me know, to start running. When I heard the whistle, it was my turn to excuse myself, joining my brothers and the three of us running as fast as we could and at the same time licking Seppi's arm. In the background the storekeeper was running after us with his arm up in the air, yelling, "wait till your Mother hears about this. Just wait." Out of breath, and far away from the town's edge, we stopped running and licked off every drop of that delicious honey. We laughed, as we looked at each other and said," Did you see the look on the storekeeper's face? That was so much fun," Uncle Pete said, "well you know in those days with so many of us boys in the house, we had to do something."

"Oh, my goodness," I said, "What did Oma do to you when she found out?" "Well, what could she do?" My uncle said. "It was already done. Oh, but my Mother, oh I loved her very much. Only one time, we had a problem, my Mother and I." "Tell me, Uncle Pete" I urged him on. "You know Katie, when I married my first wife, your Aunt Bervi (Barbara), you know I was only twenty years old. In those days it was not unusual for people to marry young. Bervi was pregnant at the same time that my

Mother gave birth to your Mommi, only your Mommi was six months older than my Johnny. One Sunday morning early, my Mother appeared at our door step unannounced. When she found Bervi and me still in bed, she was upset and said. 'Why are you still in bed? The cows and chickens are waiting to be fed." Uncle Pete said, " I had to say something, now that I was married I felt it was necessary, but I didn't enjoy it. So I said, "Mother, first of all I didn't invite you here this morning. This is mine and Bervi's house now. If all you can do is criticize us, then you're not welcome." She seemed speechless and in a huff left without saying good bye.

"You know I was her first born," with a little conceited smirk, Uncle Pete continued. "Well you know back then even if we were married, we still shared many chores with the homestead. For months, Mother pretended as if nothing was wrong, with one difference, she didn't come to visit and told me she was not setting foot in my house again." "You told me I am not welcome," she reminded me. "But Mother," I said, "you won't come even when our baby is born?" At the Baptism Mother broke down. I invited her a week before, only with no answer. I simply said, "Mother, come. Your Grandson needs his Grandmother." On the day of the Baptism, she didn't join us for dinner, and I was sad because my Mother and I, we were always close. Sometime, late in the afternoon between coffee and cake, a knock at the door, there in the doorway stood Mother, over her arm a blanket folded over, and she said, "I had to finish the blanket I knit for my first born Grandchild." "We joked many times about my Mother's ways, but I felt complete again that day," Uncle Pete said with much love that even I felt in his tone.

Uncle Pete talked with much love about his Mother, "You know Katie," he said, "Mother ran the household. She did everything from disciplining us kids to working out in the fields. My father, your Grandfather, had an easy going personality and he liked his wine. On many an afternoon, my Mother needed my Father, with so many kids, just to find him in the cool cellar sleeping away the day. So what could I do," Uncle Pete said, "she needed help, so I did everything I could with her. Changing and bathing the young ones, feeding them and even cooking. We worked well together, and we talked a lot."

"Oma told me some of your childhood stories too," I informed Uncle Pete. "You know, Oma spent a lot of afternoons in bed. On a rainy day, Susi and I sat on the edge of the bed and listened and couldn't get enough of these interesting stories of your childhoods." I was happy to tell Uncle Pete this story in particular.

Top: Peter Onkel & Mischko Onkel
Center: Hans Onkel
Bottom: Joschi Onkel & Martin Onkel
Missing: Seppi Onkel

"Oma started, 'you know my Mischko, Joshi, Seppi and Martin, my four boys. They ranged from fourteen to seventeen years of age. Hearing many stories of my four Uncles that I never met in person, somehow I felt a connection spiritually with them. Oma told me this story about her four boys that I found so amusing. One weekend, Oma said, my four boys decided to walk to town which was quite a walk since we lived in the country, to a Gasthaus to have some fun. I told them, "you better come home at a decent time or else. They knew what I meant. It was well into the night when they stumbled home. Scared of me, they decided to sleep in the barn, so I wouldn't know when they arrived home through the night. Early in the morning they grabbed their clothes and quietly tried to slip into the house. But, knowing this, I hid behind the door, with a broom in my hands waiting for them. Well you should have seen the look on their faces when they saw me." "What did you do?" I asked Oma. "Well, not much," she said. "The boys surrounded me and held my arms, and made me promise, that I won't hit them, if they let go. I promised, but I didn't mean it," she said. "Although I got a few hits in, but when they told me they loved me and gave me kisses, oh well," she said, "by this time they were already too old and strong." From what I know, my Oma was a strong and tough woman so their respect outweighed the strength of her boys. My Oma never saw her four oldest boys again, after the First World War. It made me sad and I wondered how my Grandmother must have felt on that day when her boys left for North and South America at such a young age, unthinkable to me.

Uncle Pete and Aunt Katy had a loving relationship, the kind of home with love, humour and respect. One time in particular I remember watching my Aunt in the house looking out the window. She was patiently observing my Uncle losing his temper with the lead cow called Leni. His efforts to control Leni that evening became comical when Leni went every which way except where Uncle Pete wanted her to go, the barn. As he walked in the house my Aunt immediately said in a loving tone," Leni is stubborn today, come Pete," as she grabbed his arm," come and have a coffee." I know my Uncle Pete was devastated when he lost his first wife, Barbara, after more than twenty years of marriage, and their daughter, within six months of each other. It took him many years to find love again, but got a second chance with Aunt Katy. We often commented that he had two marriages that were beautiful when some people never have one.

My Uncle Pete was a strong man, physically and mentally. His high cheek bones made me think of an Indian Chief. He also had most of his hair and very little grey. I will always remember these 3 things he told me. Dress every day as if you are going to work. Never worry about things you cannot change. Every day without fail, drink one ounce of whiskey. He was a secure man and way ahead of his time in understanding feelings. He inspired my life and I not only learned trust, loyalty and love from him, but also enjoyed his company.

Uncle Pete

I stopped writing to Frank that fall. My memories and thoughts of him were fading with every day that passed. Just once in a while my longing for what used to be took me back to Frank, to Kikinda, to the barracks, but as time went by the pain lessened and finally I left it all behind, or so I thought. Live in the present, start planning the future, and don't think back, that was my wish. All too often my wish didn't work but it wasn't for lack of trying. And so it was, we slowly adapted to our new life in America.

Our Uncle was instrumental in finding Karl a job. We owed Uncle Pete the money he paid to sponsor us. To pay her brother back was a big concern for our Mother. Uncle Pete said it many times, "Don't worry about it, there is plenty of time." But, that was not our Mother's way. Uncle Pete had friends in Detroit and after a few phone calls arrangements were made for Karl to have an interview with the Studebaker Car Company. Karl returned after a few days with some good news. Monday, the beginning of that week, was to be his first day on the job. It was decided that Karl would go ahead on his own, to make sure, the job was solid before we followed. By this time we moved to a small house near a small community called Deckerville. Our Mother was happy to be independent again and only ten miles away from her brother. The few months together, just the three of us, brought back wonderful memories of how it used to be, our days filled with harmony, work and laughter. Mother cooked all the noodle dishes that we loved so much that we were not able to enjoy when Karl was around. It was then that I learned how to make noodles from scratch. Aunt Katy made a special recipe that I loved called Grumbire und Nudle, potatoes and noodles. She made the dish in a cast iron pan, which she lent to us whenever needed. Mother made poppy seed strudel often at that time as well. I spotted a half unused lemon left over from the strudel, just sitting on the counter. I kept staring at the lemon for a while, noticing the sugar bowl nearby, my taste buds gravitated towards them both as I picked up the lemon and twirled and squeezed , till the juice of the lemon was covered with the sugar. A taste so satisfying that it became what I called thru the years, "food for the soul." A treat, I continued to enjoy throughout my life, from time to time.

Every weekend Karl returned home late Friday night and we were reminded of how dysfunctional a family can be. They argued almost the moment he walked in the door. Whatever triggered this, we never did figure it out. During those few months our Aunt and Uncle made weekly visits. Because we had no vehicle, they took Mother for groceries and anything else that we needed.

That summer the farmers needed help with their fields. So we picked weeds from the fields of wheat, sugar beets, and whatever else grew in the area. The work was hard and boring, but on the weekends, Susi and I dressed up, the white blouse especially attractive with our tans, and no place to go. By this time, both Susi and I cut our hair to shoulder length.

Our Aunt and Uncle arranged a visit one weekend with a family that just happened to have two boys, one nineteen and the other twenty two years old. They knew each other, were old friends and also of German descent. At first, a once a week visit, but it wasn't long before Nick fell for Susi right off. I had feelings for Henry, the younger of the two. Mother was not happy, for she, like so many parents, felt we could do better. Living on a farm in the country was not the plan Mother had for us. Get a good education, a good partner, and take your time. We didn't hear her. Our youthful years had been anything but comfortable and time was the one thing we didn't want to waste anymore. The more she talked, the more determined we became not to listen. There was no reasoning with us for Mother's example of life didn't hold anymore, or so we thought.

We didn't have a car so this meant walking to town for everything. Susi and I, for a weekly outing, walked to town for odds and ends that Mother needed. On one of those trips we met our new country boys, Nick and Henry, just riding around. Of course, in no time at all we found ourselves sitting in a booth, sipping a milkshake, as we enjoyed laughter and good conversations. It made carrying our bags all the way home easier, for they gave us a ride close to home. "Please drop us off here," which was far enough away from the house, we asked. They did reluctantly and said "see you next week."

Mommi would be very upset if she knew we were with boys. To be treated so nicely by these boys was something we craved and liked. As time passed Mother extended our stay in town, with allowing us to enjoy a game of bowling. "No boys, you hear me," she threatened us on the way out the door. But it was no use, every time we walked only part of the way, the brothers showed up. What could we do? We didn't do anything wrong, and besides we liked each other, we are just friends, we told ourselves.

These afternoons went on for a few weeks. I don't know how Mother found out, but she did. She not only found out, but she caught us walking holding hands, right there on the street. Oh, boy, a big blow up followed. I was so embarrassed, for Mother didn't care who saw us and how loud she talked. Mother was so upset, she was shaking. She ordered us to meet her at home immediately as she stepped back in the car, which I recognized as our neighbour's. Our country boys offered to stay with us for support. "Oh no," we said, "We will face Mother by ourselves." I felt uncomfortable walking down the cement sidewalk leading up to the house and the back door, knowing what was waiting for us inside. Mother asked a neighbour to take her to town and back, and I knew she was home. Oh boy, with a deep sigh, I reached for the knob, before I turned it the door flung open, and there she was, our Mother. Instantly she lashed out at us, "What are you doing with boys?" She was so upset her lips were quivering and her face red. She continued, "You're walking hand in hand, do you know what boys want? Do you?" "Mother, we didn't do anything wrong," Susi said. "You know nothing about boys," she yelled. "Let me tell you about boys, they want only one thing and I'll kill you if you ever bring me home a baby." Susi finally said, "Mother, you can say anything you like, but these boys are nice, and I like Nick. They are not like you say they are." Mother's high pitched voice became louder as she continued to express her disappointment in us.

Being excused and walking upstairs to our bedrooms, my thoughts lingered and I didn't feel good about Mother so upset with us. To my surprise Susi was pretty calm about the whole thing, and said to me, "Katie, I like Nick, he treats me a lot better than anyone. Mother is not going to stop me from seeing him." I however, became worried, now knowing that Mother is so against these boys and wished I could be a little more like Susi. After some time, Susi and I came downstairs. Mommi calmed down somewhat and she talked in a normal voice again. Susi and Mother did most of the talking. Sometimes there is an advantage to being the youngest, and this was one of those times. "But, Mother." Susi started, "Uncle Pete likes these country boys, and it is good for us to meet young people, don't you think?" "Don't be ridiculous," Mother answered, "Meeting people is not the same thing as joyriding in a car with boys. Don't let me see you doing this again," Mother threatened. Susi backed off for the moment as the evening ended in a reasonable tone. Later that evening Henry called on the party line with concerns, I whispered, "Everything is ok. Mother calmed down." "Boy, she was mad." Henry said, "Will I see you next week?" "I don't know," I said, as I hung up.

During the week, our Aunt and Uncle visited and on the weekends when Karl was home, we visited them. With Uncle Pete around, Karl seemed more civil and treated our Mother better. We felt Karl didn't show his true colors when Uncle Pete was present. They both knew the Hungarian language and spoke it every chance they had along with my Mother. Karl respected and liked our Uncle, and that was a good thing, we agreed. However when Mother complained about us girls disobeying their wishes with the country boys, the conversation became heated between Uncle Pete and Mother. Uncle Pete the first one to point out in a nice way, "Uh, Kati, you have two beautiful girls, and they are good kids. They do their chores, they never say no to anything you ask them to do. Don't you think they deserve a little free time and a little fun?" Mother answered, "Well, Pete, fun yes, but not with boys."

It was clear to see that this was a cultural difference between sister and brother. Uncle Pete had lived in the United States since the 1920s. He and Barbara raised two children together, in a country different from ours. Uncle Pete and Mother had similar values, certainly no difference there, but the freedom to make choices was a different issue. These were hard times for our Mother. She not only struggled with the language and to find work, and now, with us becoming Americanized so fast, it scared and worried our Mother for our futures.

That September we started high school nearby. The school was large in size, not at all like our small country school we left behind. Susi and I, feeling a little out of place, became inseparable and kept to ourselves at least the first few weeks. We attended the same classes and took the same subjects. However, it took time to make good friends and we told ourselves we didn't care. Every day for one hour we ended up in a large room they called the study hall. In this room we did our homework or goofed off. I tried so hard to be serious and do my homework, but the boys sitting nearby had mischief on their minds. I don't know how many times paper planes flew by, or one of the boys next to me kicked my shoe, or winked from across the room. It made concentrating difficult. I thought these actions were so childish and ignored them. At the end of one of those study halls, one of my classmates caught up to me, and said. "Do you know how many boys like you?" "Oh, go on," I replied. "No, I guess you don't" she said, as the crowd in the hall separated us. I dismissed her comment, for I wasn't interested in these boys. Besides, I liked Henry. In this school I learned to play basketball and volleyball, and enjoyed watching our team play other schools. I yearned to play on the team too, but was way too shy, to let anyone know about my sporting abilities.

Something was missing in this school. Although we made new friends, in general the school had cliques, the popular girls and boys, and then us. Most of the time it was okay, except when we heard of a weekend party that we were not invited to. On Mondays the elite group huddled together and relived their weekend fun, as we could only listen and feel envious. It didn't make us insecure, but bothered, that's for sure. However as time went on this all changed, a little. In the summer months Susi and I worked hard in the farmer's fields. For the first time, we could keep enough money to buy some new clothes for school. Through the summer months every spare moment we had we read romance novels. I found myself reading these thin books while eating, while walking, being talked to, without missing a line, Susi right alongside of me, doing the same.

On those sunny days, the sky blue and the wind blowing gently through our hair, we became more and more American girls. We learned from these novels, perhaps, how to feel sexy, and needless to say we learned of love, the kind between a man and a woman. Oh, sometimes it seemed so gross to read about what they were doing, but of course it was only on paper, I thought. Oh, if Mother only knew, what I read, I don't think I would be reading anymore, I thought to myself.

Sometime that fall Mother gave us some of the money that we made over the summer, so we could take our clothes that we so carefully picked out, out of layaway. We returned to our high school with a different look. The dark tan complimented the white lacy blouse which I wore that first day, the red full skirt with white bobby socks and shoes to match, very attractive. We did get a few stares, but it was the boys that took notice. Oh, what a waste, for we were not interested in these boys, too immature and for us too young. Susi and I were more mature than our classmates, but just fitting in with girls is what we wanted most.

Henry and I started dating when I turned sixteen that year. Mother was not happy at all with this and told us so, every chance she had, of her disapproval. But our Uncle Pete was much more liberal with us. Every opportunity we had, we stayed with our Aunt and Uncle, seeing our country boys whenever visiting them became routine.

Henry taught me how to bowl. He could throw a ball down the lane pretty accurately and I learned quickly. After awhile, I gave him some competition and that was fun. The four of us, Susi and Nick, Henry and I, double dated all the time. Well, I mean, maybe once a week. There was no question we had fallen for each other. Our once a week dates were simple outings. In the summer, swimming in the nearby dug out gravel pit. Visiting Nick and Henry's grandparents and enjoying homemade desserts. It was especially welcoming to see the old Grandpa sitting on the porch, puffing on his long pipe, as he greeted us with joy. An occasional drive-in-movie was fun, and of course we socialized with friends in the cars near to us. That felt like a real American date. Oh, how can I forget "The Drive-In" restaurant, the one where the good looking girl's roller skated to our car. They brought the burgers, fries and root beer on a tray and connected it to our window. Just like on Happy Days. The cars lined up and we socialized with one another and that was also considered a date. The drag racing that followed on those country roads with the loud mufflers, were dusty, exciting, but fun. Henry enjoyed little ponies, and a good rider he was, too. While exercising his pony, I'd lean on the wooden fence and watch him walk the pony around and around, while he talked to me the whole time.

However, the time had come for us to move again. Karl was now certain of his job, and in late fall we moved to Roseville, a suburb of Detroit. Mother and Karl found an upstairs apartment on Twelve Mile Road and Gratiot. Susi was deeply disappointed by this move and informed my Mother of her plans to stay behind and live with our Aunt and Uncle. On the other hand, our Mother was extremely happy, for this move meant a separation from our country boys. "Oh, no," Mother replied to Susi's request, "you are coming with us, and that's my final word." When Susi and I looked so sad, Mother said, "We will visit every chance we have, I promise. You will see. It'll be okay," Mother tried to reassure us.

For me the city held promise, and in a strange way I was looking forward to the move. Besides, coming back like Mommi promised once a week sounded good to me. We settled into our new apartment over one weekend. We didn't waste any time. Susie did stay behind for a short time. I enrolled at the Roseville High School. It was a long walk to and from school, but I was used to walking. Our city school was very different from our country school. Most of the time sitting in a large classroom, it was very disruptive. The young, attractive teacher could not control the fresh sixteen year old boys. The English language was still difficult to write and to fully understand and the extra help I needed was just not available in class. Still too shy to ask for help, I fell behind, and lost interest with every day that passed. Being at school was still better than being at home, so for now I made the best of it. I gave it a real good effort.

It didn't take long to notice the different groups in our school, very similar to our last school. All the popular girls with their well groomed long hair, their full skirts and penny loafers all seemed to be in one group. I made friends, but I missed Susi and wondered when she would come back home from the farm, for Mother allowed her to stay only a short while.

Pond of Plum Dumplings

When Susi returned our concerns always shifted to the home front, our conversations of disgust about Mother and Karl's life together. We longed for a normal home life; it left us with a feeling of being helpless. With Uncle Pete far away, Karl returned to his old ways. Mother found work by this time, working four days a week doing housework. That meant that Karl was home already when we arrived home from school. Two hours alone with Karl everyday was stressful. When we entered the room, he sat by the table playing solitaire and talking to himself with his boxers on like before. It frightened us, for we didn't trust him. So many times, as Susi and I changed our clothes after school in our bedroom, the door flung open, just to hear Karl say, "Oops, wrong door, I thought it is our bedroom," he said. Of course we knew what would happen if we told our Mother, so we kept silent.

One time Susi and I did approach our Mother. "Just one more time, we will tell her," we said to each other. Mother listened to our concerns, and she said, "Ah, never mind. He will never touch my children." The following evening, Mother did question him, a major fight broke out and Karl hit our Mother again. There is this sick feeling in your stomach, when you witness this kind of abuse. He screamed from the top of his lungs. "I'll teach you who the boss is, and who brings home the money." He slammed the door so hard, the whole apartment shook. Mother held her face, as we surrounded her to give support.

All three of us sat at the table as our Mother swore this would never happen again. She called him a few names in Hungarian and ended up by saying, "I am going to throw him out." We were not too confident for this had happened before. Mother gave in, and took him back. Susi and I couldn't understand how our Mother made this choice in her life. Oma and Uncle John were against this union. We wondered how she didn't seem to understand how it affected all of us. Selfishly, we wished he would not return. But that didn't happen. Sometime during the night he returned. Susi and I woke to a squeaking sound from their bedroom. Every part of my body felt uncomfortable, I just wanted everything to stop. We took our pillows and squeezed them tight to our ears, so we couldn't hear anything. I hated her, how could she do this to us. Selfish wants poured out combined with a lot of anger that night, till the noise finally stopped. In the morning Mother and Karl were already gone. We were relieved.

"That's enough," Susi said "I am going to live with Aunt Katie and Uncle Pete, for good this time, Katie, I can't take it anymore. "Susi, what about me?" I questioned. "Well," she said, "you can come too." That day after work, Mother and Karl were exceptionally nice to us, although Susi and I were not nice back. Our answers to their questions were short and sharp, and we were not amused with their new mood. When they left that evening our unending complaints didn't have any solutions, but it made us feel better to talk.

Back at school, I made some friends, but I longed to belong to the group of the popular girls. My clothes didn't look or feel classy. My seventeenth birthday was coming up in the summer and I thought maybe then I would get a job and buy some new clothes. I was confident of my looks and figure, but I needed more, or so I thought. That summer Susi and I joined a German Youth Group. We danced until our feet could not move anymore. Susi and I danced together at the beginning, but became popular quickly. We had no shortage of boys asking us to dance. I had broken up with my country boy by this time and decided not to go steady with anyone for awhile, for breaking up with Henry was too painful. I loved Henry still, but I also knew that I was not a country girl, and that kind of life was not for me. Mother was relieved when I told her.

"Now, finally you have gotten smart," she said. "I am glad Katie; it's for the better, you'll see." It took a long time to forget Henry, but in time I realized many things. Susie, however, was not interested in the new German boys, for her heart was with Nick. She saw Nick often, for our weekly visits to the country continued way into the winter.

When I returned to school, another summer had left me with a tan and a new hairdo. I felt and looked glamorous, or so I thought. Susi and I worked at odd jobs throughout the summer, so both of us had a few brand new outfits. That summer we discovered the Toni Perms that we gave to each other to make our hair curly. Oh, that smell so strong, but it was fun anyway. The next thing we knew, the whole neighbourhood came for us to give them a Toni.

Back at school my first day, I wore a navy blue, tightly fitted skirt with pockets, a crisp white coloured, soft cotton blouse with special stitching around the collar and cuffs, to finish the outfit a five inch red leather belt. The looks from the boys that day was extra special. Even Rosalie, nicknamed The Beauty Queen, gave me a second look.

That afternoon, my wish came true. Rosalie walked right over to me in the hall, and said, "Hello Katie." "Hello" I said, surprised. After a short pause, she asked, "What are you doing after school today?" "Just going home," I answered. "Well would you like to meet me for a soda after school today?" "Okay." I said, barely being able to control my joy. "See you at four at the soda fountain," she smiled and left. I was so excited all afternoon, I couldn't concentrate. My eyes watched the clock for I surely didn't want to be late. After the last bell rang, I met my neighbour friend and told her that I would not be walking home with her today." There will be plenty of time to tell her of my good news when I get home, I thought to myself.

As I turned the corner on Gratiot, I already spotted the elite group congregating outside like they did every day, waiting for each other. Inside the store, I paced up and down the aisle pretending to look for something to buy, while waiting for Rosalie. Outside the Drugstore I spotted Diane, Blanche and Ruth, but I made sure they didn't see me. I kept looking at the clock and Rosalie was already five minutes late. I made a decision right then, that I would only wait ten more minutes before I'd leave. All of a sudden, a blonde head appeared. I stepped forward to find out it was not Rosalie, it was Linda, her best friend. I stood there a bit embarrassed as she looked right at me with a smile on her face. I opened my mouth to ask her, when at that very moment Rosalie walked in.

Rosalie walked right by me only looking at Linda, not even acknowledging of my presence there and they started to laugh out loud. I knew immediately this was a cruel trick. I turned and walked out, without saying a word. Although my heart crushed, I wouldn't let them see. My feet kept walking faster away, and I didn't look back. I could hear them laughing and based on the chatter amongst them, I knew the group outside was in on this cruel joke, too. When I reached a place that I knew was safe and I was alone, it was then I cried bitterly and I could hardly breathe. I cried silently all the way to the stairway that led to our apartment. I sat down on the bottom of the stairs to collect myself. The picture of Rosalie's face kept coming up, and I felt so much pain, and just couldn't understand people like that. After awhile Susi saw me and came running down the stairs. She took one look at me, and asked, "What's the matter, Katie?" I could barely bring myself to tell her, but I did. Susi was angry,

"Wait until I see that snob." "No, no Susi," I pleaded, "Don't say anything. Besides, I am not going to school anymore anyway."

It was a relief to learn that Mother and Karl went to their Wednesday night movie and left for the evening. That evening, I felt cold inside and became disillusioned with people and something changed.

A few times in my life I wanted to be alone and this evening was one of those times. I sat on the side of the bed for the longest time in silence. I asked the same question over and over again. How could Rosalie be so cruel as to humiliate me like that? So many emotions blended together in an instant to make me understand mistrust. Unresolved feelings that night and as always, when the outside world became unbearable, I could count on my sister. Susi came and sat next to me and we planned the following day together.

The next morning, Susi walked with me to the entrance of the school as I walked through the hall straight to my room and Susi took the bus to work. Rosalie and her friends passed me in the hall. I was uncomfortable, that's for sure. With the dignity that I had left, I walked with my head up high, right on by all of them without a word. It was definitly not comfortable, but not as hard as I thought it would be either. I never spoke to Rosalie or her friends again. It left a lasting feeling for me, and maybe even taught me a lesson, that some things are not worth having. It took a long time to overcome this experience, but time has a way of helping us forget and understand.

On the home front, Karl had his way with Mother, most of the time. He demanded all her time and we knew our place well by now. The less we said the better. It would only lead to a fight anyway, so we remained silent most of the time or spoke of our feelings only to each other. He demanded meat for all meals and forbade my Mother to make meals with flour that we loved, like noodles and crepes.

I remember one day in particular. Karl called Mother to tell her that he was working late, maybe ten or so in the evening.

Mother took the opportunity and made a dish we had not eaten in a very long time, plum dumplings. Susi and I helped peel the potatoes for the dough. It was like old times, all of us in the kitchen working and talking. The breadcrumbs roasted with a little sugar added, to cover the dumplings right before serving, was my job. Just as Mommi placed the pan with the delicious plum dumplings on the table, the door flung open, and there he was. Without so much as a word, Karl looked at the dumplings and said, "You call this meat?" Mother stood in front of the stove, surprised, and said, "What are you doing home so early?" as she walked over to the table. "Oh, that's why you made these dumplings behind my back, ha!" "Karl, don't."

With much anger in his eyes, Karl picked up the pan and dumped the dumplings on the floor. Mother became enraged and started screaming, "What are you doing?" Mother walked over to him and lifted her arm ready to swing at Karl, but as quick as she was she was no match for Karl. He grabbed her arm. Mother started to scream, that's how hard he squeezed her wrist. Susi and I immediately dropped to the floor and tried to make peace, "it's all right, Mother. It's all right, please stop," as we collected the dumplings from the floor. A terrible fight broke out. Karl again lashed out at Mother and hit Mother in the face, not once but twice. It was the only time that I can remember Mother trying to hit him back, when he hit her again, this time really hard. Oh, it was so disturbing for the rage in his face at that moment is hard to describe. At that particular time, we feared for all our safety. To our relief he walked to the door, slammed it and left.

Mother locked the door behind him and she held her face. Her cheek swelled quickly, as we looked up from the floor. The feeling of relief slowly changed to anger which started to build inside Susi and me. Susi and I remained on the floor on our knees as we moved around to pick up the scattered dumplings. It was at that very moment something inside me changed. With every dumpling in my hand my anger built into a clear vision of outrage and a solution of my own. We rinsed the dumplings under hot water and arranged them nicely back on a serving platter back on the table without the breadcrumbs. We sat silently staring at each other, and the dumplings. The dumplings remained on the table, untouched. We didn't eat and we didn't talk. With so many mixed feelings that night, I knew the time had come for us to act. Something hardened within us both, as we picked ourselves up from the floor that evening.

The evening for the three of us that night was sad, disturbing, long and sleepless. Mother made the usual threats and it was clear to see she was extremely angry. As Susi and I walked up to our bedroom it seemed with every step we took our plan became more firm in our minds. It is time to involve our Uncle Pete. Karl respected him and perhaps, he would be the only one that could make this madness stop, we thought. We knew Uncle Pete would help, we were certain of that, but not so sure of what would happen to us when all was said and done, but it was worth the risk.

Karl returned home that night banging on the door till Mother finally let him in. Although it seemed Karl spoke normally, we didn't sleep that night and Mother did not want him in the house. Mother held her ground for a few days, but gave in when Karl promised to never hit her again. We, however, were not convinced and began to put our plan in motion.

That weekend, on our weekly visit to the farm started in the morning with a good breakfast and then we took the two hour ride in the country. During the drive, our thoughts consumed in our plan, Susi and I could hardly relax. We somehow managed to lure our Uncle in the barn and started with our complaints. Uncle Pete was shocked and angry as he listened to our pleas for help. He reassured us that he would take care of us and this problem. "Don't you worry, leave it up to me. I'll make him understand," he said, and we knew from his tone that he meant it. Sometime that afternoon, Uncle Pete made his move and took Karl to the basement, as we listened with much fear, upstairs.

"Karl, what is this bruise I see on my sister's face? A real man doesn't hit a woman." Uncle Pete proceeded, "Come on, if you want to fight someone, come and fight me." "Awe, you old man," Karl replied. Later, Uncle Pete told us he grabbed Karl by the collar and lifted him off the floor a few inches and said, "If you ever touch my sister or those girls again, Karl, I'll deport you. I brought you over here and signed for you, but I can also send you back. Do you understand me? Don't think, I won't do it," our Uncle threatened. They shook hands, as both men made this agreement. The best of all, Karl never knew it was indeed Susi and me that told Uncle Pete.

We bid our goodbyes as Uncle Pete whispered in my ear, "Everything will be okay; don't worry. You call me anytime if he ever so much as lays a hand on any one of you." It was a stressful day for Susi and me. We were scared and so uncomfortable. We saw no sign of anger from Karl and that was a relief. Karl never hit our Mother again, but the nature doesn't change entirely over night. He found other ways to be cruel. At least the hitting stopped and that was better than what we had.

Susi, by this time, was silently planning to marry Nick. When Mother found out she was not happy. Susi stood her ground and wouldn't listen to Mother anymore. Mother and Karl threatened not to sign for her since she was not eighteen yet. For now anyway, Susi remained at home. In some ways to see Susi married to Nick would be great. I really liked Nick and we had a good relationship. On the other hand, it meant I would be left alone in the house and that made me nervous. Selfish thoughts, for sure, and I was happy when Susi stayed a little longer.

Mother cleaned houses for rich people, or so we assumed, like so many immigrants in the fifties who did this kind of work. Mother left at eight in the morning and returned with the bus at five in the evening. She felt lucky to have such nice people to work for. They trusted Mother with their children and in some cases Mother became very attached to the children. In the evenings when she shared her day with us, it was obvious this made her happy. "I cook for these kids," she said, "and they eat everything, to their Mother's delight." The money she received for her hard work was fair, but not great. Karl, on the other hand, made good money at the Studebaker car factory. Karl liked to carry cash. You could say he enjoyed flaunting bills of money around every chance he had. It was clear to us that Karl was not only undesirable to us, but to others as well. Mother and Karl didn't have any friends.

Our neighbours that lived below us, also of our heritage, did not socialize with Karl. We felt the judgment of this family, towards us girls, and once again so many times, we struggled to belong. If it wasn't for our looks and our good manners, we would have easily been dismissed in this cruel world as losers. Outside of Karl, we felt confident in ourselves and that was a big help. Because of our family situation bringing newly made friends home for acceptance was totally out of the question. Our Mother didn't like company at this time and didn't offer any invitations either. When Susi and I had an invitation from one of our friends for dinner, the parents gracious and friendly, it made us long for that sort of a home life. We made this thinking so important in our minds that it consumed us and wasted much of our precious youth. The time came when we shifted from wanting changes to running away from them. In the 1950s, it was a time of judgment, a time of ignorance, a time to heal, a time to forget, and a time to love again, all rolled into one confusing time for me.

That fall I decided not to return to school. At that time, 1953, a grade ten education was enough and many girls worked in a dentist or doctor's office as a receptionist before getting married. Mother was disappointed and tried hard to convince me to continue, but I refused to listen. By now my English reading and writing were up to standard, so I thought it was enough. Besides that, I didn't feel any connection with our school and that didn't help. From the very first day I felt like an outsider. I made only a few friends. I mostly felt the pain of being a foreigner and heard words behind my back, like Kraut and DP (Displaced Person). Our principal was very concerned and caring when I told her of my decision not to return. She asked, "Why? We are happy to have you." and other similar questions. I just answered "I don't know" to every question she asked. She then realized it was too late, for my insecurity closed my mind to anything she tried to tell me.

Susi and I accepted positions as salespersons, I at Neisner's Dime Store, Susi at Kresge's on Seven Mile Road and Gratiot. We tried to get the same hours so we could ride together on the bus. Since we lived on Twelve Mile Road, the buses ran regularly and were dependable. Our hours varied through the week, but we adapted well. The job I was assigned to was tedious but easy. The notions counter, like needles, buttons, etc. had to be stocked and neat at all times. Friday was the best day of the week: payday. Having money for the first time in our lives was exhilarating. Although there was not much left after we paid Mommi room and board and of course our daily bus fare. It didn't matter. It was still a whole new way of life. I spent all my spare money on clothes. I loved beautiful things and quickly had the reputation of being too extravagant in the family. Mother was upset when I brought another shopping bag home with something new inside. So, what could I do with the bargains so attractive and cheap, I had an eye for the best style for the money, so I snuck the packages in the house every chance I had. When Mommi asked "Is this something new?" "Oh, no," I'd reply, "I bought it a long time ago," and it worked. Mother gave us many lectures about saving money. There wasn't much left to save so "Why bother?" became our reasoning.

It seemed from the moment Mother found out that I broke up with Henry she changed towards me. I believe it was the first time Mother and I sat across from each other at the kitchen table, just the two of us, and talked. Her praises for my decision to break up with Henry made me see Mommi in a whole different way. I always knew underneath that stern exterior there lived a big heart. She gave me some advice that I still repeat often, "You really don't know someone truly" she'd say, "until you sit on the same table sharing bread day after day with them. Many people seem so nice." Her pessimistic side was showing, I thought to myself, as I continued to listen to her, "When you are courting, faults are little. When you marry, the same faults become bigger faults. Just remember in the exciting years everything is rosy, but everyday living can be very different," she tried to advise me. I, of course, thought that all this advice didn't apply to me.

Mother, like I said before, was not a fancy woman, but orderly and clean that's for sure. One of her teachings became my biggest lessons in life. When you use something, put it back when finished. If you break something, replace it. Don't do to others, what you don't like yourself. Don't expect anything for nothing, work for it, you will appreciate life more. And, never go into someone's fridge, except family. That was a big mistake if anyone came to visit and did just that. Mother brought this up after they left, as a lack of manners, and didn't let us forget it. Susi and I laughed for we thought it was so unimportant.

Besides our work and our German dance group we grew fond of our life in America. My name on my citizenship papers I changed from Katharina to Catherine, the American spelling. We had found a new country and I wanted to make sure I didn't stand out with a German name. Our beloved Kikinda was now a faded memory. I could hardly remember my room or the city. Deep down in my mind I never forgot my doll, my dog and that feeling of home. But, memories of Austria held on much longer, for most of my youth was spent there. After all, our sister Margaret, as we now called Grete in the American way, had given birth to a son. Oma and Hans Onkel also lived there still. We worried about their well being and how they were coping without us. From letters abroad we discovered Oma's health was failing and it was only a matter of time before Hans Onkel could not take care of his Mother anymore.

In our dance group there was no shortage of dates. Still feeling the pain from Henry, I became selective. What I really enjoyed was dancing. Compliments poured in from the young men about my dancing, "She is so easy to lead," things of that sort. I heard this, but I felt uncomfortable and had trouble accepting compliments. Mother taught us to be modest, and not boast about ourselves, and we didn't. I'd polka and waltz until I couldn't breathe anymore. There was much laughter and joy at those dances.

As time went by there was no doubt of the popularity I had with boys. But, I started to notice girls distancing themselves from me and it was troublesome to me. My knack of adding a flower, or a bow, or a special color of shoes to make an outfit more striking was easy and normal for me, the same for my hair, a different hairdo daily. With my natural deep wave, my shiny, flowing hair fell into place very easily. I thought it looked attractive and sexy. The best part of all, I didn't spend much time trying to look attractive. Perhaps that was the reason the girls treated me that way, I told myself.

In many of my private hours, I visualized a fashion show from beginning to end and the collection was all mine. This kind of thinking was only in my dreams, for after all I was just a girl during a time when most women were not expected to have big career hopes. Typically marriage and kids right out of high school was the choice. I didn't want this for myself at that time.

Susi, however, did. Marriage was certainly something she wanted. Right from the very beginning, she felt a real connection with the country and the people in it. On July 3rd, 1954, Susi married her country sweetheart Nick. Susi glowed in her beautiful satin wedding gown. The train, made with the same satin material as the dress, followed her all the way up to the altar. With her hair so beautifully set and the flowers held in her hands, she walked up to the aisle to be united with Nick. Mother and Karl, however, did not hide the fact that they disapproved of this union. As the Maid of Honour, I was right by Susi's side and we carried on as we had many times before, pretending and ignoring all the facts around us, deep inside just praying that no one will notice of our dysfunctional family. "*Please God*," I made my case to God, let there be no trouble today.

Henry didn't stand up with me. So it was some time since I seen him, it was so good to see Henry again. We had parted as friends and the two of us were comfortable with each other and it showed, especially to Mother and Karl. The white tuxedo jackets and black pants looked attractive on the two brothers. The strapless light blue toile dress I wore hugged every part of my upper body and showed off my small waist. The full skirt all the way down to the floor with matching shoes peeking through made me feel elegant. I was proud at my sister's wedding and my first chance to be a Maid of Honour.

We sat down for dinner and I placed my bouquet of flowers in front of my place setting. At that moment I caught a glimpse of Karl looking at me. I had seen that look many times before and it started to invade my enjoyment of this lovely evening. I tried to push it back in my thoughts, but it just kept surfacing, like a bad weed. Henry was seated next to me. He leaned over and whispered in my ear, "Are you okay, Katie?" Our eyes met and it felt great to see how compassionate and kind he was. "I am fine," I answered quietly.

When we raised our glasses and toasted the Bride and Groom I realized it was my first time tasting champagne. I didn't like the taste too much, but that didn't matter. When Susi and Nick took to the dance floor for their wedding dance it wasn't important that Nick was no Fred Astaire, they looked great. After our dance, Henry and I walked out together to the bar. I finally said to Henry, "Do you notice something about Karl?" Reluctantly he answered, "Yup, he is worried maybe you and I will get back together again, he wouldn't like that." "You think," I said jokingly.

"Would you like a drink?" he asked. With that, Henry half serious but still smiling, I said, "Maybe a little bit more champagne." He squeezed my hand. "Great idea," he said, and with that Henry laugh, he turned and headed straight to the bar. I followed him with my eyes and in the distance Karl came in my view, not far from Henry. It seemed as if he was waiting for Henry. If I hadn't known any better, I would have said he planned it that way. My eyes fixed on the pair standing together. I didn't have to be there to know they were talking about me. From the movements of their mouths I knew the conversation was not pleasant. All through my body I felt that familiar uncomfortable shaking inside that I had felt many times before. My pleas to God were so many, I was afraid he might not hear me anymore, but one more time, please God, I asked. Henry moved away from Karl and headed towards the bar, Karl followed him. Henry carried our drinks in both hands, and had to pass Karl to come back to me, when it happened.

Karl flung his arm and knocked the drinks out of Henry's hands unto the floor. Without hesitation Henry launched at Karl and punched Karl in the chest. Before Karl returned the punch, intervention by several young men around held them apart. I stood paralysed with my hands over my mouth, and I cried out in disgust. A crowd gathered quickly, but it was broken up as quickly as it started. Out of the crowd walked Henry, straightening his jacket and brushing himself off walking over to me. Silently we walked outside and sat on a cement ledge. He finally said, "Boy, Katie, I tell you, it felt good," his lips still quivering from anger. "That maniac, how do you live with someone like that? How do you do it?" he asked.

We talked for the longest time. It felt good to speak from the heart and to know you're totally understood. If only Mother and Karl could trust me, there would be no need to worry, for my mind was made up, and Henry and I were not to be. Although

191

I knew that Henry felt differently, I couldn't prolong and hurt a person like Henry any longer when I knew my heart was not his anymore. I watched the two brothers sitting together from a distance and discussing the whole episode, as I walked away and joined my sister. The embarrassment was so public that it lingered on in some people's memories much longer than in ours, as they reminded us from time to time. Mostly, we learned to believe in ourselves and on occasions, like that, it was hard to do.

In those times, in the 1950s, things like social status and money divided classes of distinction. It was obvious to me that to rise above the level where I found myself, I needed to possess these things. I wasn't looking to push aside the important values I already had, that carried me through, thanks to my family, I told myself many times. After all, I was not related to Karl. Monetary possessions, without manners, never impressed our family. Being a good person and working hard for what you want and never expecting anything for nothing, these were the values instilled in me then, and remain the same to this day. Still, I felt I needed more.

Being without Susi was a challenge for me. For the first time in my life I felt alone. What am I going to do without my sister and my best friend? I asked myself. I was depressed for a long time. Sitting in the bus by myself, I missed the togetherness. As I sat aimlessly with my face pressed against the glass on the bus, I saw a large sign that read, "**A time to make a friend is not when you need one.**" Every day, I passed this sign and I read it, every day. Letter by letter it became very meaningful in my life.

When Mother and Karl left in the evening for a movie, and I was home alone, it was then I'd sit on the window sill and daydream the evening away. On one of those times I started drawing, first movie stars, then landscapes. Mostly I was lonely. I didn't need or want anyone besides Susi, or so I thought. When the phone rang and it was Susi, I was happy. That summer I made plans to spend my whole vacation with Susi and Nick. My week with my sister and brother-in-law was like old times. We had a great time. But, on my way home, I realized that nothing will ever be the same again. It made me sad and I didn't want to move on. With every turn I made in my mind, I reached the same bump. Slowly over time, others walked into my life to fill the void.

Somehow word came of a German girl that was looking for a girlfriend to go to dances with, because her best friend was getting married and no longer available. Her best friend just happened to live in the downstairs apartment from us and she gave her girlfriend my phone number. When Catherine called on the telephone, I felt comfortable for she was easy to talk to. We agreed to meet the next day to see if we were a fit. I was relieved when she wanted to meet at her house. Her name was Catherine, just like mine. Catherine was an only child. Well, she did have an older brother who was long gone from home when she was very young. You could say she was the only one, especially since her brother and family lived far away.

Catherine stood by the front door, waiting for me, as I walked up to the porch. With a certain laugh she said, "Hi, I am Catherine," as she held out her hand to me. "I'm Catherine, too," I said joyfully. She pushed her glasses up with her finger. Her dark eyes and a slightly cross eyed look, is when she said to me, "Come in and meet my parents." It didn't take long to figure out that we were a perfect match. Catherine had blonde hair and a very good figure, especially her legs. She was secure, and I was balanced and steady. We both shared a good sense of humour, and were almost the same height, I possibly a bit taller.

After awhile her Mother, Mrs. Wagner, called for supper. That same selfish familiar feeling, it never did go away, if only I had such a home life. The table set beautifully, the dishes matched the tablecloth which was light peach. Catherine was very helpful to her mother and they served us tea and dessert together. I could only sit and watch with envy, until I asked,

"Can I help?" "Yes, of course you can," Mrs. Wagner said, and handed me a sugar dish. "Fill it up for me please," she asked. After the meal, Catherine and I offered to help with the dishes. Her Father piped in, "No not today. Go and visit with each other, and ask your new friend if she wants to come to the dance with us on Saturday night," he said with a smile. At that moment, I felt comfortable and relaxed for they let me know that they approved of me, and I began to be myself.

It was a wonderful evening. Their house not large but in a well groomed neighbourhood. The outside of the house with light brick perfectly laid, the driveway cemented and the attached garage took up the allowance of the whole lot. The inside was tastefully decorated; the feeling reflected the warmth and easiness of their ways. Catherine's room in peach and off white, clean and elegant, and I loved it.

It was starting to get dark, as I said goodbye to my new friend and ran to the corner to catch the bus. My ride home was short, but I did have to transfer once. Walking toward our apartment I knew Mother and Karl were home. I wanted this feeling to last, so I lingered and sat on the landing of our stairway. My thoughts still with my new friend, maybe I'll be happy again and I won't be so lonely anymore. As the slightly cool breeze filled the evening and the leaves on the trees could be heard making a rustling sound, the air was so warm just like my heart. Maybe there will be good times ahead. With that thought, I walked slowly up the stairs, making a pause between every step. When I reached our landing on the top, I turned once more and took a long look over our neighbourhood. The door opened quickly and it was Karl with only his undershorts on. "What are you doing out here," he asked. "Nothing, I'm just coming in," I answered. He moved over to let me walk past him. "Where have you been?" "Oh," I said, "didn't Mother tell you? I went to meet my new girlfriend." "Well do you like her?" he asked. "Yes, I do," I answered.

It occurred to me that there was a possibility that I was

alone with Karl." Where is Mother?" I asked. By this time, I was already a little nervous, he said, "She is gone to help out at the neighbours, she'll be right back." I sat by myself, across the table from him, and pretended to be busy with some bookwork. There was no way I was going into the bedroom to change. Karl played solitaire the whole time, talking to himself. It seemed forever, when Mommi finally came through that door. I excused myself without talking to my Mother and went into my room to sleep, since I was tired and 6 o'clock came early in morning. Many things had changed and Mother trusted me much more now than ever before. There wasn't anything said, but their rules softened as well as their tone towards me. I took full advantage and stayed out later as often as possible.

During the week, Monday through Wednesday I worked during the day. Monday evenings I had to catch up on my sleep, which meant going to bed early. Tuesday evening I did odd jobs and cleaned my room. Wednesday, my neighbourhood friends as a group went to the movies. We'd gather at our apartment, walked fifteen minutes and had just enough time to find good seats before the movie started. It was on Wednesdays, at the movies, when they handed out dishes with every ticket. Mother agreed to let me go and was happy that we finally had some nice dishes. The dishes felt strong and sturdy and white with a brown rim. Some of my friends didn't want the dishes and offered them to me and that did speed up the set of eight.

No matter what, Mother's strict orders to be home at ten left me never knowing the ending of any movie. I tried hard to convince her that it was unfair, but she wouldn't hear of me staying out later than ten during the week. Knowing that she gave me much more leeway on the weekend made me give in. Thursday I worked in the evening until nine. This meant that by the time I rode the bus and made the transfer I arrived home about 10:30pm. I had just enough time to put my hair in rollers, relax a little and call it a night. By the time I reached eighteen, Mother and Karl felt comfortable to leave me home alone often.

I had no regular boyfriend so there was really nothing to worry about. Friday night I went through my closet and picked out just the right dress and the shoes to match to wear for the Saturday dance the next evening.

I usually worked on a Saturday, so that meant I had just enough time to come home and get dressed, before meeting Catherine at her house. I took one last look in my mirror to make sure, the seam on my nylons were straight. My turquoise crepe dress with a flared skirt, very appropriate for dancing, fit perfectly. This being my first time going to a dance with my new girlfriend, Catherine, I wanted to look special. I was happily chuckling as I said out loud to myself, "Let's go and do some dancing." That first time Mother and Karl agreed to drive me to Catherine's house and that really helped. "Now Katie, have a good time and remember your manners." "Yes Mother," I answered under my breath.

Catherine's Mom and Dad drove us to downtown Detroit where we took the tunnel under the Detroit River over to Windsor, Canada. We showed our identification papers when questioned by the Customs Officer, not as big a deal as it is today. When we entered the dance hall called the Teutonia Club, my heart began to pound so loud, I felt it all way up to my throat. "Two dollars, please," the person at the door said, as we walked up to the desk. Catherine looked at me as we paid our entrance fee and gave me a smile, "Don't worry just follow me. We'll look for a table." We worked our way through the crowd, as I noticed people following our movements with their stares, as if they noticed that I was someone new. I became shy, but not uncomfortable, as we found a table. Another family sat across from us and they introduced themselves to us.

By this time, I settled in my chair. I lifted my head and had a chance to glance through the crowd. Catherine poked me and said, "Oh, Catherine, look there," pointing her finger, "there is the group that I know." At that moment they spotted each other and motioned hello with a nod. My eyes moved slowly through the crowd as I saw many good looking young men. I was beginning to feel quite comfortable, mostly because Catherine was right alongside of me. I turned to her and said, "I like this hall, I am glad you asked me to come." "Just wait till the music starts, you'll really like that, and I'll introduce you to my friends then." "Oh, good," I said.

I jumped as the Polka band began the evening with a peppy beat. The dance floor filled up quickly and through the crowd two young men appeared and came to our table. "May I have this dance?"One of them extended his hand to Catherine, and the other young man, to me. We nodded yes and walked ahead of them to the dance floor. I turned with his outstretched arm and laid my hand in his. We danced a waltz. "What's your name?" a blonde, 5ft 9in, fair haired, young man asked. "Catherine," I answered. "Oh, so you are Catherine's new friend, huh?" he grinned. "Oh, you know Catherine?" I asked. "Oh, yes for quite a while, but she didn't tell me you dance so well." "Go on." I blushed. "And not bad looking either." Before I said anything else, he said, "You can call me Matzi." "Ok," I said.

This young man was definitely not my type, but he could dance. We danced three dances together, a waltz, a tango and a polka. Walking me back to the table, Matzi made me a promise that he would teach me the hopping polka. I was in good hands for Matzi was the best dancer in the group. It was sort of an unwritten rule, I could say, in dancing that if one enjoyed a partner, three dances gave the welcoming sign for a repeat performance. Just one dance meant one didn't enjoy the dance, and usually was not asked again.

By the time the intermission came along I met most of Catherine's dancing partners. We stood together in a group talking while the band took a fifteen minute break. I felt the curiosity of some of the remaining friends I had yet to meet as Catherine introduced me to them as they joined in. A great group of young people, I felt lucky to have this chance to be part of them. We ended up on the dance floor talking throughout the entire intermission. When the band started with a waltz, I was asked to dance by a new young man and Catherine danced with someone, as well. The time came for the song to be played that signalled the last dance, *Aufwiedersehn*. We moaned. We wanted this evening to last forever. And so our friendship began, Catherine and mine.

In the fall we made another move. Mother and Karl had a chance to manage two small apartment buildings. Karl was now out of a job, for the Studebaker Company closed their doors and everybody lost their jobs. For maintaining these buildings, the rent was free and the apartment fully furnished. Mother thought it to be a good deal, so we moved once again. For me it meant I wouldn't see Catherine as much as before. I wasn't happy to move from Roseville, on the east side of Detroit, way over to the west side on Grand Blvd. and Linwood.

By the time we settled in our new apartment, the cold and brisk air had set in. The trees were bare and not pretty. I had to change my job, for the bus traveling to my old job, took 1 ½ hours each way. I read an ad in the paper that appealed to me. It said, **salesperson needed, customer service, dealing with people helpful.** Sanders Bakery and Candy Store, not far from our house, was looking. I applied that day and was hired on the spot. The first week of work, I trained to work in the Chocolate and Candy Department upstairs. I learned the different names of chocolate, and also how to neatly pack the chocolate into attractive boxes for every occasion possible. But, I longed to work downstairs.

The following week, my wish came true, the fountain counter, needed someone and I quickly learned how to make hot fudge sundaes. After a few weeks of training, I enjoyed coming to work. My working buddies became very dear to me. We served the hot fudge sundaes and cream puffs to the same older ladies every week. It was their outing and we knew them well enough to call them by their names. That was so sweet. Through the day my new friends and I passed each other behind the counter, with a little gesture of humour, all day long. It was lots of fun. Six of us girls worked on a counter for an eight hour shift. Our supervisor assigned each girl to a counter, each counter seated between six and twelve people. Marianne and I for some reason never got a six chair counter, ever. After some time we asked our supervisor, "Why?" This was her answer, "I am sorry girls, you both are my fastest girls, and you do such a good job. Unfortunately some of the other girls can't handle so many chairs," she said, "but I'll try."

Marianne, Millie, Darlene and I had the counters next to one another most of the time, and we worked together like a well-oiled machine. When caught up with our own booth, we simply moved on to help out on the next one. And so the unfairness we felt disappeared, instead friendships began. The four of us became such good friends, that at least once a week we planned something. Mostly we enjoyed talking to each other about our growing pains, but once in awhile, a movie for a treat. For me life was good. I had my work that I enjoyed and my friends on the weekends, oh, yes, dancing with my friend Catherine.

On a weekday with my work friends, at Darlene's house, my friends taught me a dance that I didn't know, "The Jitterbug." I was dying to learn this naughty dance. My German friends wouldn't dance such a dance for it meant you were loose. Can you imagine? I loved the twirling and the sassiness of this dance, as we laughed and giggled the night away. Only Darlene from the four of us had a serious relationship with her long-time boyfriend of five years. That was the only sad times we had in this group. One morning Darlene didn't show up for work, we knew something was wrong. When we changed into our brown uniforms that morning, stuffing our long hair in the hairnet, we expressed our concerns to each other. Every spare moment we had, we talked amongst each other about our worries. At lunch, we walked to a payphone twice, but no answer each time.

We made up our minds to make a visit to Darlene's house after work.

Darlene didn't want to open the door. "I look terrible," she said, through the crack of the door. "Open the door, please Darlene," we pleaded. "We're not leaving." When the door opened, she turned away and walked to the far side of the room. "Darlene, please talk to us, please look at us," we asked. When she finally faced us, she looked awful. The side of her face bruised and her eyes puffy and so sad. We tried so hard to help her, but she looked broken. Rory, her boyfriend, broke off their relationship and it left her devastated. When she ran after him and they argued, is when they started hitting each other, she explained to us. It was clear to us that Darlene lost her self esteem, and felt lost without Rory. The fact that he found someone else already kept Darlene in this pain that she couldn't overcome. We did what we could that day, put her to bed after a hot meal and a cup of tea and left.

After work for the next three days, we took turns checking on Darlene. One of us made sure she dressed for the day. The other got her hair washed and set. I opened the blinds, the windows and made a small homemade meal. Chicken and dumplings, which I knew by heart, was easy. By the third day the bruise had faded, but Darlene still in a lot of pain. Our supervisor informed us, knowing we were good friends, "if Darlene doesn't return soon I can't guarantee her job. I hope you know it's out of my hands, I am sorry," she said. The three of us worked hard to pick up the slack for Darlene. We knew it was just a matter of time before Darlene would return.

On the fourth day, as we reported for our shift, Darlene walked in. We stopped for a second and then we all clapped for her. In the weeks that followed, Darlene went through a deep depression from time to time. We all agreed that it was no easy task for her to get over Rory. We remained friends and looked out for each other, always.

My time at home much more at ease, perhaps not spending

too much time in the house, or perhaps being older and stronger was the reason. The few times that I was home, I was angry at my Mother. Mother started smoking. All these years, Mother preached to me about drinking and smoking and boys. Now that I am truly living the way I was taught, to have to endure the opposite from my Mother, was very disappointing to me. When I approached my Mother, she said, "You know Karl smokes, so you know when he drives in the car I light his cigarette so I might as well join him and smoke too." "Mother, what if I do that?" I said angrily. "Well, well you know better." I walked away, it was no use. What could I do? I shook my head as I started to understand life a little better.

Catherine and I remained friends. If we didn't see each other during the week, Saturday night dances were for sure, Sunday we'd take the bus together to the Detroit Tunnel, hopped on the Tunnel bus and went to Windsor, where some of our friends there picked us up. Once there, we then decided to either drive to Leamington to a hall called HiY, where every Sunday afternoon a dance was held, or, sometimes, the Rose Garden in Kingsville. We really didn't care, we just wanted to dance. Catherine was a very good dancer and popular equally with girls and boys. Me, on the other hand, boys loved dancing with me and some girls gave me the cold shoulder. Although girls didn't welcome me nearly as much as boys, I had Catherine on my side. She trusted me and didn't feel intimidated. Anyway, I was getting used to girls being that way, and convinced myself it didn't matter.

In those days I lived for the weekends and for the time I'd be old enough to have an alcoholic drink in public. I'd sit by the window sill on a Monday night before bed for hours and relived the weekend gone by while at the same time planning my wardrobe for the weekend. During the week without fail, Catherine called to tell me of our plans for the following week. On a rare occasion her parents had other plans and couldn't drive, we asked each other, what are we going to do? "I'll see if Mother and Karl can drive for a change," I reassured Catherine.

It was different driving with Mother and Karl, but we didn't care. By this time Catherine and I became selective with boys and wanted to start practicing how to turn down a boy and simply say no, when he asked for a dance. Our timing couldn't have been any worse.

When Catherine and I walked through the large dance hall with our noses up in the air, as if we were better than everybody there, and my Mother following behind us, we were in for a real shock. Both Catherine and I sat across from my Mother as this young man that I didn't think was cool came immediately and asked me to dance. I said, "No thank you, maybe later." However, moments later, a good looking guy asked me to dance and I said "yes." I caught my Mother's look in her eye and I knew what was coming. When I returned to the table, Mother put her finger in my face, and she said, "You turn down another boy that asks you to dance, then consider this your last time here." She added, "Every boy is good enough to dance one dance with, and don't you forget it." Mother, was one of those people that you heard when she spoke. I just rolled my eyes, got up and went to the bathroom, and Catherine followed.

Our regular group arrived late that night, so our evening turned out better than we first thought. Almost at closing Catherine and I spotted two young attractive men standing by the entrance door. We learned they lived in Kingsville about twenty miles from Windsor. As I danced past them, I could see them watching me move across the dance floor with my partner. When I came closer and could observe them better, I noticed them whispering to each other, and of course I was hoping they were talking about me. Catherine and I couldn't wait to meet at the table after our dance so we could talk about these two guys. Catherine had seen them before and liked the one they called Johnny, and I of course, the taller one, called George. The sophisticated one definitely caught my eye. One thing for sure, they were not just outstanding looking, but also older than the young men in our group, maybe twenty two or so years old. We lost sight of them for awhile, then through a little opening in the crowd, I noticed them dancing with other girls. Our hopes shattered, they didn't notice us after all, we thought.

Toward the end of the evening, as the band played a beautiful tango, these same gorgeous guys stopped at our table. "May I have this dance?" they asked and both of us, in sync, lifted ourselves out of our chairs and joined them on the dance floor. We flowed over the floor with every beat of the music. "You are new here," he questioned me. "No, I've been here a few times." "Well," he paused, "my name is George, and I know your name is Catherine," as I nodded yes. At the end of the tango, we spotted Catherine and Johnny and we walked over to join them. By the second dance with George, I learned he lived in Kingsville and was indeed older, twenty three to be exact. I was only eighteen at the time.

George's charming way and good looks held my interest and also an immediate attraction. Something I hadn't felt for awhile. The band announced the last dance and I was disappointed. The night flew by again and I wasn't nearly ready to stop dancing. "Thank you for the dance," George said, as he bowed his head. Catherine and I talked about George and Johnny all the way home. Our anxious questions, of what did he say, or are they coming next week? Neither one of us knew anything for sure, except that we counted the days, the hours, till the following Saturday and hopefully we would see them again.

The following Saturday turned out to be our regular group only, George and Johnny were not there. Although disappointed, dancing every dance is what we lived for. From time to time, a new young man would come from nowhere and ask us to dance. As time went by we became familiar with many different young people. The following week we chose the Teutonia Hall, our favourite band, The Hetzel Band was playing, that we liked so much. Catherine and I walked in like we always did with our beautiful flowered dresses, white crinolines and matching color shoes, with our slender figures and perfect skin, a pair that complimented each other. We joined our group of friends, as Mr. and Mrs. Wagner joined their group at another table, away from us. The evening began as always with a peppy song, usually a polka or a march.

After the first intermission, Catherine came running up to me, she was so excited, and pulled me to the side and said, "They are here," "Oh my gosh," I said, "really." I knew immediately who she meant. "Johnny and George just walked in and I think they are looking for us," she said. "How do you know?" I asked. "They walked down the aisles from one end to the other looking side to side." "What do you think this means?" I questioned. "Well, let's go and see," Catherine said. Before leaving the washroom we collected ourselves and started to walk proud and pretended not to notice anyone. We reached our table as the music started to play. I felt a hand on my arm, I turned and there was George asking me to dance. "Well, how are you today?" he asked. "I am fine," I replied as calmly as I could, considering that I was overjoyed to see him again. After a pause, "Where were you last Saturday?" he questioned. "Catherine and I went to the Saxon Hall on Erie St." "Oh, really?" surprised, he said. "They had a dance there, didn't you know?" I asked. I was dying to ask him where he was that Saturday, but I couldn't get my nerve up to do that. After a waltz they usually played a tango. I was hoping that would happen, so maybe he'd hold me just a little closer. There was no doubt, I was falling for George. No tango, so after our three dances we returned like usual to our table. With our eye contact, I knew this feeling I felt was mutual between us, but too soon for any other approach. When I twirled around the dance floor with different partners, and George and my eyes met, it was magic.

I looked at the clock several times as I longed to dance with George before closing at 1am. I returned to the table on purpose at 12:45am so I'd be available, just in case. When I looked over to the table where they sat, the table was empty, and everyone was gone. The look on my face was sheer disappointment, but the joy returned as I felt his hand behind me, lifting me out of my chair. We didn't talk much, except he wanted to know of our plans for the following Saturday. "See you next week," is the last thing he said to me.

For the next month, George and I tried to keep our feelings hidden. It was a no win situation. When eligible boys knew a girl had special feelings for someone, they stayed away. Until totally sure of George, I didn't want to risk it.

Defining the Dance of Life

I enjoyed dancing so much that just meeting at the dance hall once a week was safer for both of us. We never even kissed in the first month, but dancing close every chance we had was exciting. When hunting season came along, Johnny and George missed several Saturdays in a row. It gave Catherine and me a chance to dance with anyone we wished. At that time in the Saxon hall Catherine introduced me to a good looking young guy named Bill. Catherine pointed him out to me, where he sat, directly across from us on the other side of the hall.

William (Bill) Bering

"He is really nice", she said, "and my Mom and Dad like him. I've danced with him a few times already." Catherine explained to me that she hadn't seen him lately and wondered where he was. Just then the music started to play and he immediately started walking towards us. "Oh boy, he is coming to ask me to dance," Catherine whispered to me. I was so embarrassed and reluctant, for it was not the way it was supposed to be, as he asked me to dance instead of Catherine. I felt awkward. We started to waltz, he looked at me and said, "I am Bill and you are *Schwartzi* (meaning a brunette)." "No, I am not," I replied somewhat annoyed. He proceeded to explain, "Well you might not know this, but all the boys call you that." I was getting impatient with this Bill, as I said, "You should have asked Catherine to dance, you know." "I wanted to dance with you," he replied, a bit unsure of himself. I must admit, he seemed younger than I. He smelled so clean, so pure, untouched.

I made up my mind he was not my type, and just too young. The walk back to Catherine was uncomfortable for me. But Catherine had plenty of dancing partners and when she talked to both of us upon our return, I knew everything was fine. Besides, Bill did dance with Catherine when the band started again. During the first intermission, Matzi, with whom I was dancing, offered me a drink of soda. We started walking downstairs to the bar. Matzi came back with a coke and put the bottle in front of me. Bill and his dance partner, sat directly across from us. Bill, noticing that my coke was not poured, offered to pour it into my glass. "Thank you," I said, a little surprised.

At home, Mother and Karl were not happy with the apartment buildings anymore and started planning a move. They received an offer at a nunnery in Bloomfield Hills. This move was a major one, especially for me. The distance to my job now, was long and costly. I needed to take the Greyhound bus, for city buses didn't travel out that far and didn't run as often as city buses. In spite of my disapproval of this move, the deal made between my Mother and Mother Superior held firm.

Our new home was part of a large piece of land consisting of many buildings. From the highway, I wouldn't have known of this property, except for the large intricate wrought iron gate that was never closed. The first day, our driver drove us to our new home. I was curious as he turned into the open gate. The shrubs and trees on each side of the driveway led us to the main building. The three storey brick house had ivy growing alongside the walls leaving only the opening of windows exposed. It gave this building the feel of wealth and style. The two cement pedestal urns with many bright colors of flowers among the greenery, made the entrance to a large oak door, warm and welcoming. The driver continued to drive us down another path as we passed the garages to the back of the building. We passed a garden with perfectly cut cedar shrubs in a formation of a square. In the middle, amongst all the luscious greenery, a rose garden in full bloom was peeking through. We came to a stop as the driver announced, "Here we are. This is the place, these are your quarters where you will live as long as you work here," he said.

We called our new home "the cottage". The name suited this quaint little place. Lilies of the valley, now done blooming, surrounded the whole cottage grounds instead of grass. We just missed the distinct and powerful lingering perfume smell of this small pure white spring flower. The cottage was totally furnished with pink flowered furniture, a couch and a few chairs. The walls of the kitchen, decorated with small printed wallpaper in blue. Yellow dishes in an antigue cabinet rested on glass shelves seemed absolutely beautiful to me.

After placing my suitcase in my room, I took a walk around the grounds. I felt somewhat relieved by the beauty of it all. The distance was a real concern, so far from work and also from Catherine. The weekend was coming up and my concerns started to weigh on me. To call Catherine on the phone was a problem, for now long distance charges applied. We kept our conversations short and our long talks were a thing of the past.

My concerns over the weekend started to overshadow the beauty and splendour of these gardens all around me. I sat on the cement bench for the longest time daydreaming mostly, while many questions that I had went unanswered that afternoon.

It was the next day that I came up with a plan. Before saying anything to Mother, I had to check it out with Catherine and her parents. My plan was to simply stay with Catherine for the weekend as it would save time and money. Mother agreed, and Mr. and Mrs. Wagner were delighted as well. I had won my Mother's trust by now and in my mind I had confidence that I would do the right thing if away from home.

It was the following week when I made myself known in the main house of the nunnery. Mother was proud to show me off to Mother Superior. One by one, the nuns came and curtsied with a smile and said hello to me. With their black and white habits, I could hardly tell them apart, they looked so alike. It took some time before I remembered all of them by their names. My Mother was hired to do kitchen duties, and Karl to do odd jobs, like cutting the grass, sweeping the garages, etc., although his main duty was to chauffeur the nuns around. It was comical to me, such an uncultured man who is so not religious and possessed no social skills, would drive nuns about. It was interesting to me to watch and observe this experience unfold. I chuckled to myself and watched the first time Karl opened the door for a nun called Maria. He not only looked awkward, but totally out of his element. The sisters travelled in pairs, never alone. The nunnery housed about thirty retired nuns and priests.

Every evening at 7pm, the nuns held a mass in the chapel that was an extension of the large building. What I liked about the masses was the peace and serenity. Many evenings I found myself slipping into the chapel and joining in on the prayers already in progress. There was actually a time I pondered the thought of joining the nunhood, but that thought was short lived. I found the small chapel comforting on many of my idle times. The quiet moving about, only whispers spoken, gave my mind a place and a time to dream and plan my life. My zest for dancing and having a family of my own one day outweighed the thought of a life as a nun.

Mother spoke of our sister Margaret and her family often. We all did. Four years had passed since we left Linz, Austria, and we left them behind. Our Mother's first grandchild was born that Mother hadn't even seen yet, and she missed terribly. There was talk of our sister coming to join us soon and that was good news for all of us.

In the winter of 1955, commuting for hours on the bus five days a week started to take its toll. It turned dark early in the day and walking to and from the bus in total darkness to our isolated cottage gave me some scary feelings. Out of fear that someone was lurking behind the bushes, I ran home all the way down the long driveway to our cottage. The interior of the nunnery was, built strong with walls and wide hallways, however very private. The only room I was allowed to visit anytime of the day, just past the foyer, was a large sitting room. The tongue and groove ceiling was at least nine feet high. It gave the room the feeling of being larger than it actually was. Massive beams separated the ceiling in sections. The same boards extended from the floor about four feet up the wall, giving the room the finished look of solid wood. Two large bookcases filled with books covered the longest wall, with a stained glass window in between. The sofa, covered in nylon fabric for durability, was placed in front of the bookcases. The many different chairs of different sizes all around the room made picking out a book and reading easy. I did just that as I sat and waited for my Mother to finish her work. There was plenty to eat for us, for whatever Mother prepared for the nunnery, we ate the same. Mother brought four containers every day to the cottage full of meat, vegetables, salad and dessert.

Back at Sanders, many changes took place. Darlene, our dear friend, gave notice and moved away to be closer to her family. We felt she never did get over Rory, despite our many talks. By the year's end only Marianne and I remained. Work lost some of the joy and commuting so far every day didn't help. With the holidays approaching, looking for another job had to wait for now.

My weekends with Catherine remained steady and enjoyable. For some reason that I can't recall I didn't see George for awhile, until that New Years Eve. Our group decided to do something different for a change. About ten of us drove to Leamington to a dance. The evening started as usual in a parking lot. We drove in several cars and I ended up in the front seat of Bill's car, a yellow and black Chevy. There wasn't anything said, but the way we were paired up it sure looked like a date. We had so much fun at the dance, and we all danced with each other. I noticed that every chance Bill had, he asked me to dance. Bill was a good dancer and very good looking, about six feet tall, with short, dark wavy hair. He acted young and he was extremely kind. Bill shared with me that his family lived in a town about 100 kilometers away, although he worked and lived in Windsor.

Toward late in the evening, everything changed. George and Johnny walked in. With their dark suits on and their hands in their pockets, so sure of themselves, they were hard to resist. Catherine and I connected with them right away and there was no doubt they came to be with us. They had eyes for no one but Catherine and me. We left the group and did the ultimate terrible thing and let George and Johnny drive us home. I felt guilty and knew it was wrong, especially when we passed Bill's car on the highway driving home.

George and I went steady for a short six weeks. I must say, he was a true gentleman at all times to me. But away from the dance floor, we didn't seem to have much to talk about. On Valentine's Day, I received long stemmed red roses from George. With every rose that I carefully placed into the vase, I felt little excitement. I knew our love had faded away by now, because when George called and I thanked him for the roses, we didn't make any new plans. We parted so smoothly that words didn't need to be spoken. Shortly after, George's job moved to Oakville. He transferred and I never saw him again.

I returned to the Saturday night dances and decided to stay single for awhile. However, a month later, I received my first marriage proposal. A much older man, maybe close to thirty, appeared out of nowhere it seemed and asked me to dance. I knew he was older from his receding hairline and he was somewhat overweight, but well dressed. "Hi," he said, with a smile. "Hi," I said back. "I know you are Schwartzi," and before I could say anything he added, "I am John." Oh, he was light on his feet and a good dancer. We talked very little and after the third dance we returned to my table. "Thank you," he said, "I'll see you next week." "Okay," I said reluctantly.

The second week, I questioned him. "Are you new here? It seems, except for last week, I didn't see you here before." "No, I've been here, but I haven't seen you here for awhile." "Oh," I replied. "Are you going out with anyone?" he asked me. "No," I said, "why do you ask?" "Just wondering," he answered. He asked me to dance for three weeks in a row and I was beginning to get quite comfortable with him. On the last dance, this is what he said to me, "I know you don't know me well, and I am just a simple guy. I am twenty eight years old. A lot older than you, I know. But I am ready to settle down, and I have been watching you from afar for a long time. I know you don't love me, but maybe someday you will. I know you are everything I want. Would you consider marrying a guy like me?" He noticed the look on my face, and stopped. I didn't know what to say, so I said nothing, as he continued. "I have a farm and can offer you a life of luxury. I promise you a good life." I was stunned and couldn't speak. After some silence, he said, "Don't say anything, please just promise me you will think about it and give me your answer next Saturday."

The proposal consumed my every thought for much of that week. I wouldn't dare tell my Mother, for she might make me marry him, knowing that he was well off. I only told my friend Marianne. There was no confusion about my answer the following Saturday when I saw John again. When we danced our last dance together, I tried to be as kind as I could be to tell him of my decision not to marry him. He stopped dancing. He took my hand and kissed it and said, "Oh, what a shame Katie," and left me standing alone on the dance floor. I felt so sorry for him, so sure of my decision one minute and then felt so unhappy another minute. As time went by I looked for him, but he never came back to the Saturday night dances again.

At the end of March was the first time since that awful New Years Eve, I saw Bill again. I wondered if Bill was mad or if he would ask me to dance again. He wasn't there long, when indeed he came and asked me to dance. Nothing was said about New Years Eve instead he posed this question, "If I asked you to go out with me, would you?" I paused for a moment, flirting and smiling, "Well, maybe," I said. There was something about his mannerism, disturbingly patient, that had some sort of pull and made me think of him, even when I didn't want to.

In the meantime, Catherine met a young man called George, a different George, and it was just a matter of time before they became a couple. We still went to the dances together Catherine and I, for now.

In the spring of 1956, Margaret, her husband Franzi and son Reiny came from Austria to join us. Oh, it was a happy day. They stayed with us at the nunnery till Franzi found a new job. Franzi was terribly mistrustful of Karl and felt uncomfortable around him. To find a job and move was of the utmost importance for my brother-in-law. After a few months of searching, Franzi settled on a landscaping firm. A far cry from what he was capable of, with his intelligence and medical experience in the old country, but it was a job. They found an apartment in Royal Oak, a suburb of Detroit, and moved that following week. My Mother enjoyed having Margaret and family near again, after such a long separation, and so did I.

Everytime I went to the dance, which was not every Saturday anymore, I ran into Bill. He looked so well groomed from head to toe. On one of those times, he wore a white long sleeved linen shirt with navy blue buttons and navy dress pants. He was noticeably sharp looking, with the shirt ironed smooth and the pants, a perfect crease. It was a lazy summer afternoon, when the dance ended early, and Bill asked me to go for a ride with him. I had not done this before. Adventurous as I was, I said, "Sure, I'll go." "Where are we going?" I asked him, walking out to the car. "Oh, you'll see," he said with a smile. Bill took me to his house where he lived with his aunt. They both must have planned this visit ahead of time, for his aunt was well prepared with a meal, dessert and coffee.

Bill's aunt was a small lady, not even five feet, and she walked with a limp. She had a husky voice and a feisty personality. It was so obvious to me that she loved her nephew when at every turn she snuck a compliment in for Bill. I went along with this obvious plan, for wanting to impress me gave me a comfortable feeling that his aunt approved of me. Bill and his aunt whose name was also Katie, worked well together and treated me with total respect. The house they shared was small and cosy, clean and orderly, just my style.

That afternoon Bill asked me to go steady with him. He drove down a side street and parked the car. "Would you be my girl?" he asked, "I hope you will say yes?" Oh, how I hated to give up my independence, but he was beginning to win me over with his kindness, that's for sure. We sealed our commitment with a long kiss, as he dropped me off at the Tunnel bus station.

Bill and I saw each other only once a week, never on a weekday, only on weekends. Catherine and I did one of two things. Either the parents drove us or we went on our own with the bus. If we took the Tunnel bus, our guys came and picked us up on the Windsor side. This arrangement worked well for all of us. Bill and George knew each other, so that made everything even better. In the summer months, on Sunday afternoons, they held church picnics. These picnics lasted only through July and August. With good food and a good band, we enjoyed such outings and went to every one of them, the four of us.

That winter Bill and I started to go on dates just the two of us. Going for a ride relaxed us, especially driving to the country. One particular Sunday afternoon we ended up in Amherstburg. Both of us were getting hungry as the large church bell rang 6pm. We spotted a small cafe which had a sign that read, "**Home Cooked Meals.**" "What about this one, Schwartzi?" Bill asked. "Okay, it looks clean," I said. We walked inside holding hands. The waitress noticed this, seated us by the window at a table for two. I felt uncomfortable, for a moment, for my Mother came into my thoughts with her advice to me. A man doesn't like a woman that is too expensive. Remembering that, I ordered the cheapest meal on the menu, hamburger steak with onions. Bill ordered the same meal as mine. Our first meal together, I learned that he liked sweets, and liver and onions. "Oh gross," I said. "I pretty well eat everything, I am not a fussy eater," Bill shared.

On the way home, Bill reluctantly mentioned an upcoming dance in West Lorne which is where his family lived. It meant meeting his family for the first time. The dance was called a *Kirchweih* (a Church Celebration) and, in the old country, was held at the end of the harvest season. Bill seemed shy as he continued, "it means an overnight stay with my family." And, of course I knew it also meant I would need a formal long gown. "Oh, I am not sure," I immediately said. "I'll let you know, okay."

In the meantime, Bill brought up that he wanted to meet my mother. When I shared this with my Mother, she right away agreed, and Bill came for a visit that Sunday. Mother was thrilled to meet him, especially when she learned of his background, the same as ours. Of course, Bill said all the right things to a point that it bothered me. When he asked mother about staying overnight in West Lorne, hundreds of miles away,

I was surprised at her answer. Mother didn't even ask me if I wanted to go, instead gave her okay to Bill, as if I wasn't even in the room. I butted in, quite annoyed, "Pulllleeze!" "Oh, you know you want to go," she said. That evening Bill and I went for a drive. "I really like your mother," he said. "Oh, I would have never guessed that," I said jokingly. We both burst out laughing. "You know your mother and mine; they will get along well, I can feel it." I wasn't so sure about that comment. Besides, we hadn't even talked about such things as marriage, so I dropped the whole thing and just planned to go to West Lorne.

I introduced Bill to pizza that evening. "Have you ever eaten pizza before?" I asked. "No," he said, "but I've heard of it." "There is a place right around the corner called Como's Pizza, do you want to go? My treat," I offered. Bill was a little surprised. We walked down a long narrow hall to a booth in the back of the restaurant. At first, biting into the slice, Bill wasn't sure if he liked pizza, but like me, it grew on him. I knew Bill liked the pizza for a few weeks later he wanted to go to the same place again.

1956 Our First Formal Kirchweih Dance

A month later, it was time to attend the special dance in West Lorne. Bill seemed nervous as we turned into the long gravel driveway that took us to the back of the old farmhouse. His Mother immediately pushed the screen door open. "My Willi," she said as she ran around the car to Bill. They kissed and embraced, as Bill slipped his mother's arms away from him. "Come, Ma," as he walked towards me. She didn't wait for an introduction. "You're Katie. Bill told me a lot about you." "Oh, Ma," Bill embarrassingly said. "Bring your suitcase and I'll show you the upstairs," she offered.

Everything happened so fast. I didn't hear much or see much, as I hurried through the house, up the stairs. Once upstairs, Bill's mother stayed and watched every move I made. I opened my suitcase, and that's when she took over, and started piling my belongings in a drawer. "Oh, you have such fancy things, they cost money, huh," she said. I became uncomfortable, but stayed silent. Once downstairs again, I met Bill's younger brother Peter and also the man Bill's mother lived with, a strong and good looking man, and his son, Joe. A while later Bill's grandmother came into the room after her nap. I liked Bill's grandmother very much. She seemed gentle, kind and patient.

Their house reflected an old fashioned style inside and out. That evening, Bill complimented his mother, and said, "Ma," as he called her, "She is a good cook." The meal was indeed of the old country style, delicious. I did my part and helped with the clean up and dried the dishes. Ma grabbed my hands at one point and said, "Katie, such beautiful nails. You know you couldn't change a baby's diaper with nails like that." She laughed a little. My security started to fade with every moment with Ma. I was hoping for the time to pass quickly, for being in the company with Ma was starting to wear me down.

I had confidence in my dancing, as Bill's family watched us perform the traditional Kirchweih Dance. Joe was also in our group, but not Peter. The dance was performed by eight couples.

The girls wore a variety of different coloured floor length gowns. The guys white shirts, black vests and pants, and a dark hat which was decorated by the dance partner the night before with artificial flowers around the base and ribbons of all different colors hanging down the back. The lead couple walked into the hall with a march playing, also carrying a live rosemary bush about twenty four inches high decorated with many different colors of ribbons. A performance of a special dance followed. Later in the evening the couples formed a circle around the rosemary bush and it was raffled off until the alarm, set ahead of time, rang and the bid at the bell won the bush. The winning couple, holding the rosemary bush, joined the group for a final dance. At the end of the evening one more group dance as we marched off the dance floor to close the performance. Bill and I danced mostly with each other, except for a few dances with family.

On Sunday morning when I said goodbye to Bill's family, I made sure they knew of my appreciation. I left the farm with mixed feelings, certainly not with Peter and Joe, for they made me feel welcome, and we liked each other. On the way home I was quiet and didn't talk much. It took Bill sometime to notice, as he finally asked. "What's wrong?" "Your mother doesn't like me," I said, nervously. "No, that's not true," he came to his mother's defence. "You're wrong," I said, "I feel it."

Many years later Bill confessed to me that indeed his mother had had misgivings about me. Her main concern was money. When Bill asked his mother what she thought of me, this was her answer. "Oh, Willi, my child, Katie is too classy for you. If you marry her, you will never have any money. She is way too expensive for you," was her opinion of me.

Bill worked at Motor Products (a chrome plating company) for a few years before the layoffs started and Bill was handed his pink slip. Shortly after, the railroad hired Bill as a labourer, very hard work. Bill realized quickly he needed to do more with his life. In the meantime, Joe was in the same position as Bill. Joe realized quickly that he needed to move away from West Lorne to find work. Joe ended up in a thriving city way up north called Sault Ste Marie. Joe, left and found work right away, and in no time at all, he and two partners formed a construction company, sub-contracting for houses built in the Sault Ste Marie and Elliot Lake areas.

For me during the week, my life revolved around work. Not much time for fun. Bill seemed to be traveling to West Lorne more by this time, every other weekend, feeling some extra responsibility to his family. On these weekends it meant no social life for me. I was young and full of life, and didn't want to stay home, on my only day off. When Bill returned from one of his trips to West Lorne and came to pick me up, I was upset. We had our first argument. "If you think this is going steady, well, you are never here," I said. Bill had a hard time knowing what to say. His excuses inflamed the already bad feelings, and didn't do much to douse the flame. But like always, after the storm, making up was sweet.

That evening we went to the movies. I can't remember the movie; I only remember the fun we had. We sat in the balcony, practically alone. I don't know what I was thinking when I bought such a tight fitting dress. The red dress was so tight that I could barely sit down or get up. I loved the way this dress showed every curve of my body, so I bought it. Bill couldn't keep his hands off of me, and I was busy fighting him off and laughing. All of a sudden the chair broke. The steel chair made such a loud sound, that everyone below turned around and looked at us. We laughed all the way home. "See what you did?" I pointed to the seam, which unravelled about two inches or so, on the side of my leg. I took my finger and poked it through the hole, "You bad boy," I teased, as Bill laughed and said, "Yeah, those buns, wow!" We kissed often before we said good night.

In the fall of 1956, work in Windsor was at an all-time low. For many immigrants like Bill, with no trade and no college degree, and the industry in a slump, the financial future didn't look too promising. Joe in the meantime came home for a visit from Sault Ste Marie and gave Bill an offer that he couldn't refuse. "There is so much work Bill, but you know it would mean you'd have to move," Joe informed him. Since Bill wasn't sure about the move and our future together was still uncertain, he felt torn.

For the next few months or so Bill and I just had fun dating. Once in awhile we went to the movies on a Sunday when he came over to visit me in the States. Many times my sister Margaret invited us for supper with her family. If we planned ahead and had a little more time, we drove to the country to visit with Susi and Nick. By now, their little girl Christine had joined our family. My Uncle Pete's was still a regular place to stop and say hello. Bill also happened to have a cousin, Joe and his Mother, Resi, who lived in the States and with whom we got along really well.

Some weekends, Bill came to pick me up at the Windsor Tunnel and visited relatives in Windsor. One of our favourite places was his Aunt Marion and Uncle Mike. This is where I met Bill's cousin, Liz, a bit younger than I. Bill's Uncle Peter, his wife Nanschi, and their family, welcomed us, as well. There was no shortage of visiting relatives, that's for sure. It gave us something to do that didn't cost money and that was appropriate for a young, unmarried couple in those days.

One weekday in late November, just a month before Christmas, Mother met me at the door as I came home from work. "What's the matter?" I asked, as I walked past her. "Bill called," she said. "He is coming. He should be here any minute." "Oh," I said, "did he say why?" "No, he didn't," she replied, as she left to return to the main house. I was wondering what was wrong for Bill didn't usually come during the week. I was so happy to see him, as we kissed and he gave me a tight hug. He held on as if he didn't want to let me go. "Well, what's the matter?" I asked. He had a hard time to say it, "I am not going to be here for Christmas." He waited for me to say something.

After a pause, not being happy, I said, "Why?" "Well, Joe has work for me, there are many opportunities up there," he said, "It's not looking good in Windsor, that's for sure. I need the money. We can write and I hope you'll wait for me." It all came so fast, the timing seemed so ridiculous. I hardly had time to think and I didn't know what else to say, but, "Yes."

"When are you leaving?" I asked. "Tomorrow," he answered, as he brushed my hair away from my face. None of this made sense to me. Not wanting to be difficult, I swallowed, "Okay, then." We sat on the couch for the longest time that afternoon and realized our feelings had deepened more than we thought. Bill handed me a wrapped box and said, "I bought you a Christmas present. I am sorry, my timing is lousy." Long after Bill left that afternoon, I lingered in a silent mode, too numb to move. Just to be alone and private with my thoughts was a blessing. After some time, I opened the package, a black, lacquered jewellery box that played a tune I didn't recognize. It was then I became angry. I stopped crying and threw the box on my bed. In the months after Bill left, I spent many weekends in Canada with Bill's cousin Liz. I liked Liz the first time that we were introduced. Liz and I talked about everything and became good friends. I also had girlfriends from work that I shopped with, went to movies, just to pass the time.

Bill came home in April. He surprised me and just showed up. Bill stayed for two weeks and it was like old times. We danced till out of breath, socialized with the old gang, like Liz and her boyfriend, Andy, Catherine and George and many more. The two weeks flew by and before Bill left, we talked about many things. He had so much to tell me about Sault Ste. Marie, and he also told me that he was lonely, but working all hours of the day helped. Up to now, we talked mostly about the present and very little of our past. But, this evening Bill and I talked about our Homeland. The conversation came easy, the more we talked the more we realized how similar our pasts were.

Bill was born in a town very close to mine called Molidorf, only 25 kilometers away from Kikinda. His grandparents and parents made their living by farming the land that surrounded their village. When the friendly soldiers came in October 1944, the same as in Kikinda, to advise them to leave immediately, their townspeople made the dreadful decision to stay. Like so many at that time, they could not comprehend such a demand. Bill's voice seemed low and strained as he told me about what they went through next in the Concentration camp. "Oh, Schwartzi," he said, "that was a hard three years for our family." We both felt we knew what the other meant and stopped talking.

After a pause, I snuggled up to him as Bill continued, "The hardest of all came when we heard of our father's death. My father was only thirty-two years old when he was shot. The war was declared over, so my father was on his way home to Molidorf when he was killed." I could tell Bill was becoming emotional, as I asked what happened. "Well, the train of approximately 600 or so soldiers, just like my Dad," were told to board the train that would take them home to Jugoslavia. After some time, the train stopped abruptly in no man's land and all the soldiers that came from the Donau Schwaben region were asked to step out onto the field. The Officer asked all tradesmen to step forward, but my father didn't do that. He wanted to go back to his family and was afraid they might detain him if he stepped forward. A costly decision, for that decision cost him his life. Through the night, a family friend told my Mother, the barrage of guns was heard and they killed every one of those men right there in the field. My father was a chef by trade," Bill said, "but nobody knew." Along with Bill's father, his father's brother and brother-in-law, Liz's father, and many townsfolk lost their lives in that God forsaken field that night.

We both knew of the hardship of the war. For me, I left it behind and didn't want to talk about it, maybe because the rest of my family lived so much in the past. I guess the reason was that, being so young, I wasn't affected as much as my family for their pain was so much greater than mine. Everyone seemed to feel the need to talk about it more than I did.

In the spring, Mother and Karl decided they had enough of the nunnery and we moved back to the old neighbourhood of East Detroit. As much as I looked forward to living closer to my work and Catherine's house, the nunnery held wonderful memories, and I missed the gardens. I missed Bill, I missed dancing, and I missed just having something to look forward to on the weekends. Most everyone in our Canadian group was either engaged or married by now. Life was changing and I became lonely once more.

By now, Catherine and George started to plan their wedding. In those days, the weddings were large in size. Three hundred guests or more was considered a middle-sized wedding. Getting together every weekend was now a thing of the past, but every chance we had, we'd visit. I was happy that Bill and I were both asked to stand up for Catherine and George's wedding. So, I knew Bill was coming home in August.

After the move, Karl had a hard time finding a job. It was a happy day when Mother brought home a stray little puppy. This little dog, with so much energy, and those little brown shiny eyes, brought much happiness to our house and to me. The leash hung behind the pantry door, the slightest touch of that leash, she started to run through the whole house with joy. I had a hard time putting that leash on her neck, she moved so much. We named her Lillie, for we thought she was born around Easter. Lillie made my after work hours so pleasant. Instead of being in the house, I'd take Lillie for a long walk. Once on the sidewalk, this little dog showed her appreciation by running back to me constantly. Her eyes and bark spoke to me like any human could.

Karl loved Lillie and with so much time on his hands, he taught Lillie many tricks. However one of those tricks so cruel, I walked out of the room every time. Karl lit a cigarette, puffed on it a few times and stuck it in Lillie's mouth and she couldn't drop it until he said she could. Lillie was so uncomfortable and kept looking at me when it happened the first time and I told her to drop it. It was not good for Lillie, for Karl hit her and scolded her, and she was crying. But in spite of it all, she loved all of us, including Karl. Lillie loved the car. When she heard the name car, in a flash she stood by the door, waiting.

We received the news that our Oma died in Austria, where she was in a nursing home. It was a sad day, especially for my Mother. Shortly after my Oma's passing, Hans Onkel came back into our lives. I was overjoyed. Hans Onkel felt lost without his Mother. His whole life he spent taking care of her, especially when we left and she was bedridden. It was hard for Hans Onkel because he did not speak the English language, and over 65 years old. Seeing my mother and me working made him uncomfortable. However, he was a big help to my mother and the household. He tended to the yard work and prepared whatever he could for the meals. He also felt lonely. Karl and Hans Onkel being alone together all day, worried my mother.

A fight was brewing when Mother confronted Karl. Apparently, Karl lied to Mother for weeks about looking for a job. Mother somehow pressured her brother into telling her the truth about what Karl did during the day. Looking for a job was not what Karl did. Karl was furious, when he found out that Hans Onkel told Mother the truth, we didn't know that the following day Hans Onkel argued with Karl over his laziness. "How can you lie around all day long, and not lift a finger around here, while your wife is out trying to make a living." Hans Onkel told him. They argued and Karl pushed Hans Onkel into the wall. That day, Hans Onkel had an epileptic seizure for the first time in years. Mother was convinced that these attacks were triggered by being upset and emotional. I wasn't home, but my sister Margaret was.

"Oh, Katie," she told me afterwards, "it was awful." Our uncle was weak and quiet for a few days. Sleep followed until he had his strength back. Of course not knowing what happened here the day before, Hans Onkel made me promise not to tell Mother or Uncle Pete about the fight. Our uncle might have been a gentle man, but he was no pushover. Underneath that easy going personality, stood a solid background of knowing right from wrong and standing up for his beliefs.

Twice a week I worked late which meant I'd arrive home when it was dark out. It took only once for Hans Onkel to hear me say that I was scared to walk home alone in the dark. My next shift, climbing off the bus and seeing my uncle waiting for me, made me feel protected, like a father I never had. I put my arm in his, as we walked the long blocks home together. On one of those walks, I asked him, "Hans Onkel, how come you never married?" "Well, I was married once, in my early twenties, for two years," he said. I continued, "What happened?" "My epilepsy, you know it scared my wife, and I just couldn't see her, or bear it, to watch her so afraid. Before the medication, the attacks came more often, so after two years together, I asked her to leave." "Oh, I am sorry," I said. "Oh, my child, I couldn't put another woman through something like that again, so I decided to stay single."

For months Hans Onkel met me twice a week at the bus, and each time we talked all the way home. On one of those talks he brought up Karl. Hans Onkel knew that Susi and I endured a lot, and that Karl's treatment of our family affected us more than we let on. "Don't worry about Karl," he tried to reassure me. "Karl is a man that left his family when he was just a boy," he continued, as I listened to every word. "You know, Katie, Karl and I have so much time together home alone during the day, so we talk, especially when Karl is in a good mood. Karl also likes the fact that we can speak Hungarian together," Hans Onkel said to me. "Karl told me of his past only once, and I'll tell you what he said," he went on, "Karl's mother was a woman of deep religion. When his mother made him go to church all the time, he hated it. All that Latin, he didn't understand, and when the priest turned his back and faced the altar, instead of him, it made him mad. His father, a policeman, didn't like church either, which made everything easier for Karl. There was much conflict in the house, for his mother accused the father of influencing the son. His mother was deeply troubled and disappointed in him. When Karl was older and his father caught him stealing, his father turned ugly, and punished him. When Karl turned seventeen he decided to leave, for he had enough of his father's rules. Karl took all the money that his mother hid in the pantry and left without a word to his parents. He hasn't contacted or talked to his parents since."

"Oh my gosh," I said, "that is terrible, his poor mother, she must have been sick with worry." "Well, you know, Katie, that's the kind of person he is," Hans Onkel continued, "Karl is an angry man, and unfortunately lets his anger out on your mother and us. We are the only family he has. I know you are so young, my child, and you have gone through so much already, but I hope knowing this about Karl will help somewhat." When I heard sad things like that about Karl's parents, in some small way I felt sorry for this man that caused our family so much grief. I matured somewhat that day. Little by little, my heart began to understand others as well as myself.

When Hans Onkel experienced loneliness, our talks turned back to a time long ago. "Oh, my child," with a deep sigh, he started, "oh, Katie, do you still remember that day when we left Kikinda?" "Oh, yes, I remember everything, but most of the time I don't want to think about it anymore," I answered. Hans Onkel continued, "I never dreamed that our lives would turn out this way. Oh, it is so hard to make roots in another country, especially when we planned out our whole life in Kikinda. War is terrible. Oh, that war made us go through hard times. I think of the peace I felt in Kikinda, that feeling of belonging, something we could call our own. I miss that. When I walk past so many houses here and I know no one, and no one knows me, everybody so busy, and you know speaking German, doesn't help. Oh, that war made many enemies." "I know, Hans Onkel."

I snuggled up to him, like I always did, as we reached our house and walked up the sidewalk together.

My Hans Onkel was tall and slim with salt and pepper hair, deep waves, parted on the side and for his age, a full head of hair. His blue eyes were deep with lines on the forehead and cheeks, but it is his unending patience I remember most. As children in the Refugee Camp, Susi and I made Hans Onkel sit on a chair and we would play barber. We combed his hair every which way and giggling the whole time while he pretended to be amused. As I said before we didn't kiss or talk about love much in our family, but I remember Hans Onkel's hands. When he took my hands and put them into his, before I fell asleep next to him every night, I felt safe and protected.

During this time, I received the occasional letter from Bill. In one of those letters, he made a request that I couldn't turn down. "Come to visit me, I miss you," Bill wrote. "Come and stay with Gwen, Joe's girlfriend. She is really nice, and I asked her parents already and they said you are welcome to stay with them while you are visiting me." It sounded good. I got approval for a week off and made my plans to visit Bill.

Early July, I took the Greyhound bus in downtown Detroit and headed north. The bus made many stops, like Flint, Bay City, and many small towns along the way until we reached Mackinaw City. A ferry was needed to cross the straights in Lake Michigan to reach the other side, the city of St.Ignace. It was a lovely sunny day to enjoy the deck of the ferry and have a bite to eat. The ferry took some time to cross, several hours for sure. "One more hour," the bus driver announced before we reach Sault St.e Marie. A ferry crossed the river, called St. Mary's in the two Sault Ste. Maries, one in Michigan and one in Canada finished the four hundred mile trip for me.

I saw Bill through the shaded glass of the bus, and I was excited. Bill saw me and stood by the door and grabbed my hand. I almost fell into his arms, the steps were so steep. We kissed and hugged over and over again. "How was your trip?" he asked. "Well good, but long," I said, "but I don't mind." "Where are we going?" I asked. "Gwen's house," Bill answered, "they are waiting for you." Bill filled me in about Gwen's family. Gwen and I connected quickly and liked each other. It didn't take any time at all for me to meet the rest of the family. Only being there for one day, I knew this to be a family of integrity and respect. I observed the movement of the family, of everyone knowing what to do, and how to act, without saying a word. This made my stay with the Shell Family truly interesting and enjoyable.

Bill and Joe usually worked on Saturdays, but on the day of my arrival they didn't. The four of us just sat and talked that evening. The following day, it was decided to make a picnic lunch. Gwen and I made ham and cheese sandwiches with pickles on the side in a glass container. Mrs. Shell (Gwen's mother) offered chocolate chip cookies. "They are easy to pack," she added. Our picnic basket full of goodies, we then drove to a park called Point Des Chene, a beach front park outside the city on Lake Superior. With our blankets spread on the sand, we realized our guys were not interested in getting a tan or relaxing in the sun. They were restless and playful. Besides building sand castles and spraying us with water or sand, so we could not relax, we decided to join them. We played like little kids, playing tag, and of course a kiss here and there for a reward when caught. Sometime late in the afternoon, two little bear cubs ran into the water nearby and started to play. I can't believe we did the unthinkable and joined them. We didn't actually touch these little cubs, but for sure they were not afraid of us. All of a sudden, a loud roar came from the bush behind us, as we scattered away from the cubs. Lucky for us, the mother bear had no interest in us, only interest in protecting her young. What an experience it was. It made for interesting conversations to come.

That night, Gwen and I, in her bedroom upstairs, talked for the longest time. In the morning, being a Monday, Gwen left for work at Lawrence's Drug Store, with the promise that she would take off early if possible. Bill came by mid-morning, for he took the day off to be with me. That made me happy. "Let's go for a ride," he said. "Where are we going?" I questioned. "Well, I thought I'd show you the beautiful country around here." We drove north of the City, the scenery breathtaking, the cliffs, the formation of rocks at every curve with the sparkling water peaking through, made this ride memorable. Bill stopped and parked the car near a huge rock. We sat on the large rock overlooking the lake, as Bill started talking about the future. He told me about wanting to go into business for himself. "The houses that Joe's construction company worked for needed lawns, so I decided to go into the landscaping business. It will take some time yet before I can make good money. What do you think, Schwartzi?" he asked. "You will do well in whatever you do," I answered. "It's beautiful here," I said. You know I need money before we get married." "What?" surprised, I said. He grinned, as if it slipped somehow.

To dream of a future on the beautiful rock that day, was truly unforgettable. The water so peaceful with the rolling waves as far as the eye could see, blue-green and so clear. The many maple trees that grew super large leaves were big and bushy. The miles of evergreens in the distance in clumps of all shapes and sizes multiplied in the hills. Along the lakeshore, quaint cottages filled with activities of summer people. Bill spread a blanket nearby, and I laid in his arms, way too close for comfort. We teased each other and laughed a lot. When the laughing and touching turned into much more, Bill became aggressive with his love for me, but I held back and didn't feel I was ready to go to the next step. We stood up, pulled ourselves together and decided it was getting late and returned to the car for the long drive back to Gwen's house.

I left the Soo with mixed feelings. On the way home in the bus, reality set in. I thought of the distance, so far away from family, this beautiful Sault Ste Marie. My thought switched to the rock, and I felt warm and comfortable. Oh, so torn and confused, I faced my future plans with many unsolved questions. One thing for sure, when Gwen and I promised to write and stay in touch, I knew I had made a friend. Besides, I knew I'd see Bill again soon, for Catherine and George's wedding was in August.

Everything around me was changing. Catherine and George's wedding was a festive evening, as they celebrated their love for each other with friends and family, good food and of course, dancing. I was proud to be part of their beautiful day. Realizing my best friend is no more, I was left feeling somewhat lonely. For when a woman married in those days, her life became all about her husband and home, with no place for single friends. And so, my life went on without Catherine.

Bill, in his tuxedo, looked so attractive and so young. Although we stood up with different partners, I with Andy and Bill with Maria, it didn't matter for we all knew each other well. At the church ceremony, walking down the aisle, knowing all eyes were on us, we felt uncomfortable and proud all at the same time. Afterwards we all lined up next to the newly married couple as the formation of congratulations continued till every last person had their turn. Cars, decorated with white paper roses, lined up close by the church waiting for us to climb in and drive through unknown streets blowing the horn following each other, caravan style.

For the longest time after Bill left, I was depressed. I cried about everything. Hearing of someone I didn't even know dying triggered a crying spell. When my family referred to me as being too sensitive, I felt criticised and misunderstood. I withdrew once more, and tried to live up to everyone's opinion of me, pretending to be happy when I wasn't, pretending to be easy going when I was upset. One day sitting in the bus, with so much time to think, it came to me. For some time now, Margaret and Franzi had spoken of me coming to live with them. I know Margaret would welcome my company, I was sure of that. I took off work the following day, so I could look for a new job. I heard of a new shopping mall called Northland that was hiring for their grand opening. I applied at a store called Chandler's Shoe Store. Within days, I received the news that I was hired. My job was to be a cashier and also behind the counter selling nylons and shoe accessories. Margaret lived close to the mall, so to room and board with them made sense to all of us. I welcomed the thought of being so close to my job.

At my new job, it took only a few weeks to feel comfortable in my new position. In no time at all the salesmen and I worked together well as a team. Franzi drove a Volkswagen which we agreed to share when I moved in. We also took turns with the expense of the gas. In the morning, I'd drive Franzi to work, than get ready for work myself. I worked late twice a week, so on those days Franzi managed to get a ride home from a co-worker. We got along well and this schedule worked for us.

In my new home the atmosphere was pleasant, the consideration and the kindness in the house, made me feel so safe. The household ran smoothly, with Margaret at home with their son, Reiny. Margaret was a good cook, so the meals were delicious and so tasty. But it was the baking of special tortes and squares that when Franzi and I returned home, to the smell in the house, absolutely delicious. On the weekends, a neighbouring theatre started showing German movies on Sunday afternoons. So when I had no plans I'd join my sister and family for the afternoon. It was good for Margaret and Franzi to see these movies, for they missed Austria.

I worked different shifts so when I didn't make it home for supper, Margaret kept my meal warm in the oven for me till I came home. For the first time in my life I could come and go as I pleased, still staying within our family rules which I knew well. On Sundays, as a family, we attended the Catholic Church nearby. I welcomed this tradition. Before moving to Margaret's, I went to church on my own. Mother and Karl didn't go to church regularly, only on special occasions such as holidays, weddings and funerals. I still chuckle to myself, when Karl told me how he felt about church. "You know," he said, "if I pass an open church door, and the wind blows my brand new hat off my head and that hat flies into the open door, I wouldn't step one foot in there to get it, I'd walk right on by." "Oh gosh, what a thing to say," with a grin, I replied.

I settled in quite nicely with my new arrangements, in my little cubical built into the wall where I slept with the curtain drawn. I felt safe and that meant so much to me. With the summer behind us, and autumn setting in, I was looking forward to dancing again. Bill was coming home in October for a Kirchweih dance. In the meantime, I had a lot of time to work on my wardrobe which had a style all of its own. I worked well with colors and had no trouble to mix colors in unusual ways. Like the cashmere rust blazer with a lot of detail and shaped tightly to my body, I wore with a fitted charcoal skirt with rust pin stripes. A black turtleneck sweater made the outfit not only unusual, but my favourite. Every time I wore the outfit to work, rich and fancy ladies that came to the store, complimented me. If for some reason, or by some chance, I would have pursued my dream to be a designer, I would have succeeded. It was not meant to be. Mother's words didn't leave room to dream of such things, for after all I was always told, "girls are meant to be mothers and learn to cook and sew.

When Bill returned in late October, and we danced again, I felt alive and happy. I suppose the dancing, being so close to one another, made up for the forbidden dreams we couldn't yet experience. I didn't know then that Bill came home for a special reason, until after our Kirchweih performance. We performed the dance before so we didn't need much practice. Having my blue formal gown on and standing next to Bill, we made a striking couple, walking into the hall to perform. On the way home Bill wanted to stop at his aunt's house, he said he forgot something. Instead of walking into the house, Bill took out a little velvet box and handed it to me. "What's this?" I asked. "You know, I knew I would marry you the first time I saw you," he said and I quickly replied, "You did not." "Yes I did," he said, "I told my mother that weekend that I found the girl that I am going to marry, and her name is Katie." I opened the box and took a look at the ring. A beautiful shiny diamond set in gold. I took it out, as Bill slipped it on my finger and asked. "*Will you marry me?*"

The following week Bill and I started to plan our wedding. Considering Bill's new business, we decided April 12th 1958 would give Bill enough time before the busy landscaping season began. The band and the hall had to be finalized before Bill returned. I could take care of the photographer, church and flowers on my own. Our family offered and took care of the food, and that was good for us, for we paid for everything else. A few disagreements along the way definitely made planning our wedding difficult at times. Bill's gentle nature, with his easy going mannerism and my sensitive, competitive nature, gave me some concern. Everyone that I talked to told me these feelings are normal, and also guys are different than girls, my married friends told me.

I had a lot of time to take care of our wedding plans, for Bill wasn't coming back for six months, the longest time, we been apart so far. I wasn't looking forward to planning our wedding on my own, but shopping for my dress I loved. I shopped forever, until one afternoon in a little shop I found the perfect dress. White tulle full skirt and tiny buttons all down my back, with satin swirls throughout the full skirt, a fitted bodice, and the neckline in a deep v. A waist length veil, attached to the tiara, finished the total outfit.

I looked forward to Christmas every year, especially in 1957. The decorations in stores were so festive. I walked through the mall everyday just for the decorations. The mall was full of shoppers, hurrying to find their last minute gifts. The mood of most, friendly and cordial as they passed and nodded a hello to perfect strangers. I saved all my extra money, so I could buy everyone a gift. I went a little overboard, but I didn't care. I loved the cold air as I stepped out to the parking lot. My red full length coat with a large collar and wide belt kept me in style and warm. My arms full of packages and snowflakes falling onto the pavement so lightly, created a Christmas spirit for me that lasted all through the holiday season. On my way home I noticed my gas gauge read empty. I remembered the gas station, just down the street, on the corner by our house. I drove to the pump and a young man walked toward my car, and said, "Hi."

"Five dollars please," I said, as I struggled to roll my window all the way down. I watched him in my mirror the whole time. He took my five dollars and said thank you and I left. All the next day, off and on, my mind travelled to the gas station. I looked forward to gassing up each week. The following week, he walked up to my window and said "Five Dollars?" I was impressed that he remembered the amount. "Yes please," I said. This time he noticed me watching him in the mirror. "Do you live around here?" he asked, "Yeah, just down the street," I said, as I handed him the five dollars. He smiled enough so I noticed his white perfect teeth and he said, "Come again." The third time I stopped for gas, he lingered by my window and devilishly asked, "This shiny thing you are wearing on your finger, does that mean your'e taken?" Teasingly, I answered, "Maybe."

After a month or so, before my afternoon shift, I put my red dress on that I liked so much with matching suede high heel shoes, fixed and fussed with my hair until just the way I wanted it, and drove to the garage. I parked the car and nervously walked into the large, open garage door. All I saw were feet sticking out from underneath a car. "Could I use the phone? It's a local call," I asked. Margaret didn't have a phone, so I thought it was a good excuse. He rolled the dolly out enough to look at me. "Sure go ahead," he said, raising his eyebrows. I learned his name was David. There was no doubt in both our minds that we were drawn to each other. It started by taking longer after every fill up at the pump, most of the time the conversation ended with a customer waiting for me to move. He acted on his feelings for me, when after work one day I found a note pasted to my car window. It read…

Dear Kate,
I was wondering if you would meet me tomorrow after work.
9pm.
David

I was so tempted to stop by the station on my way home, but I didn't. I was afraid of what I felt when David was near. The following morning I did stop in. I met David's father, a gray haired, slightly overweight man with a deep voice. "You must be Kate," he said, as I approached the desk. "I am David's Dad, and you must be looking for David." I nodded yes. "He'll be in soon." "Well ok," I said, "I'll see him later," and I left.

Although my shift was over at 9pm, every once in awhile, depending on how busy, we'd stay after work to finish the bookkeeping for that day. Bernie, one of the Salesmen, unlocked the door for me and watched me walk toward my car until he knew I was safe. I looked in the direction where my car was parked and I saw David. I waved to Bernie, and said "See you tomorrow," David leaned on my car with his arms folded in front and watched me walk toward him the whole time. He didn't move until I reached the car. "Hi," he said quietly. "I know a place close by where we can go for a bite." I hesitated, "Oh, I don't know." "Oh come on, you must be hungry." We talked so much, the hours passed so quickly. I wasn't aware of the time, as I jumped up and said, "Oh, my gosh I have to go, my sister doesn't know where I am, she will worry." He drove me to my car and took my hand and said, "Thank you for meeting me." "You're welcome, it was nice," I said.

When Mother found out of my new interest, oh boy, she talked to me every chance she had. It was different now with Mother, we could discuss things. "Mother," I said, "I am too young to stay home every night, besides David knows I am engaged." After a pause, Mother asked, "What nationality is he?" "Well, I am not totally sure but I think Irish and French." "Oh, yoy yoy, oh my goodness," I thought for a minute she was going to faint. "A Frenchman, you know they don't make good husbands." "Oh, Mother," I said, "where did you hear that? Besides, he's American." "No, no, not true, remember, the apple doesn't fall far from the tree, trust me Katie," she pleaded. After bickering back and forth for some time, I finished the conversation by saying, "I like David, and Bill is not coming back for four months. I'll tell him I go for coffee with a guy." "Oh, you wouldn't do that. Oh, you are so naive, Katie," she said, rolling her eyes. I gave my Mother a great deal of grief at that time, but I was absolutely sure of myself, or so I thought.

Mother and Karl accepted a new positions working at Hutzel Hospital, downtown Detroit. Karl was hired as a parking lot attendant and Mother as a cleaning lady. They were happy with this opportunity, for the benefits were good. I don't know why on my day off, I found myself missing my mother. Living with my sister, and working all hours, mother and I didn't see each other enough. So I thought I would surprise her and drove to the hospital on my day off. I walked through the long halls of the Hospital with doors on each side and sick people everywheres. I searched for my mother, looking from side to side. When I saw a pail of water in the hall, I looked around the corner and there stood my mother, wiping down the mirror. I stood behind her and before I said something, I noticed my mother was crying. Tears streaming down her face, as she moved her arms up and down the mirror with a cloth. Quietly, I said, "Mother?" she quickly turned and seemed embarrassed, "What are you doing here?" "Never mind that," as I asked, "What's the matter, Mother?" She didn't answer me right away. After a deep breath, she said, "Oh, it's nothing." I moved closer and wiped her tears gently, "It's something, don't say it's nothing. What's the matter?" I urged her. She replied, "You know I am just feeling sorry for myself, you know sometimes, when these moods come, you know." "Yeah, I know," I said.

I didn't leave, but stood for awhile, watching my mother from afar. My heart felt heavy, as I remembered a time when her destiny took a cruel turn. Because of circumstances that were none of her doing, to see her go from her humble, yet meaningful, beginnings, to this low point in her life of cleaning toilets, was heartbreaking. She never complained about the work, and never missed a chance to say, this is a good country, this America. But, the loss of her homeland, the life she left behind never left her. She longed for family togetherness and especially, missed her mother.

In the next weeks, I looked forward to meeting David, if only we sat in our cars, talking for hours. I learned many things about him. He and his family lived on the west side. David was an only child, but his parents adopted a girl, a few years younger than David, when they found out they couldn't have any more children. His father, not in good health, depended on David to take over the gas station one day. I learned of David's dream of wanting to be a commercial artist one day. He brought a few paintings to show me, and I was impressed. I must say his art took me by surprise, it was that good. There was no doubt in my mind, that if David chose this talent for a career, he would succeed.

When David asked me to his once a year Cadet Ball, I was thrilled. "Is this a date?" I teased him. "Well, I sure would be happy if you say yes, and besides you'll get to see my uniform," he answered me. "Is it a yes?" "I'll go," I said with a grin.

I wore a bright yellow, chiffon cocktail length dress, with matching yellow high heels. A pearl necklace and earrings. My hair, just touching my shoulders, with a deep wave partly covering my face, made me feel attractive. David looked tall and slender in his white uniform, with stripes on the pants and hat. The evening began with introductions at every turn. When the band started to play, David turned to me and whispered, "You know, Kate, dancing is not my thing." I whispered back, "Oh, but it is tonight. Why do you think I am here? Oops, that didn't come out right," I tried to apologize. He grinned and said, "Well in that case, let's dance."

We slow danced every dance, with his arm totally folded around my waist, as feelings started to take hold. When the band played a jitterbug and I tried to teach David the dance that was asking for too much in one night. He managed all right in slow dancing, but his idea of dancing the jitterbug was to hold my hand while I did the dancing and he did the looking. We had so many laughs throughout the evening. I could tell he was happy that I came. When one of his Cadet buddies came and asked me to dance, David's jealousy showed. He didn't like it, so I only danced one dance, but I liked the fact that he minded. At one point through the evening, he said, "Wow, where did you learn to dance like that?" "Well, Bill and I always dance like"...... I stopped talking. "Yeah, I know," he answered.

We walked hand in hand to the door of the apartment. "It's a beautiful night," he said, to break the silence. "Yeah, look at all the stars," I said, as we both looked up to the sky. I faced him and said, "Thank you David, I had a wonderful time." Looking in my eyes, he asked, "I suppose giving you a good night kiss is not allowed?" I remained silent as he bent over and kissed me on the lips. "Our first kiss was short and the perfect ending."

That night I lay in my bed awake for quite some time. I rolled my engagement ring around and around and wondered what was happening here. Bill kept creeping into my mind, and I couldn't dismiss the feelings I had for David. The need to live in the moment was stronger than the distance with Bill, so I slipped the ring off my finger. David noticed the ring off my finger right away, as he said, "With this ring off your finger does this mean what I think it means?" Sincerely, I said, "I am not sure." Needless to say my family did not approve of my actions. I listened patiently to their concerns. But, by now, my own mind made decisions for me, so I distanced myself from anyone that I thought didn't understand me.

I found another note on my car window a few weeks later.

Dear Kate,
I have a surprise for you, meet me on Sunday. Please
call me.
David.

When I asked David about Sunday, all he said was, "dress casual," and, "tell your Sister it will take most of the day. You have to wait," he said, "It's a surprise."

His car was so shiny and clean as he picked me up mid morning, right after Church. We drove over to Port Huron and crossed over to Canada, at least two hours, before he turned into a narrow driveway that led to a cottage by the lake. "Here we are," he said, "This is our summer place. I love this camp. My family comes here every chance they get. But today, it's just you and me." He turned the key and the door opened. The sand came right up to the door, so I took my shoes off and David did the same. The camp smelled from firewood, rustic and comfortable. "Would you like a cup of tea," he said, "before I show you the rest of the camp?" "Okay," I replied. A cold day, so hot tea sounded like a good idea. We sat on the couch sipping our tea, laughing and clowning around for some time.

We went outside and started walking along the sandy beach near the water's edge. It was then I saw the full beauty of the area. Their summer camp was in a small settlement called Ipperwash. With the smell of the blue water, the high carved cliffs, and miles of sand, we felt playful. I started to pull away from David, but it wasn't long before he caught up to me. We embraced and kissed passionately for the first time. He moved my hair away from my face and he quietly said, "You know I am falling for you." "Oh, don't do that," I jokingly said. I turned away from him and started walking back to the camp. Quietly David followed me, "I am sorry, I shouldn't have said that." "No, no," I answered "I am glad you did." Guilty feelings surfaced, as

I asked, "I hope you don't think I am leading you on." "Well, I think it is too late for that," he said.

Deep down inside, I wanted to have fun and enjoyed David's company. I didn't plan to have feelings for him. After that afternoon at the camp, David tried to make light of his feelings and told me that he had a love interest. Apparently, a girl at their summer camp, they had a thing for each other. David didn't mention this girl often, but he didn't have to, for I never forgot. I purposely stayed away from the gas station for two weeks. I was surprised when I stopped to get gas David's father told me, "David's gone on vacation. He will be back in a week and I'll tell him you came by." "Oh, ok," I said and left.

The following week as I walked through the crowded parking lot to my car, deep in thought, I didn't notice David leaning on my fender. "Hi," he said. We just looked at each other in silence for awhile. "You want to go for a ride," he asked me. "Okay," I said, as I hopped in his car. We drove without a word, until he turned into a dead end street and stopped and turned the motor off. Awkwardly, I asked, "How are you?" "Well, ok I guess. No, not really," he answered. "Why?" I asked, concerned. "You know why. I went to the camp to do some thinking and to have some fun." He paused, "but all I thought about was you. Then my mother tells me I shouldn't feel this way, my Sister tells me things I don't want to hear, and I am sure it is the same for you." "Yeah, I know what you mean. My mother is against you too, because you are French." I said. "Nobody would be good enough for my mother, but a Schwob." We both started to laugh, as David said, "What's a Schwob?" "Oh, never mind," I said.

David's face expressed warmness even when he was so serious, as he continued, "Kate, I know you have feelings for me, gosh it feels so right. Kate, do you feel it too? I made up my mind let's just spend more time together as friends. I just want to be with you. Whatever happens just let me know when the time comes." "Okay, I will," I said. "You can count on that." We talked about everything that evening, including religion. David was not

Catholic like I was and that seemed to pose a problem. In the 1950s, differences like those put pressure on everyone concerned. David took my hand in his, and gently stroked every finger, and then he gave me a compliment. "You have beautiful fingernails, Kate. I meant to tell you that a while ago." "Thank you, how thoughtful of you to notice," I said. Devilishly, he answered, "Oh, that's not all I noticed," And we both laughed.

David and I held back our feelings most of the time, with the uncertainty that lay ahead of us, except for one time. We didn't date as such, but instead met for a hamburger at Big Boy's restaurant. We sat in each other's cars for hours, went for long walks, hand in hand, and every opportunity David had, he'd give me a short kiss or squeezed my hand. On one of those walks through the park, David steered me off the walkway to a large tree trunk that was lying on the ground. Flirting came naturally to me, as I said, "Wow, what a beautiful spot. It looks like you have been here before." "What do you mean by that?" he questioned. I sat on the flat part of the trunk and moved my legs over to the opposite side. David sat tightly next to me and grabbed my hand. David's face became serious, as he said, "I've been so happy, Kate, you have qualities, well, you've got something. I won't pressure you," he said with a sigh and he stopped talking. He leaned over, touched my face, and we embraced extremely tightly. David kissed me passionately, only one kiss, a kiss that lasted way too long, and told me everything I needed to know about his feelings for me.

I agonized for days and time was running out. Every waking moment I thought of my decision. In some ways I knew David well. His sensitivity to me and his understanding of feelings had a profound pull for me that was hard to overlook. Bill, on the other hand, made me feel safe; he was kind, gentle and ambitious. In many ways mature beyond his years, also the same background which was huge for me. Never did I think I would have such a decision to make, just before my wedding. Strong feelings for two men at the same time, and I couldn't and wouldn't talk to anyone about this. God forbid, if anyone besides my family knew about this.

A few days later, I called David and asked him if he'd meet me at the gas station after my work. We found ourselves at the edge of a graveyard, the only private spot we could find, sitting in the car waiting for one of us to break the silence. "Well, Kate, tell me. You have something on your mind, I know," he finally said. He took my hand and slid his hand over mine several times. I searched for the right words, as I finally said, "Bill is coming home soon and I have to plan a wedding. Oh, I am so sorry." I could hardly stop my voice from cracking. After a long pause, I said, "Say something," as I started to cry. Looking at me, David said, "Well, was it the kiss the other day?" "No, no," I answered. "You know, I was hoping it would be me," he stated. "David, you are a great guy and I want you to know I never planned to have these feelings." In a state of pain for the both of us, he said, "Oh boy, I didn't think it would be so hard." With a deep sigh, David said, "some lucky guy, that Bill." "What about you David? That girl in Canada," I asked. He didn't answer that question, but instead said, "I'll be fine. Here's the fingernail polish you left in my car." Those are the last words he said to me, before I closed the door, and he sped away in the darkness.

I went directly to my cubical, drew the curtain and cried myself to sleep. My heart was in so much pain that I called in sick the next day and stayed home. Some time through the day, when I was alone, I took the box with my ring out of the drawer and slowly opened it. For the longest time, I just stared at the ring, before I closed the box and put it back in my drawer. The thought of hurting David was burning in my chest. The meaningful conversations we shared throughout these few months, was hard for me to dismiss. It takes time to shift gears in the human heart, and I really believed that in time, I would be able to put this behind me. I spent much of my time deep in thought, at work, at home, on my day off. I couldn't concentrate for deep down I knew what needed to be done.

I took out a piece of paper and started writing a letter to Bill. It took several starts, but after about the 5th try, I sealed the letter and walked down to the nearby post office. I never did send the letter. On several tries, walking away and then back again, my letter remained unopened back in my room. There will be time, I told myself, soon enough.

The next few weeks, a total blur for me. So much talking all around me and everyone had an opinion about my wedding, but me. Everything came back into focus for me the day I went for my last fitting for my wedding dress. I stood in front of the mirror for the longest time, and visualized Bill next to me, and I felt a feeling of warmth, security and love. That night I took the little box out again and once more stared at the ring. I twirled and twirled the ring between my fingers several times. I held the ring for some time before I slowly slipped it on my finger.

The first night when Bill arrived, it was hard. For some reason, I knew he found out about David. I believe my brother-in-law told him and I knew I had to tell him myself. When Bill asked the question, "what have you been doing with yourself since I've been gone?" I took the opportunity and said, "Well besides work, I spent some time with a guy I met at a gas station down the road." "What do you mean a guy?" Bill questioned. When I didn't say anything, Bill asked, "Do you have feelings for this guy?" "Well, yes," I could hardly get the words out. Bill wasn't noticeably upset, and after a pause, said, "Do you still want to marry me?" I felt relieved in some strange way.

In the weeks to follow so much needed to be done. With last minute planning for the wedding, Bill and I had little time together, he stayed out at the farm in West Lorne with his family and I returned to my mother's house.

On April 11th 1958, the night before my wedding, longing to be alone with my thoughts, I walked upstairs and sat on the window sill, and started daydreaming. I glanced over to my wedding dress hanging behind the door. I pictured Bill next to me and I wondered if I would be a good wife. Then I took my veil and draped it over my lap and my dreams took hold. I visualized a small house, beautifully decorated with fine fabrics and comfortable furniture. Bill and I are laughing and enjoying romantic evenings with cake and coffee. With lots of flowers, especially pink roses, Linden trees with crooked trunks, lilac trees in every color, and, oh yes, a big old cherry tree. Children running around, yes, definitely children, a boy with blue eyes and dark hair, something I always wanted, and a girl, just like me. I will give them so much love and security and always keep them safe. Not like my childhood, that's for sure. We will celebrate birthdays and Christmases, something I longed for so much, a family of my own. Single handedly all my dreams became so real in my mind. There was no doubt at all, that my wishing would make it so.

For a moment, I thought of David and asked God to help me to forget. I thought of my doll and still the memories linger. Our beloved Kikinda, and the delightful smell of cherry blossoms, the gathering in the evenings on the porch. The culture of that time stripped from my memory most of the time, gave me sadness when allowed to return.

On that evening, a few tears cascaded down my cheeks, as twenty years of my life played like a movie, in one hour, as I entered a brand new promise, perhaps the most challenging of all, marriage.

Uncertain, I entered into this new life and a new country, Canada, but I was absolutely sure that I learned lessons from my own family and I would not repeat the same mistakes, or so I thought.

After all, what is life without dreams, I told myself. Hold on tight and never let your dreams die and surely when tomorrow comes if I work hard enough and give enough, all my dreams will come true.

The End

Epilogue

It's a lovely summer afternoon and I'm turning 73 in a few days. Peace and tranquility fill my heart. I sit back in my red chair, overlooking my beautiful courtyard and taking it all in. I daydream that I am surrounded by the people that I love, the sounds of the water splashing softly on the shoreline. The leaves on the trees rustle as the wind blows so softly, and birds serenade in the background. I take a deep sigh. Bill opens the gate, it's time for our afternoon coffee, and I realize I am where I want to be, and I whisper to myself, I am finally home.

AUTHOR'S COMMENTS

To understand and for a better insight to my culture and the old Jugoslavia, I found this article so beautifully written by Frank Schmidt. He so graciously gave me permission to share it with you.

WHO ARE THE DANUBE SCHWABIENS!

Although we Danube Schwabians are predominantly of German stock, we do not come from Germany, but from former homelands on the Danubian Plain in Hungary, Jugoslavia and Romania.

Our history begins in 1683, in that fateful year the Ottoman Turks, who had subjugated Hungary 150 years earlier, were threatening to expand their empire into central Europe. Their army suffered a crushing defeat at Vienna, and with their subsequent expulsion from Hungary the Islamic Tide in Europe had receded.

To develop the recovered Hungarian domains, the Austrian Imperial Council launched a great colonization scheme. It was intended to transform the depopulated wasteland into cultivated and productive fields.

Among other nationalities, German speaking people from south-western Germany and the eastern township of France were encouraged to take up homesteads in Hungary. As there were practically no roads in Eastern Europe at the time, the settlers boarded specially-built barges in Germany. These floated downriver with the current. At their destination they were quickly dismantled to provide the roofs for the settler's homes.

Because there so many Schwabians among the earliest arrivals the Magyars dubbed all Germans who came to the Country after the Turkish, wars as Schwabians. That was fine as long as we were isolated in east-central Europe. But, when contact was established with Germany after the last war, where there are still plenty of Schwabians, a name had to found to distinguish us from them. So, because of our long and special Relationship with the river, Danube was chosen-and, that how we became Danube Schwabians!

Under the auspices of the Austrian Court, Danube Schwabians established more than 1,000 agrarian Villages and numerous homesteads on lands bordering the middle Danube. These Models of 17th Century rural planning were purposely scattered across the entire Danubian Plain so they would be emulated by other ethnic groups.

The expertise of German, i.e., Danube Schwabian craftsmen, merchants and professional people set the standard for the development of the Cities and Towns. Just how much impact they had is shown by an old guide to Budapest. Most of the noteworthy structures listed in the book are the work of Danube Schwabians.

Urban Danube Schwabians were better educated than their Country Cousins, but they contributed far less to our culture. Either of our own violation, or more often due to official pressure, many took Hungarian names to further their own social or financial aims. After a time they did identify, with their own ethnic group-only the Country People, with some notable exceptions, remained Danube Schwabians.

The heart and soul of Danube Schwabians life were the villages and towns of 1000 to 8000 people. Though they were widely scattered there was a similarity and unity about them, which is not surprising, considering they were all designed by people in Vienna in the 17th and 18th centuries. Almost without exception they were founded as agrarian villages.

An agrarian Village-some grew into sizeable towns, is one where homesteads with the requisite barns, sheds, etc., are grouped together in a town. Like a hundred farms side by side. The acreage belonging to these homelands was of course, in the country-sometimes a few kilometers away. The focal point and most conspicuous landmark in these towns was always the Church. Invariably the facade would be in the settlers' baroque style. Its bell tower would contain a clock facing the four parts of the compass, and would be topped by a bulbous steeple.

Streets were unusually wide and straight, and whitewashed houses had tile roofs (just like those in Baden and in Alsace). Many streets were lined with Mulberry trees, which once supported a thriving silkworm industry.

The Kirchweih (church dedication) was our most important local Holiday. In spite of past religions links it was a purely secular holiday, devoted to fun and games, reunions, and dancing far into the night-to sounds of an oompah band, of course.

Our dialect is an amalgam of Palatine and Schwabian, plus a hint of Viennese. Due to archaic word forms it is not readily understood in Germany.

After centuries of living in east-central Europe, Danube Schwabian women adapted some feature of local costumes. German pioneers in Hungary wore tricorn hats. In this century, this had changed to the Peltzkapp (Fur hat).

All the peoples of the Danubian countries borrowed from each other to create the foods which have become associated with the area. The bratwurst, with the generous addition of paprika, became the Hungarian sausage we can buy in local stores.

Just when our flourishing communities had become more cohesive, due to better communications they were torn asunder by border changes after WWI when large parts of Hungary were awarded to Romania and Jugoslavia.

Although, we lived in peace and complete harmony with our neighbours for centuries, in the aftermath of WWII we lost all rights (such as they were), all our property and became victims of mass expulsions.

The first Danube Schwabians arrived in Canada 100 years ago, long before the troubles in Europe. The first arrivals settled in the west. There was a great influx in the 1920s and again in early 1950s when many refugees sought a safe haven in Canada. Since Danubian Schwabians who have come to this Country have adapted so well that they have hardly been noticed.

Danube Schwabian Clubs in Ontario and Quebec foster the culture, customs and tradition of a lost homeland. Above all, they promote good citizenship.

As an ethnic community we are thankful for the peace and freedom we have found in Canada, and are mindful of our enduring obligation to this Country.

By Frank Schmidt

About the Author

Katie Bering was born in Kikinda, Yugoslavia, and immigrated to America when she was fourteen. She now lives with her husband Bill on St. Joseph Island in Canada, where she enjoys painting, decorating, and photography. They have two children and five grandchildren. This is her first book.